Shooting Sports
for Women

Shooting Sports for Women

Laurie Morrow

and Steve Smith

St. Martin's Press ⚉ New York

Design by Richard Oriolo
Original drawings by Christopher Smith

Library of Congress Cataloging-in-Publication Data

Morrow, Laurie.
    Shooting sports for women : a practical guide to shotgunning and riflery for the outdoorswoman / by Laurie Morrow and Steve Smith.— 1st ed.
      p.   cm.
    Includes bibliographical references
    ISBN 0-312-14733-3
    1. Shooting for women. I. Smith, Steve. II. Title.
GV1158.W65M67   1966
799.3'082—dc20   96-22850
                                             CIP

First Edition: October 1996

10 9 8 7 6 5 4 3 2 1

To our children
Tommy and Winston
Amy, Chris, and Jake
who, along with their generation,
hold the future of the shooting
sports in their hands

Contents

—

Chapter 1

Some History of Women and Shooting in America   1

In pioneer times, a gun was the tool that put meat on the table and ensured a family's safety; here are stories of a few uncommon women who were "confidential" with a gun.

Chapter 2

Proper Handling of Firearms and Shooting Safety   15

A thorough understanding of firearms safety and the operation of your gun is the first step in becoming a responsible shooting sportswoman.

Chapter 3

Outdoorwear for Women   28

Comfortable, practical, and even fashionable women's outdoor clothing is an investment that will greatly contribute to years of enjoyment in the out-of-doors.

Chapter 4

What Is a Shotgun?   40

What is a shotgun? How does it work? How do you go about buying your first one?

Acknowledgments

—

The authors wish to thank Susan Zeckendorf, our agent, who neither shoots nor hunts but is one hotshot little lady who stood behind this book from the beginning and never lost sight of the end; Anne Savarese, our editor at St. Martin's Press; Sue King, who by example sets the standard for good sportswomanship, and her husband, Jerry; Sharon Borg Wall, a devotee of the shooting sports; and our invaluable typist, Bonnie Ainsworth.

We also wish to thank the Women's Shooting Sports Foundation, the National Shooting Sports Foundation, the Congressional Sportsmen's Foundation; the U.S. Fish and Wildlife Service; Cindy Marlenee of Safari Club International; Deborah Horn and her husband, Peter Horn, vice president of Cougar Corporation, a subsidiary of Beretta U.S.A.; *Black's Wing and Clay; Shooting Sportsman* magazine; Christopher Forbes and Leonard Yablon of *Forbes* and the staff of Forbes Trinchera Ranch; Jim and Tudor Austin of New England Arms Co.; Filson's; Sorel/Kaufman of Canada; Lisa Winkels and *Gun Journal;* sportsman Dial Dunkin; firearms experts Steve and Julie Coates, David and Martha Bichrest, and Ann and Morris Hallowell; Gordon Hinds and Dunn's Supply, Inc.; writer Michael McIntosh; photographer Don Hoffman; stylist Diann Fiebig; George Hickox of Grouse Wing Kennel; Pheasant Ridge Preserve; Mt. Blanca Game Bird & Trout; and Hawkeye Hunt Club.

Our respective spouses and children have stood by us in this, as in all things, and their love and support shine through these pages.

Tom Morrow selflessly imparted to us his immense knowledge and love of firearms and the outdoors. His passionate enthusiasm and interest in our work carried this book to its timely and happy completion. To him we are most especially grateful.

Foreword

—

Timing is as important in the publication of a book as it is in the shattering of a clay target. Laurie Morrow and Steve Smith's new book on women and the shooting sports comes at perhaps the most opportune moment in the history of sport shooting. Women are taking up this recreational skill at an increasingly faster pace. Indeed, in the decade or so since I have been involved in the variety of sporting challenges that shooting offers, female participation in these activities has been rising at the rate of 500,000 per year.

My own involvement in sport shooting began in 1985 when I met a man who was an avid hunter. He wanted to share his hunting knowledge and expertise with me so that I, too, could experience the peaceful solitude of a deer hunt, the friendly banter in a duck blind, and the exquisite allure of a frost-covered forest aglow with the rose and salmon hues of a sunrise. That man—my friend, my mentor, and my inspiration—became my husband. Together we have traveled inside and outside the United States, partaking in some of nature's most wondrous moments, viewing some of her most beautiful creatures, trekking some difficult and dangerous terrain, and meeting many interesting and talented people. All of those experiences have created a vibrant and vivid fabric of life woven on the loom of sport hunting and shooting. They have created for me a way of living that is dynamic, fun, and rewarding.

The rewards have been many. One in particular was starting up the Washington Women's Shooting Club in the Washington, D.C., area with four friends. The club has been a great success, attracting women of all ages and levels of income and education. Other rewards have been in the association I have enjoyed with such hunter conservation groups as the Congressional Sportsmen's Foundation and Safari Club International, on whose boards I currently serve. The members of both of these organizations are dedicated hunters and conservationists who contribute their money and large amounts of time to ensuring that our wild resources are well managed and maintained. In fact, one of the greatest lessons I have learned since I first held a shotgun in my hands is the true meaning of conservation.

Conservation is not preservation, which excludes the human element. It is not a fad concept to be stuffed away and resurrected only for some fund-raising purpose. Conservation is a continuum. Along that continuum are plants, insects, reptiles, birds, beasts—and humans. The demands of an increasing population for better services, larger networks of roads and highways, and more modern suburbs and cities encroach on plant and animal life. To maintain a proper balance between the competing needs of these two "societies," care must be taken to monitor and maintain our natural resources, as well as to manage the problems of growth created by our own society. Most of our citizens recognize the need for conservation, but precious few dedicate themselves to the effort. All hunters, however, contribute to conservation through the purchase of hunting licenses and state and federal stamps, and through excise taxes when they purchase firearms and ammunition. Most important, hunters are directly connected to our woodlands and wildlife. They are keenly aware that their efforts to sustain game and nongame wildlife and habitat are necessary to offset the vagaries of nature and the pressures of progress. That is why so many sportsmen and women willingly volunteer their time to specific conservation efforts in their towns or states. Today there are healthy game populations of white-tailed deer, Rocky Mountain elk, wild turkey, and Canada geese, to name but a few. Robust populations of these species exist primarily because of the long-standing and concerted efforts of hunters to improve habitat and increase the numbers of our indigenous game animals.

These lessons in conservation, the challenges of becoming skilled in the use of firearms, the opportunities for greater involvement in the natural world, and the friendliness of the shooting community are treasures that I enjoy sharing with other women. To that end, in 1991 my husband and I began conducting a once-a-year, all-day seminar on shotgun handling and hunter ethics that includes clay target instruction and culminates in a late-afternoon duck hunt. These private seminar/ duck hunts at our farm on Maryland's Eastern Shore quickly became a hit. Twelve women participated the first year. That number grew to fifty-five by the third year. In 1995, as we prepared for our fourth annual "women only" duck hunt, we took a different tack. We joined forces with Sue King, executive director of the Women's Shooting Sports Foundation, which conducts the WSSF Ladies Charity Sporting Clays Classics across the country. These events attract all levels of women shooters, from beginners to experts, and benefit such important women's causes as breast cancer research and spousal abuse shelters. The hunt consisted of a small group of experienced women shooters, along with representatives from Maryland's Department of Natural Resources, the U.S. Fish and Wildlife Service, and members of the press. This afforded us an opportunity to bring to the attention of state and federal officials, as well as the general public, the phenomenal growth of women in the shooting sports, and to pique the interest of all segments of the population in this fast-growing pastime.

Sport shooting means personal challenge and enjoyment for millions of men, women, and children. It also translates into regional and national economic growth, greater understanding and support for our American heritage, and a desire to pass along to posterity a respect for, and love of, this legacy. Laurie and Steve's *Shooting Sports for Women* will help perpetuate this legacy. Indeed, it is destined to become a part of the history and heritage of the shooting sports.

—SHARON BORG WALL,
   Chairperson, Congressional Sportsmen's Foundation
   At-large Director, Safari Club International
   Life Member, Safari Club International Sables
   Member, Women's Shooting Sports Foundation
   Cofounder, Washington Women's Shooting Club
   Member, Board of Directors, U.S. Shooting Team Foundation

—

Why We Hunt, Why We Shoot

There are precious few stories of women who were given their first
shotgun or rifle by their father and learned to hunt at his side. No
woman I know tells of sitting on her dad's knee in front of a blazing fire
on a wintery night, seeing, through his eyes, woodcock spiral skybound
on wind-snapping October days, or deer askitter in naked November
woods come first snowfall. Such is the domain of men. This is the
legacy an outdoorsman passes on to his son, the very ritual he, in turn,
received from his father before him. Women, in turn, have had their
own special legacies, left to them by their mothers and grandmothers.

Most women who hunt or shoot learned to do so from their husbands, male friends, or lovers. In many cases, it was an act of default—attempting to share with him his passion for the out-of-doors and discovering, surprisingly, that the passion was addictive. Today many women shoot and hunt, and in ensuing years many more of the distaff side will join these ranks. It has much to do with sport, little to do with killing, absolutely nothing to do with the women's liberation movement, and everything to do with exploring nature and one's God-given abilities to the fullest and within the confines of that most valuable commodity of all—time to enjoy living.

There's a big picture you must try to see before you enter the shooting sports. It focuses on the fact that women in the shooting sports is no fad and nothing new. In fact, the very first woman to shoulder a gun was Queen Christina of Sweden who, sometime in the 1600s, fired a fulminate air gun and shot a partridge. Even the ancient Romans worshiped an outdoorswoman, Diana, goddess of the hunt. Women's participation in shooting and hunting is as old as the ages, but currently there's an appreciable surge of interest in these activities by women and—even better—by men and women together.

Hunting as sport in America is only three or four generations old. Prior to that, it was purely a matter of survival.

Robert Ardrey wrote in his book, *The Hunting Hypothesis* (New York: Atheneum, 1976), "If among all the members of our primate family the human being is unique, even in our noblest aspirations, it is because we alone through untold millions of years were continuously dependent on killing to survive. It is *because* we were hunters, *because* we killed for a living, *because* we matched our wits against the whole of the animal world, that we have the wit to survive even a world of our own creation."

So when we talk about the future of hunting, we wax lyrical and that's about it. Mankind has hunted for twenty-five generations times twenty-five and beyond. Why do we hunt? Because we are human. And neither government nor sovereign nor religion, in this generation or any to follow, can change that. It is, quite simply, the nature of things. As Ardrey writes:

> At an hour quite desperate in terms of any intelligent estimate of future survival—at an hour so confused by so many threats to our existence that we cannot put our minds without distraction on any one of them . . . our temptation must be to find refuge in nostalgia, in romance, in a remembrance of things past that never were. Only by turning our remorseless backs on such temptation, only by seeking the reality of a human past that still invests us, can we discover the origins of those characters of courage and cooperation, of inge-

nuity and wit, of cunning and adaptability, of affection and human bonding, that without our hunting past would have been a natural impossibility.

Why do we hunt? Because we were meant to. Why do we shoot? Why indeed.

—LAURIE MORROW,
Freedom, New Hampshire

Some History of Women and Shooting in America

*In pioneer times, a gun was the tool that put meat
on the table and ensured a family's safety;
here are stories of uncommon women
who were "confidential"
with a gun.*

Whether it is the cause or result of things, the mass production of firearms in America during the second half of the 1800s coincided with our country's fieriest, wildest, and most expansive decades. So it makes some sense to begin our search for stories of women and guns here.

Pitifully few stories have been passed down of women who brandished weapons in war, or cried "Westward ho!" pioneering trails through the virgin West. Yet colorful women such as Molly Brown, Big Nose Kate, Rose of the Cimarron, and Calamity Jane are lesser known in American folklore and legend than their male counterparts, Butch

Cassidy and the Sundance Kid, Wyatt Earp, Doc Holiday, or Wild Bill Hickok. Famous, infamous, common, or uncommon, women played vital roles in the founding of our country. History gives too little credit to the notion that both sexes, pulling together, supported one another through the trials and tribulations of that monumental job.

By the end of the nineteenth century, the American frontier was officially declared closed, settled by homesteaders, prospectors, cattlemen, railway workers, miners, Indian fighters, businessmen, outlaws, whores, and tycoons. They came from all walks of life and most of them had to cross an ocean to get here. The land of the Indian was no more, and only came alive when Buffalo Bill and his Congress of Rough Riders enacted the code of the West to the enthusiastic applause of sell-out crowds. Of the banishment of Native Americans from their land, the words of surrender of Chief Joseph of the Nez Percé tribe sear our conscience: "Our chiefs are killed. . . . The old men are all dead. . . . The little children are freezing to death. My people, some of them have run away to the hills and have no blankets, no food. No one knows where they are, perhaps freezing to death. I want to have time to look for my children and see how many of them I can find. Maybe I can find them among the dead. Hear me, my chiefs. My heart is sick and sad. From where the sun now stands I will fight no more forever."

The East Coast was now a mere train ride from the West Coast. A bloodless uprising had taken hold of the nation—the Industrial Revolution. A young rancher in the Dakota Territory named Roosevelt was thinking of returning home to New York and entering politics. It was a vibrant time . . . a time when legends were made.

There were real-life legends like railwaymen Casey Jones and John Henry, who put their lives on the line, and lost them, to win a point of honor. One verse of the folk song of John Henry, the great, black "steel-driving man" who drove the spikes that held the tracks that built America's railroads, goes:

> *John Henry had a little woman;*
> *Her name was Polly Ann.*
> *John Henry took sick and he had to go to bed;*
> *Polly Ann drove steel like a man.*

Why? Because if John Henry was sick for more than a day or two, he'd have lost his job. Things were like that in the Old West. Hard times for men and women alike—and it took both of them to make a go of it. Fictitious heroes like Pecos Bill, the cowboy who rode twisters and embodied the spirit of all real cowboys, lassoed the West. Paul Bunyan, the giant lumberjack from Michigan, scooped out the Great Lakes with his bare hands so his blue ox, Babe, could have a drink of water.

The code of the West was a creed unto itself.

West of the Mississippi, Main Street U.S.A. was lined with boarding houses, gambling halls, saloons, and brothels. Men wore six-shooters on their hips and women stuffed derringers down their cleavage or in their garters. These were fightin' men and women. There was no organized law to harness this untamed land, and the letter of the law was usually punctuated with shots from a Colt revolver or a Winchester rifle; or tied nice and neat by a lariat knotted high enough up on a cottonwood tree so a hanging man's feet couldn't touch the ground.

As towns grew, wholesale lawlessness became big business for gunslinging, masked horsemen who were looking to make a hefty withdrawal from small-town banks. The bigger towns had marshals and

Since the days of this 1907 magazine cover, the number of women active in the shooting sports has increased dramatically.

(DRAWING BY ALBERT HENCKE)

sheriffs; the smaller ones had trouble. A woman walking down the street often carried a pocket pistol in her purse. These were a cautious breed of women. They had to be. Today a woman might carry a Beretta .25 automatic for personal security. Back then she carried a derringer in .22-caliber. It was none other than Susan B. Anthony, leader of the suffragist movement, who said in 1871: "Woman must not depend upon the protection of man, but must be taught to protect herself."

There were two kinds of women. One was the pioneer wife. She made her living from the sweat of her brow and worked relentless hours to put honest food on her family's table. She raised her children and loved her husband—to the letter of the Bible. Her story was everyday, but upon it was built the very foundation of *who* we are and and *what* we are, and that is a society that, despite the odds, still centers on *family.*

The other type of woman was more akin to Mary Magdalene than Mother Mary. She was called many names: "soiled dove," "gilded bird," "painted lady," but no matter what you called her, a whore made a profession of her God-given attributes. It stands to reason that "the world's oldest profession" produced the world's first businessperson.

Her place of business was a bordello. For a certain type of man, a whorehouse was a place as close to home as he was ever likely to get. Miners, cowpokes, trail hands, railwaymen—they were all transients, and home for any man was wherever he happened to lay his head that night. If it was on a soft, feminine shoulder, so much the better. But such comfort did not come cheap. It could cost an ounce of gold dust just to buy some time to sit and chat with a prostitute. Additional services, naturally, cost a lot more. In those early days of westward expansion, women, let alone willing women, were a rare and valuable commodity.

But both types of women worked to survive. Mark Twain said, "Work consists of whatever a body is *obliged* to do." He may have arrived upon this sentiment after his own adventures in the West as a young man. There was one difference between the whore and the pioneer woman. The madam's derringer was engraved and nickel-plated. The pioneer woman's was plain. Both served the same purpose and were equally effective in brave hands.

When we ponder the history of women and guns, places like El Paso, Dodge City, Laramie, Cheyenne, Deadwood, and Virginia City spring to mind, not the poor prairie farms and isolated Texas ranches. It's in those hustling, bustling towns that sprung up along the cattle trails that we associate the most colorful stories of the West. After all, no story's worth the telling unless it captures the imagination and sets it on fire.

Here are a few stories of some notable American women. Like Casey Jones, they too were real people, but like Pecos Bill and the cyclone, some of their stories may be cut from whole cloth. But they're what we've got—and I, for one, need heroes and heroines and choose to believe them.

Pauline Cushman

A woman raised in the East, who survived Confederate lines
in the South as a double agent for the North and went on
to make her mark in the American West

I was drunk as a coot," wrote an Arizona pioneer in 1884,

when I met her on the corner of Top and Bottom Streets. The Major—that's what we called her—stopped me and asked me if I had seen that "long-legged husband" of hers, Jere Fryer. I replied I didn't keep track of other women's husbands. No sooner had I said this when she yanked out that damned forty-five of hers, cocked it and stuck it in my belly.

"I asked you a civil question," she said real mad like, "and I want an answer due to a lady."

It seems I got sober in a hurry with that damn gun in my belly and I swept off my hat and gave her a bow.

"No, ma'am," I said, "I haven't seen your illustrious husband, Mr. Fryer."

"Now that's the way to answer a lady," she said, and to my great relief took that forty-five away from my grub sack.

This firsthand account is a dandy introduction to the spirited Civil War heroine, Pauline Cushman. Pauline was a dark-haired Creole beauty born in New Orleans in 1833 and raised in Grand Rapids, Michigan, where she became an adopted daughter of the Chippewas and was called Laughing Breeze. She rivaled any Indian or frontiersman with a gun or astride a horse, but after she refused the love of an Indian chief named Leaping Thunder, she fled Michigan for New York, where she became an actress. While traveling in Tennessee in 1863 with a troupe of actors, Pauline became enmeshed in a Secret Service conspiracy and accepted the real-life role of a Confederate sympathizer.

She became a Union spy and was notorious as the femme fatale of the Civil War. She was described by one observer as "a woman of magnificent physique, with large, lustrous, sloe black eyes, raven ringlets falling almost to her waist, with the profile of a Madonna and a voice as melodious as a lute." Her immense popularity as an actress and entertainer filled the house with hoards of Confederate soldiers; her beauty commanded the attention of Rebel officers from whom she charmed military secrets. She became the toast of wherever she went—Louisville, Nashville—and her public appearances were carefully and secretly arranged by the Union Army's intelligence network. It was during "an undertaking of unusual and extreme danger" that she crossed Confederate lines to successfully spy on Rebel movement at Shelbyville, Wartrace, and Tullahoma. Ultimately she was captured, court-martialed, and sentenced to be hanged.

Pauline's charms saved her life. General Granger interceded on personal grounds, scolded his "willful, naughty girl," and pardoned her. The Union declared her a heroine and presented her with the honorary rank of Major of the Cavalry. The *New York Herald* proclaimed her "the gallant Scout of the Cumberland who did such noble work for the Union in Tennessee."

She met and married Jere Fryer, fifteen years her junior, and moved with him to the small town of Casa Grande, Arizona, where they opened an inn. In 1880 the Southern Pacific Railroad made Casa Grande a terminal. The population of the town exploded and so did the Fryers' business. In tandem with the railway boom came the usual social outbreaks—gunfights, bar room brawls, horse thievery—and Pauline unofficially maintained law and order and refereed gun duels with a Colt .45 slung on her hip over her velvet gown. "'The Major' was known as a 'square shooter,' an excellent nurse in taking care of anyone injured by bullet wounds, and a woman who wanted to see fair play," reported one resident.

Pauline vowed that Casa Grande would become no Tombstone. In a well-documented gunfight between two ranchers with bad blood between them, Pauline confronted the men as they were ready to draw their guns on each other. She drew her revolver and stood between them. "Let them kill each other but you [boys] keep out of it," she warned the thickening crowd. When the dust settled, one rancher was down with a slug through his stomach and Pauline declared fair play was done. She returned her .45 to its holster and preached a few last words over the deceased. "This was the kind of timber our dear old lady pioneer was made of," one man reminisced, "afraid of nothing, open and above board in every way, and always ready to help her fellow man out. No one ever went hungry or wanted a bed while the Major was alive."

In another incident, Pauline threatened a teamster who refused to unhitch a string of twenty mules that he left to board overnight at her corral. They had been brutally overworked, were undernourished, and were suffering from bleeding sores.

"Those mules aren't in working condition," Pauline accused the teamster. "You won't take these animals out of my corral in this condition."

"I'm going to take them out of this corral and what are you going to do about it?" the teamster sneered and walked into a nearby saloon.

Pauline grabbed a box of cartridges and loaded her Winchester rifle.

"Hey, Major, you going hunting?" someone called after her.

"Yes," Pauline replied. "For a skunk."

Pauline burst into the bar, leveled her gun at the teamster, and demanded, "Unhitch those mules. or I'll shoot you down."

"Damn, a man can't even run his own team," he grumbled—and did as she said.

When Pauline died, word got out and a huge crowd of men in faded blue uniforms followed her casket to the cemetery, where "The Major" was buried in the Grand Army plot. Her marker read: Pauline Cushman, Federal Spy and Scout of the Cumberland.

The *Arizona Daily Citizen* ran a front-page headline: PAULINE CUSHMAN IS NOT FORGOTTEN.

Julia Bulette

The greatest madam of them all was Julia Bulette, a Creole from New Orleans whose Virginia City brothel, Julia's Palace, was legendary even during her own lifetime. Underneath her purple velvets, white satins, and sable capes it seems there did indeed beat a heart of gold. Julia was immensely popular and loved—no doubt by many men—for far more than her exceptional beauty and talents. Flushed by the activity and wealth generated by the nearby Comstock Lode, Julia conducted business at the Palace with an elegance not associated with houses of ill repute. Her clientele was served meals prepared in the French manner, accompanied by wines and champagnes. No roughhousing was tolerated in this fine establishment.

As much as Julia was admired by men, she was bitterly scorned by women. Yet no one could repudiate Julia's civic generosity. When epidemics swept through Virginia City, Julia provided food, clothing, and nursing. When the Paiute Indians attacked the mining camps, Julia remained to nurse the wounded, refusing to flee to safety with the other women. She rode atop the fire engine in Virginia City's parades, and whenever there was an alarm, Julia was already at the scene with food and hot coffee for the firefighters. A railroad car was named for her, and a Comstock mine, too.

Julia Bulette's moral and immoral accomplishments came to an abrupt end on January 20, 1867, when she was found strangled in her bed. A hue and cry for the murderer resulted in the hanging of John Millain. Women were delighted that the greatest whore known to the West was no more and viewed Millain as a hero. This caused a sizable rift between spouses but did not keep every man in town from accompanying the funeral casket of their beloved Julia. The crowd at Millain's hanging the following day was even larger. Forty special deputy sheriffs armed with Henry rifles stood between the murderer and the murderous crowd. Millain was hung and buried in the hallowed ground of St. Mary's Church. Julia was buried at Flowery Hill. The church would not permit her to be laid to rest in their cemetery. After all, Julia Bulette was a prostitute.

Although the kind of gun Julia carried is not documented, there is little doubt that she was armed whenever she went about her business. She most probably carried a derringer, a pocket pistol, a palm-size pistol that nonetheless, and quite often, could fire a deadly load.

Western historian R. D. Miller wrote, "Julia was more than a common prostitute. She was more than a common woman. This tall, dark-eyed beauty possessed characteristics necessary for the civilizing of the West—sympathy, generosity, understanding and compassion. She was indeed a great lady of the line."

As towns like Virginia City grew and prospered, successful miners and cattlemen became wealthy businessmen and land barons. Their wives celebrated their newfound success with splendid, costly, ostentatious wardrobes. What did they buy now that they had the means? The same satins and silks their tainted sisters had long been chalking off as a legitimate business expense. The only difference was that wives kept their necklines high and their corsets covered.

This was the heyday of gambler Poker Alice and lady bandit Belle Starr, "the female Robin Hood." There was "Cattle Kate" Watson, who was hanged from a cottonwood tree for rustling cattle, and Oklahoma's most desperate woman, "Rose of the Cimarron." There was Pearl Hart, the last lady road agent. But that swaggering female in boots, britches, flannel shirt, and gun belt who'd barge into bars and announce in a throaty roar, "By Gawd, set up the house!" was none other than Calamity Jane.

Calamity Jane

Vivid, colorful stories paint Calamity Jane as a legend, even in her own time. Yet history can be color-blind when it comes to an accurate picture of the heroes and heroines of the wild and woolly American West. Jane's is tinted in shades of gray. Her real story became clouded with the passage of time, wrapped up in contradictions; and although it survives to this day, the legend of Calamity Jane has more holes in it than a slice of Alpine Swiss cheese. Some western historians even contend that her autobiography fails to tell a single truth. Well, maybe that's the beauty about legends. They can lie and get away with it—as long as they remain larger than life to us mortals.

Even if one-tenth of her story is true, Calamity Jane was nothing short of extraordinary. Born Marthy Jane Cannary on May 1, 1852, in Princeton, Missouri, even the date of her birth is sketchy. Jane maintained, at various times, that she was born in 1848, not 1852; a United States census records the year of her birth as 1846; and one legend has her born during an Indian raid at Fort Laramie in 1860, where her parents were scalped and died. The *Cheyenne Sun* carried this episode further, reporting that shortly thereafter Jane was adopted by a Major and Mrs. Gallagher of Minder's Delight, Wyoming, in 1867.

Although these accounts are ambiguous, her reputation as a hellion is indisputable. At seventeen, Jane Cannary was described by those who purported to know her as "a young stray with the spirit of original sin" who "swears like a trooper, drinks like a sailor, and roughs it with the roughest," and was as "wild as a lynx's kitten." By her twenties, she had "raised enough deviltry to have deserved a dozen hangings." That she was capable of putting an entire town "on its ear by her escapades" was true throughout her life. Cattle rustlers, gamblers, miners, and drifters adored her; sober, upstanding folk shunned her. The staid *Deadwood Daily Champion* condemned her: "As for her [Calamity Jane] she is a fraud and a dead give away. A hundred waiter girls or mop squeezers in this gulch are her superior in everything. She strikes out and lays around with a lot of bull whackers or road agents like an Indian squaw.

Her riotous behavior did not stand in the way of her love of the outdoors—particularly hunting, shooting, and riding. In her own words, ". . . the greater portion of my time was spent in hunting along with men and hunters. . . . I was considered a remarkable good shot and a fearless rider." Numerous firsthand observers swore she could outshoot any man and was capable of "the finest demonstration of firearms" ever witnessed. She flourished a pair of revolvers or shouldered a Winchester as easily as most women twirled a parasol—something that absolutely did not interest Jane.

She was described as tall, with red hair and hazel eyes, and a body as lean and hard as a young boy's. She was not pretty and her face became prematurely haggard from hard living, the elements, and an overabundance of alcohol. She worked as a miner, cattle driver, and entertainer, including a stint in Buffalo Bill's Wild West shows. But her real career, according to her own reports, was as a scout.

Jane dispensed with womanly attire to don a solder's uniform ("a bit awkward at first but I soon got to be perfectly at home in men's clothes") and for five years, between 1871 and 1876, served as a scout and messenger during the Indian campaigns for General George Armstrong Custer. "I was considered the most reckless and daring rider and one of the best shots in the western country," she boasted. One day she became severely ill after swimming the freezing waters of the Platte River on a mission carrying important dispatches for Custer. Jane was hospitalized at Fort Fetterman where she remained fourteen days, her dispatches undelivered. They never would reach Custer; while Jane was delirious with fever, Custer led his ill-fated troops to a place called Little Big Horn.

After her recovery, Jane became a Pony Express rider and carried the mail over rough trails that skirted the Black Hills. It was then that she met James Butler "Wild Bill" Hickok, "Prince of the Pistoleers," lawman, and killer—and one of the greatest romances in the lore of the West supposedly began. Years later Jane admitted to being Hickok's wife and that he fathered her only child, a daughter. Historians remain skeptical, despite a number of letters by Jane to her daughter, and her deathbed confession witnessed by three people. What is conceded as fact is that Calamity Jane cornered Jack McCall, Wild Bill's assassin, with a meat cleaver moments after McCall gunned Bill down. Hickok was playing poker in a saloon, the only time he was known to sit with his back to the door. He held a pair of eights and a pair of aces—to this day known as the Deadman's Hand. Jane mourned the loss of her lover until she died on August 2, 1903—twenty-seven years to the day after

Hickok's death. Her last wish was to be laid to rest next to Wild Bill in Mt. Moriah Cemetery. Her wish was granted.

The generous and kindly side of Calamity Jane is seldom acknowledged. Skeptics maintain that, like everything about her, these stories are cut from whole cloth, too. Here's one worth believing—whether true or not—if only because it embraces the best of the West, and tells of hard times and hard people with soft hearts:

In 1878 a smallpox epidemic raged through Deadwood. The sick and dying were isolated in a pesthouse on a slope built high above the town. There was only one doctor and no one willing to nurse the sick or bury the dead. One day the doctor looked up from his ministrations and there stood Calamity Jane, hands on her hips, grinning. "You just tell me what to do, Doc, and I'll do it." Jane worked day and night, hoisting water up the hill, nursing the victims, and going into town for groceries and supplies. On her first trip into town, the proprietor of a store tallied her purchases and said they came to two ounces of gold dust. Jane drew her six-shooter and snarled, "Don't worry about your damn bill. I'll pay for it when the boys get better." She backed out of the store, groceries in one hand, revolver in the other. She was as good as the gold she later used to repay the debt.

Another story tells how one night, after the Deadwood epidemic had subsided, Jane reeled into a saloon and announced, "Boys, there's a man back up there (in the pesthouse) who has a wife and family back east. He has no dust. Untie your weasel skins and turn out enough dust to take him back where he belongs." As one observer reported, "The dust came liberally."

These incidents are only a couple of many selfless acts of generosity that earned Jane the devotion of the pioneer population of the West. Everywhere she went she adopted the underdog and looked out for those who were hard-up, satisfied with the barest of essentials for herself. Jane adopted a particular patient during the epidemic, a little boy. She'd cuddle the motherless child, "giving him the love that a lonely boy needs," and nursed him back to health. Her rough manner could not hide her heart of gold: "Here, you little bastard," she'd say, "drink this soup" and "Damn you, sit still while I wash your face"—a pretty contradiction of sentiments.

So when Calamity Jane died, Deadwood honored their formidable daughter with one of the largest funerals in the town's history. The eulogy was, according to one mourner, "one of the finest orations I ever heard." The Methodist minister officiating "spoke with a fervor greater than I have ever heard him use before," according to another. Her casket was sealed by the rector of the cemetery, C. H. Robinson.

Robinson was that little boy Calamity had saved twenty-five years earlier during Deadwood's smallpox epidemic.

Robinson wept. So did all of Deadwood.

Indeed, those who went West with dreams of wealth and glory happily settled for a clapboard house with a wraparound front porch. A few got marble ones wrapped around their mansions. Tycoons who made fortunes—from mines, railroads, cattle, land, or dry goods—invariably had clever wives who knew exactly how to spend them. Inspired by the grandeur of European palaces, palatial houses sprung up on and between both coasts, from Newport, Rhode Island, to Nob Hill in San Francisco, opulently decorated with the best that money could buy. *He who's got it flaunts it,* and flaunt it they did. It was during the 1880s that special orders for engraved, nickel-plated revolvers with fancy grips, and engraved, gold-plated rifles with fancy wood stocks flooded Colt, Winchester, Marlin, Smith & Wesson, Parker, and other firearms manufacturers. These were often given as gifts. More often, they were carried by men . . . and women such as Molly Brown, "The Gold Queen of Colorado."

Molly, the ostentatious miner's wife who with her husband, "Leadville Johnny" Brown, struck it rich just south of Central City, in Leadville, Colorado, dressed in the finest, most flamboyant clothes. "Demure" and "modest" were words not in her vocabulary. Molly would have agreed with Mark Twain when he said, "Virtue has never been as respectable as money." When Johnny and Molly later settled in Denver, they built a fancy house, decorated it with clunky gold-gilt furniture and feather boas, and lived to the hilt. She later cinched her reputation as one of the heroines of the ill-fated *Titanic* by instructing everyone in her lifeboat to huddle together for warmth and to row away from the sinking queen of the seas until they finally found safety in a squalid but seaworthy handmaiden, the *Carpathian.*

One story that's not quite attached to Molly but happened in her day is about two women who discovered they were engaged to the same man. Their heated argument resulted in the only female gunfight written into the chronicles of the Old West. A huge crowd gathered, and right out in front to watch the outcome was the lover of both women. The women drew their pocket pistols, paced, turned, and fired: both shooting, by sheer accident, their beloved. He was only scratched by the bullets. Both women publicly forswore their lover, the duel was declared supremely fair, and neither had anything to do with the guy ever again.

*   *   *

As the sport of target shooting evolved into America's first national pastime, much was made of organized tournaments and shooting exhibitions. Elizabeth Servaty "Plinky" Topperwein and her husband, Adolph, were a husband-and-wife exhibition shooting team unmatched in the annals of precision shooting. They met at the Winchester Repeating Arms plant in New Haven, Connecticut, where they were both employed—she in the ammunition loading room, he as an exhibition shooter. They married in 1903.

Ernie Pyle, the famous World War II correspondent and a great friend of the Topperweins, wrote of "Plinky": "Things were pretty tough for her at first. She either had to stay home or else go on those exhibition trips and just twiddle her thumbs. She didn't like it. So she made Ad teach her to shoot. It wasn't long before she was as good a shot as her husband. And then Winchester hired her, too (for exhibition shooting). For twenty-nine years the world's greatest shooting couple traveled the North American continent together. But always, the home they came back to betweentimes was San Antonio. They called her 'Plinky' because when she was first learning to shoot, she'd keep saying, 'Throw up another one and I'll plink it.'"

At the 1904 World's Fair in St. Louis, she broke 967 clays out of 1,000 at trap shooting. Pyle continues:

"As for Plinky, her trapshooting record in 1907 of 1,952 hits out of 2,000 targets was a world's record for anyone, man or woman. She shot for a total time of five hours, using a pump gun. It raised such a blister that a few days later the skin came off the whole palm of her hand."

She and her husband traveled together until their retirement in 1940, after a thirty-six-year career.

No book on American women and shooting is complete without acknowledging the greatest sharpshooter of all time, man or woman: and that's Annie Oakley, nicknamed "Little Sure Shot" by her friend, mentor, and employer, Buffalo Bill Cody, whose Wild West Show she starred in for over sixteen years. Much has been written about this little lady, who stood only five feet tall. Born Phoebe Ann Moses in Darke County, Ohio, little "Annie" learned to shoot at the age of eight by killing wild game for a hotel in Cincinnati in order to earn money to help her family get by. When she was fifteen, she defeated Frank Butler, a professional marksman, at a shooting exhibition; he ultimately won her hand in marriage. Butler became her manager and she adopted the stage name of Annie Oakley. The rest is pretty much history.

Some of her feats included shooting a dime out of Frank's hand, or putting a bullet smack in the middle of a playing card thrown into the air ninety feet away. Her most famous deed was to shoot a cigarette out of the mouth of German Crown Prince Wilhelm during one of her successful European tours. During World War I, Annie taught firearms instruction to American soldiers. Unlike the stage and movie portrayal of her in *Annie Get Your Gun,* Annie was a quiet woman who enjoyed doing needlepoint in her spare time. She died in 1926, at the age of sixty-six.

C h a p t e r 2

▬

Proper Handling of Firearms and Shooting Safety

*A thorough understanding of firearms safety
and the operation of your gun is the first
step in becoming a responsible
shooting sportswoman.*

The first step in the shooting sports is to learn these rules so well that they become second nature to you:

1. *Always control the muzzle of your firearm.* Whether your gun is loaded or unloaded, be aware of where you are pointing it at all times. When you are not shooting, keep the action open and your finger off the trigger. Be sure everyone in your group does the same.

2. Under no circumstances should you point the muzzle of your gun at anything other than your intended target. Never, even in jest, point a gun at a person. That's just common sense.

3. Never place your finger on the trigger until you intend to shoot. Don't use your gunstock as a resting place for your hand. The only time your finger should be on the trigger is when you are ready to fire.

4. Whenever you handle a gun, check that the action is unloaded and there are no cartridges in the chamber. Keep your action "broken," or open, until you are ready to take your position. *Then* load, aim, and fire. Condition yourself to do this until it becomes automatic.

5. Never rest the butt of your gun on the ground or on your foot, or with the muzzle resting on your foot. Don't lose your head—or a foot—because you assumed your gun was unloaded. You can't take a bullet back once it's been fired.

6. Always treat your firearm as if it were loaded.

Know your gun. These safe practices must always be observed:

1. You should allow yourself all the time in the world to familiarize yourself with your gun. Understand its basic operation, talk to your gunsmith and other shooters. Practice firing your gun frequently at a range or another safe, appropriate, legal place. Get used to its feel and fit. Read and reread the operating and safety instructions. Obtain books to learn about your used or older gun, and consult a gunsmith on the safety of older guns before you fire them, especially if they haven't been used for a long time.

2. Never force ammunition into your chamber or mix cartridge sizes, such as by loading 12- and 16-gauge shells into a 12-gauge shotgun. Use only ammunition that matches the caliber of your gun (if in doubt, you'll find the caliber engraved on the barrel and/or the action of the gun.) You will invite damage and danger if you use anything else. Loading ammunition that is not the correct size can bulge or rupture your barrel, irreparably ruining your gun. Worse yet, you can irreparably injure *yourself.* Even in storage, do not mix up different gauge shells or caliber bullets. A good safeguard is to keep same-size ammunition in separate shell bags, cases, or boxes.

3. If a cartridge misfires, wait 30 seconds and manually extract it from the gun. If a barrel is obstructed with mud and snow, manually clear (never shoot) the obstruction, *first making sure the gun and chamber are completely unloaded.* This happens when you are hunting, especially in the deep woods, where you are apt to slip and fall.

4. Keep your gun broken open and unloaded until you are ready to take position to shoot. This is important when you are covering uneven ground in the woods and fields, climbing over stone fences or other obstructions, or hiking over rocky, marshy, or snow-covered ground. *Unload your gun until you regain steady footing.* Always remember, a loaded gun can fire whether or not you want it to. There are many accidents on record of people whose guns have discharged as a result of a fall—some were fatal.

Practice caution in the field, forest, and range:

1. Never shoot unless you are *absolutely certain* of your target. Shots taken at a distance allow time and concentration for careful aim and for a clean and effective kill. Upland bird and waterfowl shooting, however, is fast shooting based on instinct, ability, and experience. You should be as sure of your shot in the fleeting seconds you have to point your gun at an upland bird that's just exploded from a cornfield as you would be scrutinizing a white-tail through a scope to determine a shoulder shot. Don't let the time factor rush you. Take the time you need. You'll be surprised how long those extra few seconds can seem. They ultimately cost nothing—and buy you safe and secure shooting. Again, once you pull the trigger, you can't take a bullet back.

2. Be sure you have clear, unimpeded access to your target, and be *absolutely* certain that no person, dog, or object other than your target is in range or beyond your shooting area. This is especially important, and for that reason you should be aware at all times of where your hunting partner is. If you cannot see each other, work out a voice or whistle call that keeps you each cognizant of where the other is at all times. Never hunt out alone. Always take a companion.

3. If you are at a target range and a vehicle or person enters the field, cease fire altogether until the field is clear once again. The

range manager supervises the field, but that doesn't mean you don't have a responsibility to yourself and others to keep a constant eye out too.

4. Safeties can be unsafe. *Under no circumstances* carry a loaded and cocked gun. A loaded gun on safety can misfire. There are casualties to prove it. A safety is merely a mechanical device, and no mechanical device is foolproof (only a fool would assume otherwise).

Ensure your personal safety:

1. Wear field glasses whenever you shoot to protect your eyes from low-hanging branches, debris, and gases that emanate from spent cartridges.

2. Wear ear protectors. This helps prevent damage to your hearing as a result of gunfire, especially in target shooting or driven birds, when shooting is rapid and frequent.

3. If you are on medication that makes you drowsy or impairs or slows down your faculties, do not go shooting. Drugs and firearms don't mix. Needless to say, neither do drinking and firearms: *Under no circumstances go shooting if you have been drinking alcoholic beverages.*

4. Dress appropriately. During fall and winter hunting season, sturdy, well-fitting outdoor clothing is important to keep you warm and dry against the cold and inclement weather. In warm weather, wear clothing that allows perspiration to wick away from the body, such as 100 percent cotton. Wear waterproof or water-resistant clothing in inclement weather. Comfortable outdoor footwear is a must.

   Blaze orange is mandatory in most but not all states. Your personal law should be *always* to wear at least one garment of blaze orange. It instantly identifies you to other hunters and shooters. Deer are pretty much color-blind and can't see blaze orange anyway. Turkey, on the other hand, can. If you must be dressed in camouflage, at least tie a band of blaze orange around the tree or blind you are in so that other hunters are aware you are there. Hunters have been mistaken for game—with tragic results.

5. Wear a hat and carry sunscreen lotion and insect repellent with you at all times. If you are out for the day and not in easy access of amenities, be prepared with a full survival kit.

Basic Field Survival Kit

These are the components of a basic survival kit. As you become more experienced, you will find that you'll add things that suit your personal needs. However, the following items are all important to have on hand, so be prepared:

1. A good pocket knife

2. A reliable compass

3. A plastic whistle (in cold weather, a metal whistle can freeze right onto your lip!)

4. Matches in a waterproof container

5. Another fire-making device, such as a butane lighter

6. A fire starter, such as fine steel wool, candles, or paraffin-coated cord

7. Soap (antibacterial)

8. Water purification tablets (obtainable at any drugstore)

9. Medication if you need it

10. First aid kit

11. Drinking container, such as a collapsible cup

12. Nylon cord or rope

13. An extra pair of glasses if you need corrective lenses

14. Sunglasses or shooting glasses, shatterproof

15. Hearing protection

16. A space blanket

17. A large, heavy-duty plastic garbage bag, which serves well as an emergency rain poncho or ground cover

18. Instant energy food like beef jerky, chocolate bars (if you are hunting with a dog be sure that it does not get at the chocolate—dogs have a reaction to chocolate that can be fatal), freeze-dried hikers' meals, etc. Military rations packs from army surplus stores are handy; in one compact plastic bag is everything you need for a surprisingly tasty and filling supper.

19. Sanitary napkins—not only for the obvious reason, but also to use as dressings for large wounds in an emergency.

A note about medical emergencies: Before you go hunting, be sure you know the location of the nearest ranger station or another place you can get help. A lot of hunters suffer broken bones, cuts, scrapes, and bruises, especially if they are unprepared to go into the woods. More serious are hypothermia as a result of sudden adverse weather or exposure, shock from a severe injury, and unconsciousness due to a fall. Learn the warning signs of hypothermia and stay dry and as free of perspiration as possible. If you are planning to do some serious hunting, enroll in a first aid course.

Field Etiquette

Good manners are the rule, not the exception. I read in a British magazine about a woman who attended a public bird shoot and flew into a rage when a gentleman shooter mistook her for a tea lady and asked her for a cup of coffee. "Miscreant pig!" she stormed—and of course that soured the whole day for everyone. Perhaps if she hadn't been dressed like a tea lady this outrage wouldn't have happened. This person—woman or not—should have nicely but firmly been invited off the field. Face it, the first impression anyone gets of you is based on the way you look, and we'll discuss this in Chapter 3. But the second and by far more important impression you make is by how you behave. And when your sports equipment is a gun, good manners and field etiquette are not only desirable, they are mandatory—no exceptions.

1. In the shooting sports, your equipment is a loaded gun. Whether cool or hot, any degree of temper has no place on the field, in the forest, or at the club. Stand clear of anyone who does not observe good field etiquette. Emotional circumstances could compromise others, and the offender should be invited off the field or dismissed from the hunting or shooting party.

2. Understand the *safe zones of fire* before going onto the field or range. Know exactly where your companions will be hunting or shooting in relation to your position. This should be discussed before going into the field, forest, range, or course.

3. Never, under any circumstances, shoot across another shooter. This is especially true in wingshooting and sporting clays events such as Flushes & Flurries, where multiple clays are thrown over a team of shooters. Keep a mental picture at all times of where your teammates or partners are standing.

4. Tragic accidents occur every year when hunters mistake a movement in the woods and shoot a fellow hunter instead of their intended quarry. Whether big game, upland bird, or waterfowl, be absolutely certain of your target. Discuss and plan a drive *before* entering the woods. Know where the other members of your party are starting, traveling, and ending up. Agree on a rendezvous place and time.

5. Do not release your gun's safety until you have mounted your gun. It cannot be stressed enough: *Do not assume that a safety will keep a loaded gun from firing.* A safety is merely a mechanical device and like all things mechanical, subject to breakage or failure.

6. If you are hunting with field dogs, watch where they are ranging or pointing and do not fire if they are in the path of traveling or flying game. Remember, birdshot spreads. Do not shoot over another hunter's dog without the consent of the dog's owner.

Again, the Golden Rule of Shooting is: *Always handle yourself and your gun properly and thoughtfully, alone or with others. Be a responsible outdoorswoman.*

How Do You Shoot with a Man?
(Or Anyone Else, for That Matter?)

How do you shoot with a man? By being sensitive to the responsibilities inherent to a sport where the equipment is a loaded firearm. You don't have to read Emily Post to know it takes more than good manners to be accepted on the sporting field. Those who ignore field etiquette have no right calling themselves sportsmen—or sportswomen. First and foremost, always be aware of where you are pointing the muzzle of your gun. "It's okay, the gun's unloaded" just isn't acceptable. Keep your action open and unloaded until you're ready to shoot. Honor safe gun-handling positions

Know where your shooting partner or companions are at all times. Never take a shot if you are unsure of what's beyond it. Some bullets can travel, unimpeded, for over five miles, so no distance is truly safe. Shoot only in your line or area of fire, and sacrifice your shot if it infringes on your partner's range of field. If you are in danger of swinging your gun too wide, or your partner is too near, surrender the shot. It's not worth the risk. Should someone fire a shot that you believe was too close or even dangerous to you or others, walk off the field. Report the shooter to the master of the

Gun Safety at Home

An integral part of owning a gun is being responsible for it when it's not in use. This means storing it in a safe and secure place in your home: safe from burglars, safe from those who are unfamiliar with guns, and most important, safe from children who are too young to know better. When you are not home, you want to be certain that your home is as burglar-resistant as possible. If you have a number of guns, a burglar alarm system hooked up to your local police department is a safe and practical measure.

Most people don't have gun rooms. However, that doesn't mean shoot or the range manager. You can't call back a bullet or birdshot once a gun is fired.

Pick up your spent cartridge cases; do not leave them on the ground, especially if you are hunting on private property. About private property: seek written permission from the owner of the land on which you wish to shoot. This is simple courtesy, not a written law, but it surely should be observed. Never yell or talk loudly on the field or at the range. You will distract others who are preparing to shoot and can put them off their mark. If someone's behavior is unsportsmanlike, do not confront or criticize. Again, simply walk off the field. Use courtesy and good sense. You are entering a respectable sport. Respect your companion, your gun, the habitat, and the game.

Charles Dickens wrote, "What is the odds so long as the fire of soul is kindled at the taper of conwiviality, and the wing of friendship never moults a feather!" A good sportsman or sportswoman is a pleasant person to be around. And when you're with a man you're close to, it can be so much more. You've good times ahead that may bring you closer together. You may discover things you never knew about each other—or yourself. Whether the man you shoot with is your husband, lover, friend, father, or son, cherish your days afield together. They make golden memories.

Conwiviality. Yep, that's what it's all about.

you shouldn't have a proper place set aside for the safe storage of guns. The best bet is to buy a gun safe. Gun safes are sold at sporting goods stores and many large chain stores carry them, too. You can get just about anything you want in any size, color, style, and price—the heavier the better. A fire-resistant gun safe gives you some added security.

Your guns should not be stored on the first floor of your home for obvious reasons. The basement, or a room on the second floor, is more practical against burglary. When you put your gun away, be sure you have wiped it down with a soft cloth and solvent to keep it free from rust. Check your guns regularly. In humid climates, even guns in safes are not protected from rust. Specialty gun supply companies carry rods that wick moisture from the inside of gun safes, preventing rust.

Gun safes are available from many
manufacturers, in many sizes, and in a wide
price range. This is your best home security for
firearms. Pictured here is the Winchester
Legend gun safe.

(PHOTO COURTESY OF WINCHESTER)

Insure your valuable guns. Sometimes your homeowner's insurance will not cover guns. In that case, you can get affordable insurance coverage from other carriers. Ask your local gun club, gun dealer, or the NRA for further information.

Respect these rules:

1. Never store a loaded gun. A gun must always be stored empty, with no bullets in the chamber or magazine. A gun that's loaded, even with the safety on, is *not* safe.

2. Store ammunition separately from your guns in a locked place such as a footlocker with a padlock, a file cabinet that locks, or a desk drawer that locks.

3. Invest in a gun vault. Although inexpensive vaults are available on the market, a really solid, fireproof vault is a sound investment—and will afford you some peace of mind. Your local sporting goods store generally carries, or can order, reliable gun vaults.

4. If you cannot afford the space or expense of a gun vault, a closet that locks securely is a far second, but nonetheless viable, alternative.

5. Never leave a gun under a bed, on top of a refrigerator, or in any conspicuous place.

6. Be aware of state and federal laws regarding possession of firearms—especially handguns, which require specific permits.

Children and Gun Safety

Teaching children how to use a gun is something that should be done with a great deal of thoughtfulness after a fair appraisal of the level of the child's natural curiosity and, most important, his or her ability to deal maturely with the concept of firearms. Under no circumstances should a young child be allowed to handle a gun. An older child should be introduced to firearms gradually, and always under the direct supervision of an adult firearms operator. Not until a child is well into the teenage years and past a certain level of capability and performance should he or she be allowed to handle a gun without an adult right at his or her elbow. Even then, an adult should be aware when the teenager is handling a gun, and be close at hand to supervise and lend guidance.

Never give in to the argument that a teenager is old enough to handle a gun. A teenager has to *earn the right* to handle a gun. If you are not qualified to teach your youngster gun safety, enroll him—and yourself—in a gun safety course. Go together to the local shooting range *on a regular basis,* not just once or twice, and practice under the supervision of the professional instructor there. Enroll your child in an NRA-affiliate course. Contact your state instructor of the Women's Shooting Sports Foundation (see the Directory in the back of the book) and ask her for the name of a qualified instructor in your area. Another way is to enroll your teenager in a hunter's education course. Your child can earn a hunter's safety card before the age of sixteen, at the discretion of the instructor, but cannot apply for a hunting license until he or she has reached the age of sixteen. These courses are conducted through many fish and game clubs, at public ranges, through local police departments, and at private clubs. Contact your local fish and game department, which will be able to put you in touch with the right people. Just as your child is legally obliged to take a driver's education course before he or she can drive a car, you are morally obliged to see your child gets proper training in firearms before he or she handles a gun.

There's no point sweeping it under the carpet: People have lost children to gun-related accidents. Losing a child, under any circumstance, is the worst tragedy a mother or father can know. When a child dies through carelessness, the lifelong burden of loss and recrimination must be almost too heavy to carry. But in all cases these accidents would *never* have happened if guns and ammunition had been kept securely under separate lock and key.

If you learn nothing else from this book, remember this and this only:

- A gun is to shooting sports as a bat is to baseball, a racket to tennis, a club to golf.
  A gun is also a weapon.

- A gun discharges a projectile that comes in contact with your target, be it a clay pigeon or wild game.
  It discharges a projectile that cannot differentiate between a target and a human.

- The bullet or shot will smash a clay or effect a clean kill on game.
  A bullet or shot can effect a clean kill on a human.

Guns do not kill people. People, for whatever reasons, kill people. A gun is outdoor sports equipment, like a racket, a golf club, or a baseball bat. Unlike these, however, it discharges a bit of lead. Don't be afraid of guns; *just be cautious to the extreme.* Never handle firearms quickly or without your full attention. And unless a child is under controlled circumstances directly related to a shooting sport, no gun, for any reason whatsoever, should be in that child's hands.

Parents who have nurtured their children in the shooting sports have instilled in them a sense of confidence. In turn, they've added to the foundation of their family by spending time together in a shared sport. Shooting sports help develop a child's sense of self and responsibility. That's the greatest gift a parent can give a child.

Like many things in life, owning firearms is an all-or-nothing deal. Whether or not all members of the family participate in shooting sports is up to the individual. However, if there are guns in the home, it is the responsibility of adults and older children who handle them to fully understand how they work and to keep them stored in a childproof place and unloaded when not in use. Otherwise, you either remove firearms from your household and make the decision not to enter the shooting sports as an individual or a family, or you embrace the sport, knowing that there's gratification ahead and a common thread that will bind your family in a satisfying sport. There's no gray area. There's no in-between.

Outdoorwear for Women

Comfortable, practical, even fashionable women's outdoor clothing is an investment that will greatly contribute to years of enjoyment in the out-of-doors.

An outdoorswoman needs to depend upon her clothes. Outfit yourself with quality, long-wearing attire that is well designed and made to last. There's more women-specific hunting and shooting clothing available on the market today than ever before. Here's what to look for.

The shooting sports can be a year-round activity, depending upon what and where you are shooting. The nonhunting shooting sports—sporting clays, trap, skeet, and benchrest and precision rifle shooting—can be done in all seasons. In the hunting sports, preserve shooting in most states takes a hiatus during the summer months, usually May through August. Autumn, of course, is hunting season, and some game, such as turkey, have two seasons: fall and spring.

Clothing should work *for* you and *protect* you, no matter what time of year. Here's the rule of thumb: *Dress in layers.* Layers provide the best protection, optimum warmth, and allow you to take something off when you get too warm.

Underclothes

In hot weather, a light layer of underwear helps wick perspiration and keeps you cool. In cold weather, a heavier layer will keep you warm. It's insulation, on the same premise as insulating a house. Underwear comes in many fabrics and styles designed for certain temperatures and conditions. Natural fibers, such as silk, cotton, and wool, kept your great-grandmother warm and dry and they'll do the same for you. Modern synthetics have come a long way, however, and you'll want to look at thermal garments from fibers described with such words as *polypropylene, hydrophilic, moisture-wicking, fleece,* and *rib-knit.* Although prices vary depending on what you buy, good underwear generally is affordable—and an important investment.

A number of manufacturers offer women's-sized crewneck thermal tops and bottoms in light, medium, and expedition weights to suit your needs. Glove liners, sock liners, and balaclava hoods are available in many of the same fabrics. Unisex small, medium, and large sizes work just as well for men as they do for women.

What to Wear from the Waist Down

Women complain that men's outdoor clothing just doesn't fit them. This should not be a surprise to most men who, as we all know, are keenly aware of the structural differences between the sexes.

Before 1990, a few top-drawer outdoor companies tried seriously to market women's hunting clothing, but failed. There weren't enough buyers to meet the minimums manufacturers required, and retailers were stuck with lots of items that simply did not sell. Well, times are changing. The number of women who hunt has exploded during the

1990s, and although some suppliers are still feeling a little singed from their initial foray, many more have decided to "give it a shot" once again.

Today you will find an increasingly wide range of women's field pants available in many styles and fabrics, such as thorn-proof cloth, wool, cotton duck, chino, nylon, fleece, and neoprene. There are women's-sized classic British Harris tweed shooting pants, camouflage hunting pants and overalls for turkey and duck hunting, blaze orange quilted pants for deer hunting, and khakis for upland bird shooting.

Take a look at the Directory in the back of the book and you'll find a number of companies that are presently selling clothing designed specifically for women hunters and shooters. In fact, you'll find a few companies owned and operated by women who have launched their own lines. As the women's market positions itself, don't rule out men's clothing. Some items made for men—like sweatshirts, gloves, hats, socks, most shirts, thermal undershirts, hunting vests, and even jackets in men's sizes extra small, small, and medium—really do suit women just fine. Granted, man-tailored shirts can be problematic for women (too wide at the shoulders, too long in the sleeve and tail, and too tight where it counts), but by and large you'll be delighted to see that men's outdoor clothing can be adapted to fit us, too. The message here is: Don't attach a stigma to sex when it comes to what you wear. Whether it's made for women or for men, the deciding factor should be the same as for anything you look to buy: Does it fit, is it well made, and will it serve you well in the field or forest or at the range?

For that reason, always try on hunting gear. Bend, stoop, get down on your hands and knees—make sure there's plenty of give in the knees, seat, and waist. Check that seams are double-stitched and strong; make sure your garment has good zippers and buttons, and that there are plenty of pockets that close with buttons or Velcro. Unlike your Sunday best, you're going to put your hunting apparel through its paces, and you had better be comfortable, or you'll certainly be miserable.

If you can afford to buy only one good pair of hunting pants, look for something that's three-season, like a pair of lightweight worsted wools. The lanolin in wool is naturally water-repellent and will keep you dry; add thermal underwear when you need additional warmth. Nicely tailored wool pants can be dressed up or down and look elegant. Wool breathes, dries quickly, and when taken care of, lasts a long time. A tightly woven worsted does not pick up burrs readily. You can brush off tall grass and dry mud, and you won't get drenched even in heavy rain.

You *can* hand-wash wool pants, but it's wiser to dry-clean; dry cleaning retains the construction of the garment, preserves the lanolin in the fiber, prevents shrinkage, and ensures that you'll be wearing your clothes for a long time.

If you have a wool allergy or simply do not like to wear wool, another excellent choice is thorn-proof pants made of good, sturdy cloth. You can protect yourself against extreme cold by wearing alpine-rated thermal underwear. Make sure your thermal underwear doesn't make the fit of your thorn-proof pants too tight. If so, you may want to allow an extra size (you don't have to tell anyone). Chinos are a great warm-weather fabric, and 100 percent cotton tends to dry fairly quickly.

Many of us prefer to go hunting in jeans. Jeans are briar-resistant, and if well worn are almost like a second skin. They're a good choice in informal situations *except* in wet conditions. Cotton denim is a heavily constructed fabric that, if saturated, takes a long time to dry. Wet jeans will chafe; jeans also can chafe when you're hunting or packing on horseback. For that reason, a pair of tights underneath is a wise addition. If you plan to be out all day, carry along an extra pair of jeans, just in case, or bring along a pair of waterproof chaps, which gives you the best of both worlds. For extreme cold, try flannel-lined jeans, or wear your thermal underwear for additional warmth.

What to Wear on Top

Again, layering is the key. In cold weather, start with a thermal top. Over that, choose a turtleneck, crewneck, or V-neck knit shirt in cotton, silk, or synthetic. Over that, consider a flannel shirt. Over that you could put on a wool sweater that's not too bulky. And over that, a tweed Norfolk jacket, a waterproof field jacket, an Australian outback coat, or a loden or lumberjack wool hunting coat tops it all off.

You can wear a men's soft brushed flannel shirt over a T-shirt or turtleneck, and leave the top three buttons unbuttoned. It's another form of layering, and it works. Beware of women's fashion shirts, however. Many are so snug and tailored that they don't leave enough bias to allow the arm movement you'll need to swing your gun.

Other choices are pullover shirts, sweaters, and sweatshirts. Although nothing beats a sweatshirt a couple of sizes too big to cuddle into on a cold winter's night, when you mount a gun, you can't have a lot of cloth bunching up around your shoulders. Ultimately you'll discover from experience what suits you best.

A shooting vest has a quilted shoulder pad
that cushions the shoulder against recoil.
(PHOTO COURTESY OF DUNN'S INC.)

A shooting vest can be worn over a cotton shirt in fair weather, with a sweater on chilly days, and has the value of a quilted outside shoulder pad that helps cushion your shoulder against unpleasant recoil. A vest can be worn under a roomy jacket and serves as an additional layer to ensure warmth. It also provides extra pockets for cartridges and small gear.

Selecting a field jacket is the biggest decision you'll have to make because it is the most expensive one. There are many styles of hunting coats available. including quilted jackets in blaze orange or camouflage made of Thinsulate and other weather-beating fabrics. Traditional, English-style waterproof coats are all-purpose and dependable gear, providing three-season outerwear that can be layered underneath for

English-style waterproof coats accommodate
layers of clothing in cold weather.
(PHOTO COURTESY OF DUNN'S INC.)

cold. Lumberjack or old-fashioned boiled wool coats are classics that
provide terrific warmth and dryness. The selection on the market is
pretty vast, so see what suits you.

My personal preference is somewhat unorthodox, but has served
me well, and that's a three-quarter-length Australian outback waterproof coat. It has a thin wool lining, and in really cold weather I wear it
with a sweater, shirt, turtleneck, and thermal undergarments. What I
like best about my coat is that it keeps wind and rain out; I can hunker
down and bundle up in it when I'm sitting for a long time in the cold;
and I can strap the coat around my calves when I'm traipsing about or
riding a horse. It never stays wet for long, and it moves with me. It has
no buttons, just very solid snaps; the pockets are deep; it has a cape
around the shoulders to block out torrential rain, and a good collar. The
one drawback is that these coats are brown, which is not the best color
to wear in the woods during hunting season. Therefore, you must wear
a lot of blaze orange—a shell vest, hunting hat, gloves—so you don't

look like a deer. Like all waterproofs, the coat should be rewaterproofed at the end of each season with special dressing. You can send your waterproof out to be reconditioned professionally, or do it yourself at home with special kits available through any dealer that sells waterproof outerwear. If taken care of, these coats can last a lifetime. Topped off with a matching wide-brim waterproof hat, I can go anywhere. You can, too.

If you don't like a lot of bulk, however, and prefer something trimmer, a waist-length jacket is fine, especially in fair, mild weather. Again, be certain there's plenty of give at the shoulder and that the jacket is well constructed and lined, with deep pockets and a solid zipper or strong buttons. Too bulky a jacket will hamper you when you shoulder your gun. As with pants, when you try on a hunting jacket, bend, twist, throw your arms out and up to make sure you've got plenty of room. Comfort and practicality are your primary concerns.

Once again, do not rule out men's jackets. Generally speaking, the styles you'll find in women's jackets are man-tailored styles that are sized to fit women. There are some spectacular hunting jackets on the market in men's XS, S, M, L, XL. A man's XS hunting jacket will generally fit a woman who wears size 6 to 8, and a men's Small will fit a woman who wears size 10 to 12. Again, don't be obstinate and overlook a good jacket by being a stickler for women-specific clothing. As you explore the burgeoning outdoorswomen's market, you're bound to find some great-looking, great-fitting jackets.

Hunting Footwear

Outdoor footwear comes in numerous styles and prices. Besides British-style rubber boots (called Wellingtons), you'll find traditional all-leather boots, part-leather boots, Gore-Tex boots, neoprene boots, and more. You should consider no boot that is not waterproof, however. Women's shoe sizes *do* differ from men's. Men's feet are generally wider than women's and for that reason alone you'll want to first consider outdoor footwear made especially for women. Having said that, I wear a men's size 6 upland rubber boot by Kaufman/Sorel of Canada with great comfort and easy mobility. Always allow ample room for thick socks, even if a boot is lined, as many are. Linings include wool, leather, Thinsulate, and others that factor warmth into the intrinsic construction of the boot. Nonetheless, without good socks, your feet will chafe and you will be in agony. A day can seem endless when your feet hurt.

Blaze Orange: The Intelligent Color

Hunter's blaze orange is a visual safeguard that no one should ignore. Most states require by law that hunters wear at least one blaze orange item of clothing. It is the surest way hunters can visually identify one another in the woods. Even in a duck blind or turkey stand, where hunters dress in camouflage, you should always signal your presence with some blaze, even if it's a blaze orange band or ribbon marking the tree under which you're sitting.

Topping It Off

Hats are necessary gear for hunting. Hoods, hats, caps—the style's up to you. With the exception of waterfowl or turkey hunting, choose something in blaze orange for safety's sake. If you wear a camouflage hat or a waterproof wide-brim like I do, tie a blaze orange bandanna around the brim. If it's windy, use the bandanna to tie the hat firmly under your chin.

Gloves are essential in cold weather. Many hunters like to wear thin shooting gloves in any weather, just so their hands don't perspire against the stock. That's a personal choice. The selection of handware is extensive: mittens, gloves, three-finger mitts, fingerless gloves, glove liners, you name it, in all manner of material. Men's smaller sizes will fit most women.

Wrapping It Up

Whether you are hunting all day or simply going down to the range, you'll need something to hold your equipment. A day pack or packs that strap around the waist (I loathe the term *fanny pack,* but that's what they're called) serves well to hold your survival kit or accessories. Cartridge or bullet belts are handy, or a pouch that slips onto your belt may be just the thing for your ammunition.

If you are going to the range, where you don't need to carry things on your person, a tote bag is a good holdall. A shell bag for your rounds is recommended, too. That way your shooting glasses and ear protectors won't get squashed or damaged.

Hunt Couture

Paris may be the *haute couture* capital of the fashion world, but the *hunt couture* capital is New England, home of L.L.Bean, the Kittery Trading Post, Orvis, and other fine outdoor sporting goods stores. Magazines such as *Vogue* or *Gentlemen's Quarterly* may be fashion's bibles, but catalogues from Orvis and Dunn's are the handbooks of outdoorsmen everywhere. Never before has the selection of clothing, gear, and equipment been so extensive.

Years ago, standard outdoorwear was a "lumberjack" wool hunting coat in red and black plaid and loden green boiled wool pants with red suspenders. Then blaze orange came along, providing indispensable visual security for the hunter in dense cover and forest. Today there's "tree-stand blaze," "orange mirage," "blaze horizon," and combinations of tan/blaze and loden/blaze for jackets, vests, pants, and overalls. In camouflage the color choice is even greater: "brown woodland," "realtree," "timber ghost," "brown A-P realtree," "ultimate," "universal treebark," "tree stand," "gray A-P realtree," "woodland," "all-purpose brown realtree," "bottomland," "brown camo," and more. Wool and flannel were all there used to be; today there are waterproof, breathable, insulated synthetics like Thinsulate, polyester Worsterlon, Thermoloft and Gore-Tex. You can choose pants, coveralls, cover-ups, and overalls; jackets, parkas with removable hoods and removable linings, vests with pockets for game, compasses, shotgun shells, what-have-you; and "ambush-faced," "canvas-faced," or "brush-faced" pants. There are glomitts and mitts, shooting gloves and muffs, of "neoprene," fleece, "polarfleece," and "dry-plus Thinsulate." High-top leather hunting boots with removable felt liners used to be the epitome of comfort and warmth. Compared with today's synthetic linings, they're antique. To describe the many styles of hunting shirts, hats, and underwear would take volumes.

When I think about hunters I've known, two men stand out: one a Scotsman, the other a good ole southern boy. Let me tell you what they wore.

Mr. Cook

The most sacred day of the shooting year in the British Isles is the Glorious Twelfth—August 12, the opening day of grouse season. In that mystical country of heather, highlands, moors, and lochs lived a Scotsman named Mr. Cook. A more generous, jolly, life-loving man never walked the earth. He owned the shooting rights to a massive moor thick with heather and gorse. A dozen or so guest guns made a pilgrimage of Mr. Cook's Glorious Twelfth shoot, and almost everyone in his hamlet got involved. Women made pasties, little girls served tea and coffee, boys carried the shooters' gear, and men worked the dogs, were gun bearers, or helped as beaters. The pay at the end of the day was in grouse, not pounds sterling.

Mr. Cook's head gillie spent weeks planning drives with him, like an adjutant discussing strategies with his general. Just before sunrise on the great day, the guns met at the moor. With the tradition of decades of Glorious Twelfths behind him, Mr. Cook again would open a certain mahogany box fitted with crystal decanters and shot glasses. Out came that honey gold liquid, the holy elixir of Scotland, single malt Scotch, *wee halfs* were poured all 'round, and Mr. Cook made a toast to "the wee birds who'll give us such grand sport t'day." The dawn broke to a benediction of "ayes."

Mr. Cook wore the standard uniform of a country gentleman: a tattersall shirt, tie, waistcoat and breeks of coarse tweed. Heavy, hand-knit kneesocks were cuffed over Wellington boots and he doffed the same hat, always: a shapeless tweed cap, as much his trademark as his ever present pipe. That particular morning was deadly damp and threatened rain.

It was the companionship, the vitality from being out-of-doors from dawn to dusk, and the wonderment of grouse exploding from the heather that made those shoots indelible on the memory. In the words of Dylan Thomas, Mr. Cook is "alas, no longer whinnying with us." What tribute, then, for this grand old man of the moors? First, a story:

One Glorious Twelfth, Mr. Cook came upon a bog in a faraway part of the moor. He knelt down and poured some brownish green bog water into his flask of Scotch, drank it, and proclaimed it the nectar of the gods. Carrying on around the bend, he came upon a dead sheep only a few yards upstream from where he'd drank. "It was the finest *wee half* I ever had," he recalled, wistfully.

> Under the wide and starry sky,
> Dig the grave and let me lie.
> Glad did I live and gladly die,
>   And I laid me down with a will.

> This be the verse you grave for me:
> Here he lies where he longed to be;
> Home is the sailor, home from sea,
>   And the hunter home from the hill.

—ROBERT LOUIS STEVENSON

Here's to you, Mr. Cook.

Uncle Gerry

Uncle Gerry was born and raised in North Carolina, one of four sons of Italian immigrants. All his married life he lived in Brooklyn, New York, but you couldn't take the country out of this country boy. He wore the classic American hunting outfit—a blaze orange jacket, thermal blaze orange overalls, a blaze orange flannel shirt, and a blaze orange hunting hat for deer, and had roughly the same attire, but in camouflage for waterfowl. He hunted in Carolina every weekend he could get away from the city during bird season, except when it overlapped with deer season. Then he drove to a patch of land he leased in upstate New York where he had built a tree stand—literally a house in a tree, outfitted to the hilt with game feeders, scrape drippers, spotting scopes, game finders, deer calls, and antlers for rattling. He always got a deer. He favored a Browning bolt-action rifle for deer and a Browning shotgun for bird, one of four consecutively numbered shotguns he and his brothers had bought together. When hunting season was over, Unc went fishing. He was blessed with an understanding wife.

Unc kept an English pointer in Carolina. The puppy was the runt of the litter, but grew to be strong and had all the right instincts. Unc hunted over him for thirteen seasons, until one morning.

"It's a stroke. The vet said he won't last the day, Gerry," one of his brothers said on the phone. "He wants to put him down."

Unc caught the next plane to Carolina and was met at the airport by his three brothers. His dog was with them. They set out for their favorite field. Earlier, one brother had shot a quail and dragged it. Unc carried his dog near the spot. The dog cried from the pain in his body and Unc cried from the pain in his heart. He gave the command. The dog picked up the scent and with all his might lurched forward. He tried to stand, but fell. Again he tried and fell. Then he looked at Unc, not with re-proach as he would when Unc missed a clear shot, but with the unfail-ing love of a dog for his master. With courage and dignity, he stood and pointed the quail. Unc's dog was doing what he did and loved to do best, one last time.

A shot, and it was all over. Unc cradled the lifeless body of his dog while his brothers dug a grave in the field that was their special place; they buried the dog where he last stood at point. Unc and his brothers said a prayer and remained in the field until the sun set. It set in a burst of brilliant color, the like of which they had never seen before.

These days, in my mind's eye, I can see Unc shouldering his Brown-ing, his dog at point, a quail exploding in flight from the field. Only this field is a little closer to heaven.

———

What Is a Shotgun?

*What is a shotgun? How does it
work? How do you go about
buying your first one?*

For the purpose of our discussion, a shotgun is a smooth-bore firearm that fires a *cartridge* (also known as a *shotgun shell,* or *shotshell*). A cartridge contains a quantity of small pellets, called shot, as opposed to a single projectile, such as a rifle bullet or black powder ball. Once discharged, the shot travels at a high velocity. The farther the distance, the wider the shot pellets spread. Other factors such as gauge, shot size, and choke control how shot travels.

What is a shotgun used for?

Generally speaking, a shotgun is used on small- to medium-size targets that are in motion. In hunting, this applies to small game such as upland birds, waterfowl, and in some states, turkey and small mammals. In certain states, a shotgun is required to hunt deer in areas with significant suburban populations. Shotgun shells are not used for deer hunting. A shotgun slug, which is a single projectile cast in lead, is used instead. A slug has limited range and penetrating power and is safer in populated areas—unlike a rifle bullet, which can travel more than five miles.

A shotgun also is used in nonhunting target shooting sports such as sporting clays, trap, and skeet. The target is a clay disc, or *pigeon,* which is thrown into the air by a mechanical device called a *trap.*

Depending upon the size of the shot and the cartridge, a shotshell can contain 9 to more than 500 pellets. It only takes 4 or 5 pellets to fell a target. The cumulative effect of the simultaneous hits can be far greater than that of a single projectile.

What are the different types of shotguns?

There are several configurations of shotguns, and each has its own merits, tasks, and place in the realm of shooting sports.

There are five types of shotguns: the *break-open,* or *hinge,* the *semi-automatic,* the *pump,* or *slide* (also nicknamed the "trombone" gun), the *bolt-action,* and the *lever-action.* Each type differs primarily in the design of the action. An *action* is the operating mechanism of a gun that loads, fires and ejects a cartridge. Lever-action shotguns, such as the Winchester Model 1887, were heavy and cumbersome. In fact, lever-action shotguns are no longer manufactured. Bolt-action shotguns are generally low-quality and strictly utilitarian guns. Therefore, for the purpose of our discussion, we'll look at the break-open, semi-automatic, and pump shotguns.

Parts of the Shotgun

Gunstock

The *gunstock* is the wood part of the gun. There are two parts to a gunstock, the *buttstock* and the *forestock* (or fore-end). The buttstock is the rear end of the stock from the action back. The forestock is the front of the stock from the action forward. The action of a shotgun is "hung" in the buttstock. A shotgun cannot operate without a stock.

The stock and fit of the stock are far more important to a shotgun than they are to a rifle. A shotgun must be brought to the shoulder ("mounted") quickly when the target appears. You *point* (not aim) a shotgun, then pull the trigger. Mounting, pointing, and pulling: These three steps all follow in one single, fluid motion. The shooter cannot make any adjustments in how she positions or shoots her gun. If she varies the way she shoulders her gun, she will not contact her target in the same way each time and cannot hope to connect with any consistency. The buttstock is the principal part of the gun that is subject to adjustment for gun fit.

Gunstocks are made from hardwoods such as walnut, beech, maple, birch, and cherry. Modern firearms also have synthetic stocks that are made of composition materials such as kevlar and fiberglass. Whether wood or synthetic, a gunstock must be supremely strong, since it not only holds the action in place but also absorbs the recoil. Sometimes a gun with a wood stock will break at the wrist, which is the thin part of the buttstock directly behind the action. The stock may have to be replaced, and this can be an expensive proposition.

Most gunstocks are made of some type of walnut, which is the strongest, hardest wood commonly available. There are many varieties—English, American or black, California, Claro, French, Circassian, or Turkish—and depending upon the quality of the grain of the wood, or its *figure,* the cost of a blank of wood that's used to make a gunstock can vary from $30 for American walnut to $3,000 for a highly figured blank of imported walnut, such as Circassian. The gun you buy will probably have an American walnut stock.

There are several styles of gunstock. One is the *straight,* or *English-style, grip.* A straight-grip gunstock is styled with an uninterrupted line from the trigger to the butt of the gun along the underside of the buttstock. *Pistol-grip* and *semi-pistol-grip* stocks have a protrusion at the rear of the wrist on the underside of the stock before it continues in a straight line to the butt of the gun. Pistol-grips are more common on rifles. Some guns have a *cheek piece,* although this is more common in older or custom guns. A cheek piece is an extension carved into the buttstock. Some guns are designed with a *Monte Carlo comb,* a raised portion along the top, or comb, of the gun. Cheekpieces and Monte Carlo combs are more common in rifles than in shotguns and have to do with the fit of a gunstock as well as the purpose of the gun. For example, you're apt to see a Monte Carlo stock only on a trap gun.

Buttplates and Butt Pads

The *buttplate* is a steel, plastic, or rubber pad that covers the end of the buttstock. When you mount a gun, the butt comes in contact with your shoulder. A plastic or rubber butt pad can also be a "recoil pad" and acts as a cushion to help absorb the shock of recoil when the gun is fired. An especially effective type of rubber recoil pad is the Pachmayer Decelerator, which is designed specifically to decrease recoil.

Better-made shotguns often have leather-covered butt pads, or nothing at all; instead the wood butt of the gun is checkered. Checkering is a wood finishing technique whereby fine lines are cut in a crosshatch pattern with special tools. Checkered butts are more common on British and continental guns, and best quality American guns. Checkering is common on the wrist of the stock (where you hold the gun, right behind the triggers) and the fore-end. Checkering helps you grip the gun.

Be familiar with the parts of a shotgun stock. Each affects gun fit:

Heel: the top of the butt of a gun

Toe: the bottom of the butt of a gun

Comb: the top of the buttstock

Drop: the distance at the comb and heel from the line of sight

Pitch: the angle formed by the buttplate from the line of sight

Length of pull: the measurement from the front trigger to the midpoint of the buttplate

Cast-off: the degree to the right that the buttstock is out of line with the bore's centerline

Cast-on: the degree to the left that the buttstock is out of line with the bore's centerline

Gun Barrel

The *gun barrel* is the tube of a gun through which the shot or bullet travels. There are four parts of a barrel: the *chamber,* which accommodates the shotshell; the *forcing cone,* which reduces the chamber to the bore diameter, or gauge; the *choke,* which is the constriction at the muzzle that determines the spread of the shot, and the *bore,* which is the section of the barrel between the forcing cone and the choke. In most shotguns, the bore is smooth. Modern barrels are made of fluid steel.

Some older guns have *Damascus barrels,* made up of numerous twists of iron that are wrapped around a tube and welded together in a complicated process that is largely no longer practiced. A word of warning: Damascus barrels are unsafe with modern ammunition. They were designed for earlier, black-powder loads. A Damascus gun is in danger of rupturing if modern loads are fired through it. You can tell a Damascus barrel by the identifiable pattern formed by the twists. Have your gunsmith check any older gun you may own, however; some guns with Damascus barrels have been blued at some point. Blueing masks the twist pattern, and unless you know what you are looking at, it's hard to tell whether a barrel is Damascus or fluid steel.

Action

The *action* is the working mechanism of the gun that allows it to operate. There are seven steps of operation:

　　1. *Firing* When you fire a gun, you pull a trigger. The trigger releases the hammer or firing pin, which is under spring tension. The hammer strikes the primer of the shotshell that is loaded in

SHOTGUN RIB STYLES

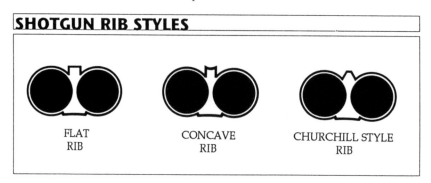

FLAT
RIB

CONCAVE
RIB

CHURCHILL STYLE
RIB

(COURTESY OF *BLACK'S WING & CLAY*)

the chamber. The force of the blow by the hammer to the primer then ignites the powder charge, which forms a gas that propels the shot down the barrel.

A double-barrel (break-open) shotgun is either a *double,* or *two-trigger,* gun, which has a front trigger that fires the right barrel and a back trigger that fires the left, or a *single selective trigger,* which alternately fires one barrel at a time.

The semiautomatic, bolt, and lever actions (also known as *repeating shotguns* because they can hold more than two cartridges in the part of the gun called the *magazine*) can fire several shotshells, one at a time, before they need reloading. This is done by pulling a single trigger.

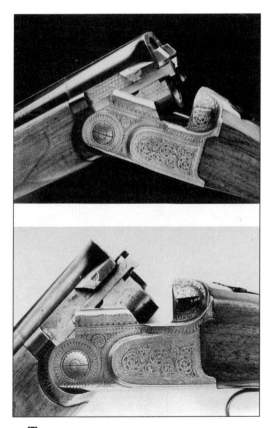

The action of an Over and Under shotgun, called a break-action gun because the gun "breaks" open for loading shotshells.

(PHOTO COURTESY OF ORVIS)

2. *Unlocking.* During firing, the breech must be securely locked so that none of the pressure that propels the shot can escape until it has left the bore. Unlocking, operated by the lever, pump handle, bolt, or operating rod, opens the gun to load a cartridge.

3. *Extraction.* The empty cartridge is removed from the chamber after firing. A non-ejector, or *extractor* gun requires you to manually pull, or extract, the shotshell from its chamber.

4. *Ejection.* An *ejector* gun mechanically pushes out, or chucks, the empty cartridge by the rear stroke of the breech bolt when you open the gun. An ejector gun is ideal when shots are fired in rapid succession, such as at European-style driven shoots, when waterfowl hunting, and in most clays shooting. It permits rapid reloading. An extractor gun, which has fewer operating parts, is best suited to field use, such as upland bird shooting. You'll find an appreciable difference in price between the non-ejector and the more costly ejector models.

   All repeating shotguns are ejector guns and automatically chuck spent cartridges from the chamber.

5. *Cocking.* When you draw back the hammer or firing pin, the pressure of the spring drives the trigger forward and starts the firing process.

6. *Feeding.* This is the term for loading a fresh, unfired cartridge into the chamber of the gun. In a pump or automatic shotgun, the cartridge automatically moves from the magazine into the chamber.

7. *Locking.* This is the opposite of unlocking: The breechblock is held secure against the gas pressure that results from firing. Most guns will not fire until they are fully locked.

Choke

Choke is the degree of constriction at the muzzle of the barrel. There are four basic degrees of choke: Cylinder (C), Improved Cylinder or quarter-choke (IC), Modified or half-choke (M), and Full (F).

Cylinder (C): The bore is a straight tube. There is no constriction at the muzzle at all. Cylinder is used for short-range shooting in thick cover where the widest possible spread is desired.

PATTERN/PELLET DENSITY & ENERGY GUIDE

Look up distance to your game for recommended pellet. Pellets appropriate for longer distances may also be used at shorter range. Use of pellets at distances surpassing their listing is not recommended

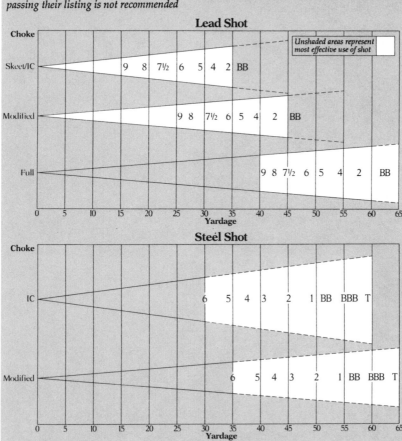

Lead Shot

Choke — Skeet/IC, Modified, Full

Unshaded areas represent most effective use of shot

Skeet/IC: 9 8 7½ 6 5 4 2 BB

Modified: 9 8 7½ 6 5 4 2 BB

Full: 9 8 7½ 6 5 4 2 BB

Yardage: 0 5 10 15 20 25 30 35 40 45 50 55 60 65

Steel Shot

Choke — IC, Modified

IC: 6 5 4 3 2 1 BB BBB T

Modified: 6 5 4 3 2 1 BB BBB T

Yardage: 0 5 10 15 20 25 30 35 40 45 50 55 60 65

APPROXIMATE NUMBER OF SHOTS IN VARIOUS LOADS

Shot Size	Shot Diameter	2 oz.	1⅞ oz.	1⅝ oz.	1½ oz.	1⅜ oz.	1¼ oz.	1⅛ oz.	1 oz.	⅞ oz.	¾ oz.	½ oz.
#9	.08	1170	1097	951	877	804	731	658	585	512	439	292
#8	.09	820	769	667	615	564	513	462	410	359	308	205
#7½	.095	700	656	568	525	481	437	393	350	306	262	175
#6	.11	450	422	396	337	309	281	253	225	197	169	112
#5	.12	340	319	277	255	234	213	192	170	149	128	85
#4	.13	270	253	221	202	185	169	152	135	118	101	67
#2	.15	180	169	158	135	124	113	102	90	79	68	45

(CHART COURTESY OF *BLACK'S WING & CLAY*)

Improved Cylinder or Quarter-Choke (IC): A slight constriction at the muzzle. IC steadies down the pattern and makes it more consistent. It, too, is a short-range choke. IC is very popular in skeet, sporting clays, and upland bird shooting.

Modified or Half-Choke (M): A general-purpose choke useful for any game that is likely to be shot up to 40 yards. An upland game gun is usually right barrel Improved Cylinder and left barrel Modified.

Full (F): This is the maximum constriction at the muzzle. It used to be popular before steel shot with waterfowl hunters, and is popular with trap shooters.

Special chokes are designed for skeet. "Skeet one" spreads the shot charge and has more dispersion than Cylinder. "Skeet two" is about the same as Improved Cylinder.

A choke common in Europe but seldom seen in the United States is *Improved Modified,* or three-quarter choke. Designed for medium- to long-range shooting (40 to 50 yards), it is widely used for driven shoots. As its name implies, the degree of choke falls between Modified and Full.

Adjustable Chokes

Many modern shotguns come with screw-in tubes that enable you to alter the choke of the gun to conform to the intended target. Screw-in tubes fit inside the muzzle of the barrel and can be visible from the outside. A small wrench (sometimes you can use a quarter) is used to install them. The tubes are easily changeable. The thickness of the barrel wall determines whether a gun that does not come with screw-in tubes can be fitted with them. Consult your professional gunsmith.

Choke for Steel Shot

The shot in cartridges used for clays and upland shooting is made of lead. For waterfowl shooting, however, the law requires special cartridges loaded with steel shot, which is nontoxic. Lead shot cannot be used for waterfowl shooting in the United States (see page 111 for further explanation). Because the hardness of steel shot under pressure can lead to bulging or splitting of the barrel at the muzzle, a modern gun should have a choke no greater than Modified for use with steel shot. Check the manufacturer's recommendations. An older gun should be inspected by a competent gunsmith before it is used with steel shot.

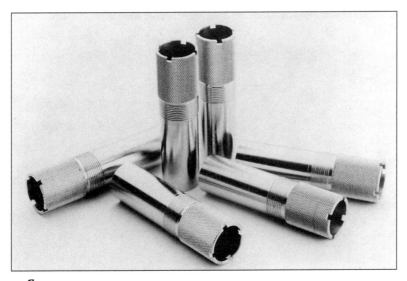

Changeable, adjustable screw-in choke tubes such as Beretta U.S.A.'s Mobilchoke choke tubes give one gun a range of performance that takes it to the sporting clays club or into the field.

(PHOTO COURTESY OF BERETTA U.S.A.)

Cartridges

Cartridges come in various sizes. Gun *gauge* is measured by the number of bore-size lead balls it takes to weigh one pound. Modern shotgun gauges are (from largest to smallest) 10, 12, 16, 20, 28, and .410 caliber.

Shotshell size also varies and which to use is determined primarily by what you are shooting.

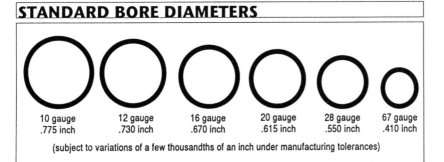

STANDARD BORE DIAMETERS

10 gauge	12 gauge	16 gauge	20 gauge	28 gauge	67 gauge
.775 inch	.730 inch	.670 inch	.615 inch	.550 inch	.410 inch

(subject to variations of a few thousandths of an inch under manufacturing tolerances)

(CHART COURTESY OF *BLACK'S WING & CLAY*)

Suggested Shot Sizes for Small Game

GAME SPECIES	SHOT SIZE	LOAD
Woodcock	9	medium to light
Skeet	9	medium
Quail, chukar, Huns	7½ or 8	medium to heavy
Doves	7½ or 8	medium to heavy
Trap	7½ or 8	medium
Pheasant	6 or 7½	heavy
Grouse	6 or 7½	heavy
"Blue" grouse	5, 6, or 7½	heavy
Small ducks	7½ or 8	heavy
Medium ducks	6	heavy
Large ducks	3, 4, or 5	heavy
Small geese	3, 4, or 5	heavy
Large geese	2	heavy
Turkey	2, 3, or 4	heavy
Squirrel	6	medium to heavy
Cottontail	6 or 7½	medium
Fox	2	heavy
Raccoon	2	heavy

Suggested Sizes for Steel Shot

Steel shot does not retain the velocity of lead, nor does it penetrate as well. The rule of thumb is to go up one shot size larger for steel.

Quail and dove	6
Pheasant	4
Decoyed ducks	4
Pass-shooting ducks	2
Decoyed geese	BB
Pass-shooting geese	T

Double Guns

Side-by-Side

The classic shotgun and all-time favorite of many upland bird hunters is the double-barrel *side-by-side*. That's precisely what it is: two separate barrels joined together, side by side, with silver solder. Each barrel fires one cartridge at a time. In Britain, this gun used to be referred to as the "horizontal gun."

Over and Under

The *Over and Under* is also a two-barrel shotgun, but as its name suggests, one barrel is fitted on top of the other. In Britain its nickname is the "stacked gun," and it is mechanically very different from the side-by-side. The side-by-side has slipped in popularity in recent years. The action of a sidelock side-by-side is more complex, with more parts, and is therefore more expensive than a boxlock Over and Under. With so

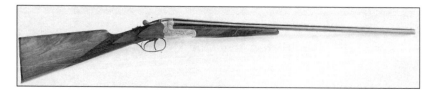

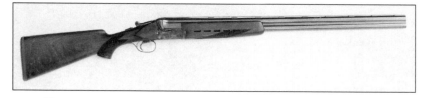

Both of these double barrel Belgian-made Browning shotguns are "break-open" guns because they break open at the breech for loading shotshells. The gun on top is a side-by-side, once nicknamed a "horizontal" gun in Britain: there are two barrels, soldered side by side. The gun below is an Over and Under, nicknamed a "stacked" gun: the two barrels are stacked one on top of the other.

(PHOTO COURTESY OF ORVIS)

many upland bird shooters engaged in one or more of the target shotgunning sports, the Over and Under is generally considered more of a dual-purpose gun more likely to be used both at the range and in the field. But the choice is a matter of personal preference—as you'll discover so many things are in the shooting sports.

THE MAIN PARTS OF AN OVER-AND-UNDER SHOTGUN

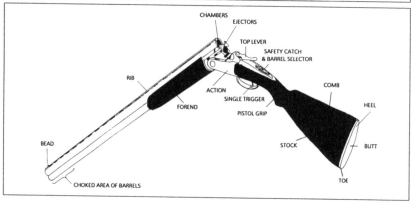

(DIAGRAM COURTESY OF *BLACK'S WING & CLAY*)

Sidelock

A *sidelock* is an action with a self-contained operating mechanism carried in two metal plates on the sides of the gun. Sidelocks are less common than boxlocks because they are far more expensive. A high-quality sidelock is considered the Rolls Royce of shotguns. It has more internal parts than a boxlock and can cost many thousands of dollars. A sidelock allows the balance of the gun to come a little more back into the hand than a boxlock. It is narrower in the *wrist* (the handgrip of the gun) and can be sleeker and more graceful than any other type of shotgun. Seldom do you see a full sidelock without some amount of engraving or extra finishing. If you're lucky enough to own one, remember: Few gunsmiths are qualified to work on a sidelock. Most are English-trained; see pages 221–22 for some qualified gunsmiths in the United States.

Boxlock

A *boxlock* is a simpler design in which the mechanical parts are all hung, or "mounted," in the action itself. This is a far less expensive gun because it has fewer parts and can be mass-produced. Any professional gunsmith who is qualified to work on shotguns can repair a boxlock.

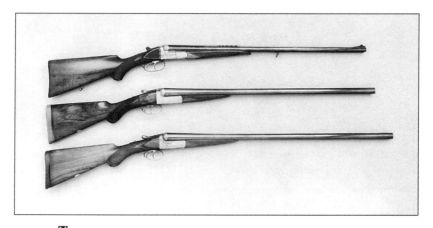

These three side-by-side boxlock shotguns are examples of a classic upland gun.

(PHOTO COURTESY OF BUTTERFIELD AND BUTTERFIELD)

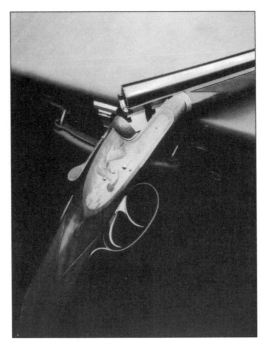

This full sidelock, double trigger, side-by-side shotgun was made in Italy. Italian guns are considered among the finest made today.

(PHOTO COURTESY OF NEW ENGLAND ARMS CO.)

Repeating Shotguns

Pump Gun

The *pump gun* has an altogether different mechanism from a double-barreled gun. It is capable of holding up to six cartridges—five in the magazine and one in the chamber. You pump the action back and forth to engage a cartridge into the chamber. The pump gun is the most widely used shotgun in waterfowl shooting. If it's used for that purpose, however, federal law requires that the gun be "plugged" so it can fire only three shells before it has to be reloaded.

Less expensive than a double gun, the pump takes steel shot, re-quired by law for waterfowl shooting. Steel shot is much harder than lead shot and is also hard on the barrels of a gun—many hunters are

Young shooter Sarah Calabi carries the classic
pump shotgun, a Winchester Model 12 in
16-gauge.
(LAURIE MORROW)

unwilling to risk their fine double guns on steel. This may soon change.
A non-steel shot called Bismuth has been granted conditional federal
approval at the time of this writing. Bismuth does not have the stress effects of steel shot, and as a result, double guns may once again return to
the duck blind. However, be forewarned: Bismuth is much more expensive than steel.

Semi-Automatics

The *semi-auto*, or auto-loader, uses the recoil of the gun or the gas from
the exploding cartridge to operate the mechanism. In other words, the

operation of the action removes the fired shell from the chamber, ejects it, and feeds in a new one. This is not the gun you'd bring to a fancy preserve down South or to a driven shoot in England. Like the pump, the semi-auto is well suited to steel shot, is an acceptable waterfowl gun, and, because of its innovative John Browning–designed action, has less recoil than other types of shotguns.

How to Buy a Shotgun

Consult an instructor. Speak to others who shoot, get recommendations. Call your local fish and game club. Go to gun shows and local gun shops. Read firearms magazines or specialty newspapers such as *The Gun List* or *Gun Journal,* which list thousands of guns for sale. We do not recommend that you order by mail until you become well versed in buying guns, and know precisely what you are looking for.

Sporting shops, gun dealers, and gunsmiths that sell firearms in America number in the thousands. When looking for a reputable dealer, be sure he or she is knowledgeable and sells only sound and sturdy firearms. A place that sells mostly used-and-abused guns is no place to shop. A good gun shop has experienced people with whom to consult.

Tell a dealer how much you want to spend. He will show you several guns. Ask questions about the differences among them. A good dealer will make suggestions that make sense to you regarding weight and fit. When you bring the gun to your shoulder (or mount the gun), you'll understand what he is pointing out. You need not buy a more expensive gun on the merit of its engraving or extra-fancy wood. Your first gun should be practical and well suited to your needs, your build, and your wallet.

A good gun dealer will be honest about the intrinsic merit and condition of the guns he sells and will not sell you one that does not suit your needs or fit you properly. You want a gun dealer with whom you can build a long-term relationship and consult regularly, and with assurance.

Second-hand Shotguns

Firearms manufacturing is generally a mass-production affair these days. Shotguns that are made by master gunsmiths and fine firearms makers such as Purdey, Holland & Holland, and Bertuzzi command staggering prices—almost always in five digits. Though guns have been mass-produced since the 1860s, up until World War II hand finishing and fitting were important parts of the gunmaking process. American, British, and continental shotguns made before World War II are not only desirable, but relatively affordable. An older gun must be checked before you buy it, however, and the *only* way you can be sure a gun is mechanically safe is to take it to a professional gunsmith who is well versed in shotguns. He will be able to tell you everything you need to know about how the gun operates. He will also be able to fit and alter the gun to your measurements and do whatever cosmetic work is necessary to restore it properly and as close to original condition as possible.

Remember, if you buy any used gun, you must have it examined for safety and fit by a qualified, reputable gunsmith. Be sure to get an estimate before work begins. That way you both know what to expect.

Buying at Auction

Gun auctions are held all over the country and are often excellent places to pick up a good sporting gun. Buying at auction is also very tricky. You have to know what a gun is worth and not overbid, which is easy to do in the excitement of an auction. You have to be able to tell if a gun is mechanically sound. For this reason, many people hire a gunsmith to preview an auction with them. Conversely, some gun dealers will work with you on finding a sound candidate, and will bid for you. A good gun dealer who can do this falls into the same category as a priest: You really have to trust that he won't betray your confidence!

So: Find the best gun you can, be sure it's sound, have it correctly measured to fit. Learn how to operate it safely. Take shooting lessons. Practice at the local range: Practice, practice, practice. A lifetime of practice is never enough. As we age, our reflexes and vision change, too, and you'll have to adjust and compensate. All this advice focuses on one thing: You want the best gun you can afford that will effect a clean, direct kill. That's the bottom line. It's how you become a responsible hunter. And it's how you become the best shooting sportswoman you can be.

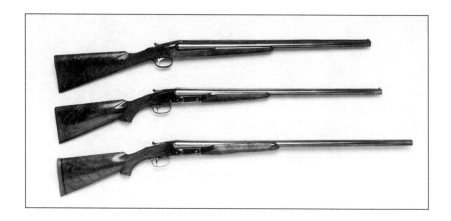

Guns range in price, depending upon make, quality, and whether they have a boxlock action, like those above, or a full sidelock, like the cased shotgun below. Boxlock prices are in the range of $1,000; the sidelock, $8,000.

(CASED SHOTGUN PHOTO COURTESY OF NEW ENGLAND ARMS CO. BOXLOCK PHOTO

COURTESY OF BUTTERFIELD AND BUTTERFIELD)

Shotgunning Philosophy and Technique

*Steve Smith, a lifelong wingshooter, wildlife biologist,
and crack shot, explains the philosophy behind
shotgunning and basic shooting
techniques.*

A shotgun is meant to be fired while it's moving. There's a simple reason for this: The target; whether bird or clay, is in motion. That's why the shotgun was developed, because hitting a flying target with a single projectile—a bullet—is just about impossible.

As a result, a shotgun, although it possesses the elements of a rifle—lock, stock, and barrel—is built differently. A rifle is meant to be fired at a stationary target, so it is constructed to allow for a steady hold on the mark. A shotgun, on the other hand, is constructed to take advantage of a human's natural coordination and movements while concentrating on a target winging its way across the landscape.

While no mechanical object has a life and motion of its own, a well-built shotgun responds to the shooter quickly and accurately, especially if the gun is constructed or altered for the individual. The inherent dynamics in the gun—its balance and weight—coupled with the individual's alterations "fit" the shotgun to the shooter in the same way a garment is tailored for the wearer. Gunmakers across the globe will design and construct a shotgun made for you alone, for a price.

On the other hand, while an off-the-rack dress may come close to fitting perfectly, a skilled seamstress, with a few tucks and tweaks here and there, can make it much more "yours" than it was before. So, too, can a gunsmith convert a shotgun that is almost perfect into one that is. Just as the dressmaker charges more than the alterations person, so the gunmaker charges more than the gunsmith. And the costs can be staggering. At this writing, the best London gunmakers charge upward of $40,000 for a double-barrel shotgun made for the individual; alterations on a shotgun you already have or are about to buy can cost anywhere from several hundred dollars down to virtually nothing—you can do the work yourself.

The first decision for a woman contemplating her first shotgun is: "What kind?" Here, we have to consider the physical differences between men, for whom most guns are made, and women.

Gauge

In an upland gun, I wouldn't recommend that a 115-pound man buy and shoot a 12-gauge, and I wouldn't recommend one for a 115-pound woman, either. A 20-gauge shotgun will handle virtually all the upland shooting and a good portion of the waterfowl shooting you're likely to do. My daughter, Amy Schultz, is a good shot, and she does all her hunting with a 20. She's a shade over 5 feet tall and weighs less than 105 pounds. The recoil of a 12-gauge would be too much for her. Recoil is a function of the shotshell's energy going forward and the gun's being driven backward into the shoulder—Newton's action/reaction law. If you tried to find a 12-gauge that wouldn't hammer you, it would have to weigh so much that after a while, you'd wish it had wheels.

The modern 20-gauge, weighing from 6 to 6½ pounds, is pleasant to carry, and the recoil is tolerable. This is important because all of this is supposed to be fun. If the act of firing a shot turns into one of punishment, you'll enjoy yourself less. You'll also miss, because in anticipation of the punishment to come, you'll grit your teeth, shut your eyes, stop looking at the target, and stop swinging the gun. But consideration of gauge only makes sense when viewed with an idea of the available actions in mind.

Action

Shotguns are built in several basic "actions": *double barrel*, in which the barrels, either side by side or one over the other, drop down and are loaded from the breech end; *pump*, in which the forend, held by your nontrigger hand (left hand for a rightie), is slid back and then forward

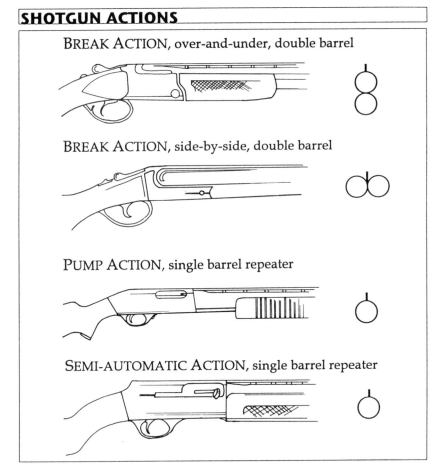

SHOTGUN ACTIONS

BREAK ACTION, over-and-under, double barrel

BREAK ACTION, side-by-side, double barrel

PUMP ACTION, single barrel repeater

SEMI-AUTOMATIC ACTION, single barrel repeater

(CHART COURTESY OF *BLACK'S WING & CLAY*)

to chamber a shell; and *autoloader,* in which a mechanism does for you what you have to do manually on a pump. Of these three actions, if the new shooter is especially recoil-shy, I recommend the autoloader, because the mechanism that chambers the next round does so via energy it has bled off from the exploding shell just fired. In other words, an autoloader uses the gun's recoil to make the mechanism work, thus permitting less of the recoil to make it back to your shoulder and face. The other actions have a "fixed breech," and the recoil is transferred directly back.

But having said all of this, a 20-gauge is not a heavy-kicking gun in any action configuration. What about the other, smaller gauges that would, of course, recoil less? The .410 is just not ballistically efficient enough for game shooting, and the 28-gauge, although efficient enough at close ranges, does not offer the wide range of ammunition options that the 20-gauge has. For example, no 28-gauge steel shotshells are made for waterfowl hunting. It's a good thing, too, because these tough birds require more shot, especially since the use of less efficient steel shot has been mandated by law. (See Chapter 7 for more information.)

The doubles intrinsically possess the best handling characteristics. ("Handling" is the ease with which the gun is mounted to shooting position and swung along the target's line.) They generally are lighter than their repeating counterparts, the pump and the autoloader. But more important, they are built to take advantage of your natural eye-hand coordination. It is interesting to note that where shooting matches such as sporting clays events or trap and skeet shoots take place, and there's a pile of money for the top performers, virtually everyone shoots a double—and an over-under double to boot.

In some circles, it is considered something of a social error to shoot anything *but* a double. On the storied driven shoots of England, Scotland, and the continent, for example, repeating guns such as pumps and autoloaders are not allowed. This is part tradition and part safety. When the barrels of a double are open, the gun cannot fire, even if there are shotshells in the chambers. No one is ever really sure if a repeating gun is unloaded, certainly not someone 10 feet away, within sure human-killing distance of an accidental discharge. In parts of the South, especially the traditional quail plantations, both public and private, doubles are considered more genteel, more elegant, and more in keeping with the mule-drawn wagon, the antebellum plantation house, and the fine pointers coursing the broomsedge and piney woods.

Gun Fit

Most good shots agree that proper fit counts more in shooting success than gauge, choke, shot load, barrel length—anything. With a properly fit gun, a poor shot can quickly learn to be a good one, and a good shot becomes a crackerjack.

A shotgun is meant to be fired while both the target and the gun are in motion. The shooter is meant to fire the gun while keeping both eyes on the target. As a result, there are no sights, as such, on the shotgun to line up, only a front bead to make the shooter aware of where the barrel is, but not intended as an aiming device.

Shotguns are pointed in the same manner as you would point your finger at an object across the room. Human eye-hand coordination is surprisingly accurate, and even the most semicoordinated of us are capable of monumental feats. Take, for example, the driving of an automobile. This huge juggernaut under your control operates at speeds capable of killing you. Yet drivers don't look at the steering wheel, and certainly can't see the tires under the car. We do it through experience and "feel."

Consider any other sport that uses an apparatus. Does the softball player look at the bat when she's hitting? At her glove when catching? Does the golfer watch her club head? The bowler look at the ball? Of course not. In each instance, the object of attention is somewhere out there, and the athlete depends upon natural ability, coordination, and experience—and concentration on the target. The ballplayer sees only the ball, the golfer only the Titleist teed up and waiting, the bowler only the one-three pin pocket.

So it is with shooting. Only it's more difficult because, unlike the other sports mentioned, the shotgunner must contend with having the tool directly in the line of sight. Other athletes have the club, the bat, the bowling ball, the tennis racket, the glove essentially hidden from their view—it's behind them or below their field of vision. Not the shooter. That gun is right up there, fractions of an inch below the line of sight from eye to target. The important thing here is to trust your instincts.

In order for these instincts to be in harmony with the gun, the gun must be fitted to your physical build. We are not all the same height, weight, strength, and so forth. Yet guns come pretty much one-size-not-fitting-all. Adjustments and alterations must be made.

The most important part of gun fit is the elevation of the eye above the barrel. This line flows from your eye, down the barrel, to the target. If your head is too high, the shot charge will strike high; too low, and the opposite happens.

In order for the eye to line up with the barrel, however, you have to know which eye. Surprisingly, a fairly high proportion of women I have instructed in shooting have what is known as "cross-dominance." (Sue King discusses this further in Chapter 10.) That is, they are right-handed, yet the left eye is stronger. If you shoulder a gun on the right, but the left eye takes over, the gun's muzzle will point to the left of a stationary target *every time*. To you, it will look spot-on, but it won't be, and a little shooting will show this to be true.

To determine if this is the case for you, here's a simple test: Poke a hole in the middle of a page of a newspaper, say a one-inch-diameter hole—jab your finger through it and it will be about the right size. With both eyes open, look through the hole at an object across the room, maybe a vase or lamp. Draw the paper closer and closer to your face, keeping the object in view within the hole. Pull the newspaper right up to your eye. If the object is still visible through the hole, and the hole is lined up with your right eye, you are right-eye dominant. If you happen to be right-handed, you're home free. If, however, the hole ends up over your left eye and you are right-handed, or vice versa, you have a *slight* problem.

Humans have binocular vision. It's what gives us depth perception. Our eyes are located in the front of our heads because we are a predator species. Look at the wolf, the lion, the bear, the eagle—they too have eyes located in front for the chase. The prey species—the deer, the zebra, the rabbit—have their eyes to the side of their heads so they can better detect the front-eye guys trying to make a meal of them.

This binocular vision is great for determining depth. The eyes triangulate with each other and the object we are viewing, allowing us to determine distance accurately. Depth perception tells predator animals exactly how much ground they have to cover before launching their final, lethal attack on lunch. It helps us parallel-park, and shoot.

Depth perception, then, tells us how far away something is. In shotgunning, in which the decision when and where to shoot is based primarily on how far away the target is, it is vital. But if the shooter has cross-dominance, there are two ways of dealing with this. If the shooter is new, has never shot before, I usually ask her to learn to shoot from the dominant eye side—switch to the left shoulder to match the left dominant eye, for example. This is quite easy, actually, because everything is new. Many of us do things with the "wrong" hand every day. Many ballplayers in the major leagues do everything right-handed except bat, for example.

If the shooter has enough experience with a shotgun that this would be a problem, I suggest a simpler method: Just shut the dominant eye when the time comes to fire. My daughter is right-handed, left-eye dominant. She keeps both eyes open when a bird flushes or a target is thrown. She mounts the gun (with both eyes open) to her shoulder, and as her cheek meets the stock, she closes the left eye and fires. By the time she closes the eye, she knows the speed, direction, and distance of the target, allowing her to establish forward allowance or "lead." It works.

Once you have established which eye is your shooting eye, you need to determine how far above the barrel that eye should be. I like to see a gun fit that will place the pattern—that is, the common center showing the closest congregation of pellets (also known as the "killing circle")—about 6 inches high at forty yards. Patterning determines the penetration and velocity of a gun's shooting performance. About 60 percent of the pattern should be above the point of aim, 40 percent below. This is because it allows the shooter to see the bird above the barrel for a good view. If the shooter mounts and fires quickly at a pattern board (or a spread of paper) with a mark in it, she'll see quickly if the shot charge is too high or too low.

The cheek contacts the stock on the top at the "comb." If the comb is too high, the shot will go high; too low, it goes low. The comb of the

BASIC SHOTGUN STOCK GRIPS AND FOREND STYLES

The straight-hand grip, also known as the "English" grip.

The splinter forend is a small wedge-shaped piece of wood.

The semi-pistol grip, also known as a half-pistol grip.

The beavertail forend curves upward along the barrel's contour.

A full pistol grip.

A deep beavertail forend on a repeater.

(CHART COURTESY OF *BLACK'S WING & CLAY*)

stock is like the rear sight of a rifle. The comb places your cheek, perfectly, in the same place each time.

On a gun made for women, the length is also important. Most gunstocks are just too long to mount and swing, so the stock must be cut off by a competent gunsmith, who can then add a recoil pad to absorb some of the kick from the shot. Where a 5-foot-10-inch man might use a stock of 14½ inches, a woman of average height needs a stock 1 to 1½ inches shorter. Determining length is easier: If the stock gets caught in your clothing when you go to mount, it's too long; if you bang your nose with your trigger hand when you shoot, it's too short.

I like to see a woman's shotgun have some cast-off—that is, a bend away from the face, both at the top of the butt (heel) and the bottom (toe). Cast-off is the degree to which the butt of the stock is set off to the right to more easily accommodate the line of vision when the gun is shouldered. Your shoulder can get pretty tender should it get whacked by recoil; this is generally the result of incorrect gun mounting, and cast-off may be the reason. A good stock for a woman veers away from the breast. In addition, cast-off aligns the eye, the cheek, the comb, and

A student shoots at a pattern board with Women's Shooting Sports Foundation instructor Lou Ann Daniels.

(LAURIE MORROW)

the barrel with the target and allows the shooter to face the shot more naturally.

A gun fits if *it shoots where you look without aiming, but by merely pointing.*

If you point your finger at an object across the room, your instinct is invariably correct—your finger will be pointing directly at the object. It is only if you leave it there, pointing, dwelling on the object, trying to be too precise, that your finger starts to waver and wander. Then, it's no longer on target. It's the same with a shotgun. Your first point is right, so the shot should be triggered then—at first point.

To determine proper stock fit, get to a pattern board at the gun club, or find an area with a safe backdrop to shoot and set up a large (about 40 inches) square board. Attach a sheet of paper (butcher paper works well) to the board with tacks, put a prominent black dot in the middle of the paper, stand back 16 yards, and fire at the dot by mounting the gun quickly and pointing it at the dot. Make sure your face is firm on the stock, but not mashed down hard.

If the pattern hits too high (above our 60 percent/40 percent perfect), the stock needs to come down on the comb. This can be accomplished with some sandpaper and a refinishing kit, but it's best to let a gunsmith do it. If it's too low, the stock must be bent upward, a complex project involving hot oil and a bending jig—again, a job for a pro. But don't do this until you check the stock length. A shotgun stock slopes lower the farther back it goes. If your stock is too long, it places your face too far back, and thus lower. Often, shortening the stock pulls the face forward and relatively higher.

If it shoots left or right, you need cast-on or cast-off, but most likely the adjustments will be for up or down, usually down. Why 16 yards? Because for every 4 inches the pattern is off at this range—4 inches too high, for example—you'll have to remove $\frac{1}{16}$ inch of wood from the comb.

Often the gun can be made to shoot dead-on by adjustment to the pitch of the stock, which is the angle at which the butt is measured from the muzzle. Pitch, in combination with pull and drop, determines the angle of the barrel when the gun is properly mounted. If the gun slips down between shots, there's not enough pitch, for example. If the stock shoots high or low, don't start sanding until you've tried adjusting the pitch. Here's how: First, if the gun is shooting high, loosen the buttplate or pad, pull the screw out from the top, place several washers over the hole in the wood between the plate and the butt, and reinsert the screw through the washers and into the wood. Tighten down just snugly, and fire again. You'll find that pushing the top of the buttplate out will cause the gun to come into your shoulder with the barrels pointed lower than before, thus shooting lower. If the gun is shooting low, try the same procedure on the lower screw.

Barrel

Barrel lengths are a matter of choice. I think 26 inches is right for both repeating guns and doubles, unless you are taller than 5 feet 10 inches, in which case 28-inch barrels are better. Barrel length is relative to the height of an individual shooter, but generally, taller shooters need longer stocks and thus longer barrels to balance the gun. Because there is an action (called a "receiver") on pump and autoloading shotguns, these guns have, effectively, 4 more inches of length than a double-barrel with the same length barrels. Some shooters prefer their repeating guns with 26-inch barrels, and their doubles with 28-inch.

Shooting Technique

The Mount

A shotgun is mounted, properly, by raising the gun, pushing it outward slightly to clear any clothing that may impede it, and then pulling it back into the shoulder pocket. The butt should *not* be out on the shoulder bone nor on the upper arm: The alignment will be wrong, and the recoil will hurt.

You should not dip your head to meet the gun, but rather bring the gun to your face, settling your cheek snugly on the comb. A word of caution here: Most newcomers to shotgunning either grip the gun too hard, thus hurting their chances at staying mobile, or shy away from the gun, holding it too loosely in an attempt to keep the recoil away from them, which results in *more* felt recoil. A shotgun, properly mounted, is held firmly but not too tight. Then, when the shot is triggered, the felt recoil is a push rather than a sharp jab. If you hold the gun away from your shoulder or face, it gives the gun a chance to get a running start under recoil and hit you hard. By way of comparison, would you rather have a professional boxer put his fist against your shoulder and push, or hold it three inches away and jab? You *know* which one will hurt more.

Your off hand, the one not pulling the trigger, should be comfortably extended on the forend, your index finger pointing parallel to the line of the barrels.

Stance

You should feel relaxed, your feet about shoulder-width apart, the weight on the balls of your feet, giving your body a slight forward incline—the classic athletic stance, whether for addressing a golf ball or preparing to return a serve in tennis. If you are right-handed, your left foot should be slightly forward of your right, but not too much.

From this position, you can easily pivot left or right. The shotgun swing is very much like the golf swing in the movement of the hips and lower body. It is a swing from side to side. If you go to the far left (again for a right-hander), you will actually find your weight shifting to your left foot, and you may even go up on the toe of your right foot; if you swing far right, the feet swap roles, the weight shifting to the right foot, and the left merely in position to prepare for the recoil, up on the ball of the foot.

Like the golf swing, the shotgun swing is a pivot about the centerline of the body on the balls of your feet. A shooter can swing nearly 360 degrees without repositioning her feet.

Shot

Now that we've examined the mount and the stance, we have to look at the most important aspect—the shot.

A shotgun is made to shoot quickly, like pointing your finger. Too often, we mount the gun, track the target, start aiming, and miss. Before any discussion takes place, a new shooter should understand the physics involved in shooting.

Essentially, if you shoot at a moving target—right at it—by the time the shot charge gets there, the target will have moved. Just as you brake your car before you get to a stop sign, so must you shoot not where the target is, but where it will be when the shot charge arrives.

A clay target moving at 50 miles per hour travels 73 feet a second. A shot charge travels 1,200 feet per second, or roughly 16 times as fast. If the target is out 40 yards (120 feet), the shot charge will travel the 120

Good shooting form is essential to making
contact with your target.
(LAURIE MORROW)

feet in $\frac{1}{10}$ of a second. So, from the time the shot leaves the barrel until it reaches the target, the target will have traveled 7.3 feet, the distance it travels in $\frac{1}{10}$ of a second.

Further, from the time your brain tells you to shoot, the message gets to your trigger finger, the trigger trips the hammer, which strikes the primer, which ignites the powder, which sends the shot down the barrel, the target is traveling. Total time for this, for someone with fast reflexes, is about G ($\frac{1}{4}$) of a second. So, counting flight time of the shot charge, from the time your brain tells you to shoot until the charge reaches the target is G + $\frac{1}{10}$ seconds = $\frac{35}{100}$ of a second. If the target is traveling at 73 feet per second, you can see that the target will have moved at least 25 feet. If you hold the gun stationary and aim at the target, and shoot when the target comes in view over your gun barrel, you'll miss by 25 feet!

How are we ever supposed to hit something, then, with a shotgun? Years ago, shooters figured this out. It's called "swinging," or more specifically, the "swing-through" method, and it works—if you trust it and use it. There are other methods, but I'm going to explain the one that works best for most people. You'll learn others as you gain experience.

Swing-Through

Essentially, when the target—let's say it's a clay pigeon—crosses your view, moving left to right, for example, you start the swing *as you are mounting the gun.* Start with the gun tucked under your armpit. This is the "ready position." You pivot on the balls of your feet along the target's line of flight, the gun butt starting out and up toward your shoulder as the safety is released. Already, the end of the barrel, the muzzle, is starting to move at the same speed or *faster* than the target. As you finish the mount, the barrels, controlled by your pivoting body, have just about caught up with the target.

Now you have the gun mounted, your cheek on the comb, your left hand extended on the forend. You will find that in order to execute this swing, your left hand (for a right-hander) does a lot of the work. This is what you want. Your extended index finger is like a pointer, pointing at the target as it travels its course.

Now you are concentrating on the target, but you are at least *aware* of the end of the barrel. Keep swinging. As you become aware that the barrel is *even with the target,* pull the trigger and keep swinging. The target will shatter.

I'll bet you're saying, "But I thought you said we can't shoot right at the target. What gives?" Well, you *aren't* shooting right at the target. Remember that ¼ second of delay between the time your brain tells you to fire and the time the shot leaves the gun barrel? During that time, you are still swinging, so when the gun actually goes off, the barrel is *in front* of the target, swinging along its line of flight. This establishes the proper "forward allowance," or "lead." It's no different from a football quarterback who throws to a receiver. He throws where the receiver is going to be; the receiver, in effect, runs into the ball. That's what you want: for the target or game bird to run into the shot.

The pattern of a shotgun does not go through the air like a pie plate. Instead, although its width increases depending upon choke and distance, the shot charge, called the "shot string," actually resembles a sausage, sometimes up to 20 feet in length. A good portion of the string can pass harmlessly ahead of the bird or target, but if the target flies into the middle or end portion of the string, you register a hit.

However, if you fire so that the front of this string passes behind the target, *all* of the shot will miss. You haven't got a chance. That's why you hear experienced shotgunners say that it is almost impossible to miss a target in front.

Speaking of misses, most come from two sources: Either the shot goes behind because the shooter stops her swing, thus placing the muzzle even with or behind the target when the shot goes off, or the shot goes high because the shooter lifted her head from the comb of the stock. Head lifting is common because we want to get a good view of what's going on. But it results in a miss when, as the head lifts, the muzzle rises with the face, and the shot charge goes over the bird.

Another cause for missing is not seeing the target clearly before you start the swing-mount-overtake-fire procedure. It is imperative that you get a good look at the target so that you are swinging along its line of flight. One way to accomplish this is to imagine that the target has a vapor trail coming out the back, like a jet airplane. Swing along this vapor trail, pass the bird, and fire as you pass through.

One saying that the British have for this method of shooting properly relates the path your gun's muzzle should take: "Butt, belly, beak, *bang!*" Start from the rear, as the gun is being mounted, swing with your whole torso, like a golfer pivoting toward the ball, catch up with the bird on the same plane on which it's traveling, pass through it, and fire when you have passed it—and keep swinging.

Types of Shots

The easiest shot for the beginning shotgunner to make is the true straightaway—the bird or target going directly away from the shooter so that no perceived lead is necessary. This is the shot all beginners hope for, and the ones good shooting coaches start off with to build confidence.

You can get a shot such as this at the local skeet range shooting the station 7 low house target, or by having someone with a target trap throw them for you. Such shots, however, are not to be discounted as too easy; in game shooting for upland birds, a high percentage of the shots you'll be offered are a variation on the straightaway, sometimes quartering away to the left or right, where little lead is needed.

The crossing shot, such as the one I've described above to show the swing-through method, are generally found in the dove field or in waterfowl shooting. We'll discuss these shots and the hunting methods for these birds in Chapters 6 and 7, but for now, suffice it to say that these are among the hardest shots to make. But with repetition, you'll make them. One fine day, the lights will go on, and suddenly your experience, muscle memory, and determination will all come together and you'll start dropping birds.

In the thickest cover for grouse, woodcock, and quail, there is little time to do anything except mount and fire. Swinging is often a cruel joke. Your gun barrel bangs against a tree; the bird cuts behind another; you hear wings but see nothing; you take shot after shot and nothing drops. Don't despair—even the finest shots do little better than a bird for every three shells in such conditions. Shooting is a complicated athletic endeavor, much more difficult to do well than play tennis, for example. But remember, it's supposed to be fun—treat it that way.

Hunting Upland Birds

*Smith discusses the various species of game birds,
their habitat, types of upland bird guns,
and how to be an effective
wingshooter.*

U pland birds are birds that don't live in the lowlands; in other words, they aren't waterfowl (ducks, geese, rails, and snipe). In this chapter, we'll take a look at the birds, the dogs, the techniques, the shots presented, and the etiquette of the upland bird hunt.

Upland birds are distributed throughout the United States and Canada, as well as Mexico. Some of the most exciting shooting is in South America; the most traditional, in England and the continent. We'll look at these birds in the order of their popularity as well as their availability for sport.

Upland birds are short-lived. Depending upon species, up to 70 percent of the birds born in the spring never see the next spring. They die from accident, predation, and loss of habitat, which prevents birds from ever being born. Biologists (including this author) tell us that hunting is a "compensatory" rather than an "additive" cause of mortality. That is, hunting takes birds that would have otherwise died in some different manner but does not add to the overall death toll. This has been shown in countless studies, some commissioned by people who would have liked the results to have been different. Upland birds are great on the table. They have not been laced with steroids and preservatives like domestic fowl. Their meat is less fatty and contains far less cholestorol—and calories—than domestic meat.

If you enjoy cooking a fine meal, as I do, then hunting and shooting the makings of a game dinner is a trip to the butcher shop or the grocery store carried one step further back. Like a gardener who grows her own vegetables, you are gathering your own meat. For this privilege, you pay in taxes, licenses, and fees, the money necessary to buy and manage land that will be the home for these birds—and countless other creatures that are not hunted. If someone asks you, "How can you shoot those little birdies?" you can tell them, "Well, you start from behind, pass through, pull the trigger, and keep swinging."

Dove Shooting

There are two species of doves hunted in the United States: the mourning dove and the white-wing dove. The mourning dove is by far the more popular. The white-wing is hunted in only a few southwestern states.

In fact, in the thirty-seven states where doves are legal game, the mourning dove season enjoys a popularity associated with your average Christmas holiday. The opening day is usually an excuse for a big gathering of the shooting community and a barbecue at the end of the day's shooting. The dove is one of the few birds more effectively hunted when a lot of people are around to keep the birds moving. Hunters wait at the edge of fields in which these birds feed and pop away at them as they pass by.

Part of what makes dove shooting so popular is that it is the first hunting season to open, set by federal law to start, at the discretion of each state, on or after September 1. This means comfortable, even hot, temperatures. But that's okay; there isn't much walking involved in dove shooting except to and from your stand, where you'll await the birds' passage.

Lest this sound a little too easy, I should hasten to add that doves are the most difficult upland bird to shoot. Statistically, more shotshells are fired at doves than any other bird that flies, upland or waterfowl. A good shot will take perhaps six birds from a box of shells. Doves are fast—up to 65 mph in still air—and they twist and sideslip with ease, often flying right out of the shot pattern before it reaches them in that tenth of a second we discussed earlier. I once shot twelve doves with thirteen shots. The next day I missed twenty-seven in a row. If you do well, don't brag—it's pointless.

The hunting usually involves finding a field where the doves are feeding or a flight path between their feeding place and their roosting cover—doves, like all birds, like to lay up during the middle of the day, feeding in the morning and evening. Once such a field or flyway has been found, shooters try to position themselves so that they will be within shotgun range—40 yards or closer—to the birds as they pass by. Concealment is not as critical as it is with waterfowl, but drab or camouflage clothing and holding still certainly help. Doves rarely flare wildly when they spot you, but they do often slip out of range, and they always light the afterburners if they spot you.

As a dove or a small flock appears in range, pick out one bird well in advance of when you plan to shoot. Keep your eyes on that bird. As it gets within range, stand with the gun's stock under your armpit, pivot with the bird, and swing through, as discussed in the previous chapter. Because doves are so fast, you may have to swing through farther before you trigger the shot, perhaps seeing a bird length or two between the bird's beak and your *moving* gun barrel. As with any swing-through shot, keep the gun barrel accelerating through the firing zone; don't slow down in anticipation of firing. You'll only shoot behind. (For your information, "shooting" is when the hunter waits for the game to come to her, as opposed to "hunting," which is to go out and actively search for it.)

Dogs are an enjoyable but not really necessary adjunct to a dove hunt. They are, of course, great company, and dove hunting gets them in shape for the seasons that will open in the fall. But be aware that the heat can get to them, especially if they're out of shape from a long summer spent lounging on your couch. Be sure to take plenty of water for them if it's not available in the field. Retrievers, or pointing dogs that like to retrieve, can help find downed birds. If you drop a dove, keep your eyes on the spot, walk directly there immediately and start searching; normally they aren't hard to find. Look for some of the loose feathers that come off the bird when it strikes the ground.

Dove Equipment and Guns

Equipment for dove shooting should consist of a gun and plenty of shotshells—a minimum of two boxes. Many experienced dove hunters prefer a gas-operated autoloader (plugged to hold only three shells—it's a federal law) because these guns soak up recoil via their mechanism and weight, especially if the gun has a recoil pad on it, which it should. Long barrels swing more smoothly, and 28 inches is about right, although you won't notice much difference with a 26-inch barrel. Any gauge capable of shooting one ounce of #7½ shot will do, and if any species can effectively be hunted with the 28-gauge, this is it. However, day in and day out, the 20 is the gauge of choice.

Doves are migratory, and the least little cold snap seems to send them south in search of warmer climes. Most dove shooting takes place in warm to hot weather, so dress accordingly. There's no need for a shooting coat or vest, because your shells and any birds you bag can be kept right next to you. You'll probably find that light slacks in muted colors and a camouflage shooting shirt with a recoil patch works fine. Although blaze orange is not required by law in all states, wearing something blaze is always recommended for safety.

Shooting glasses, which should be worn whenever you go afield, are absolutely imperative for dove shooting. Other shooters' spent shot can drop on you as you're looking up for incoming birds. On bright days, choose an amber or vermilion lens; on cloudy days, a yellow lens brightens the landscape and allows you to pick out the birds faster by increasing the contrast between brown birds and brown background.

It's a grand idea to carry a little shooting stool with you. These are commercially available for less than $20 and provide a seat and a camouflage pouch attachment that holds shells, birds, lunch, a cold drink, and anything else you may need.

If you ever get the chance to go to Mexico to shoot white-winged doves, you should do it. The Mexican limits on the number of birds you can take daily are liberal—easily twice those in the States—and the birds are present, literally, by the millions. In three days of shooting in Mexico, you will fire at more doves than you will in three years back home. But Mexico is a foreign country with its own way of doing business. If you plan to go, do so with a reputable outfitter who will handle all the licenses, permits for guns, and so forth. (See the Directory in the back of the book for sources.) To try it on your own the first time is asking for trouble.

Doves, both mourners and whitewings, are excellent on the table, offering dark, rich breast meat. Even though they're small, the liberal limits allow you to pick up enough for a meal fairly quickly. I like them barbecued with a strip of bacon wrapped around them and served with wild rice.

In all, dove shooting is great fun, the targets tricky to baffling, and the companionship of other shooters certainly a plus.

Pheasant Hunting

The ringneck pheasant is a wildlife success story, introduced in the 1880s in Oregon and later in other places. The birds found areas of burgeoning agricultural economy to their liking and moved right in, breeding like rabbits.

Pheasants are considered among the best wild game meat available—who hasn't heard of pheasant under glass? They are crafty and difficult to get into the air for a clean shot, making them something of a trophy bird. Pheasants have lived for thousands of years beside humans

Pheasant
(CHRISTOPHER SMITH)

in their homeland in China, and they brought their crafty ways with them when they came to North America. Their relatives have been slickering your relatives ever since.

Pheasant numbers reached a zenith shortly after World War II, dropping down to pitiful numbers when clean farming eliminated the permanent grasses and cover the birds need. But in the mid-1980s, the federal Farm Bill mandated set-aside acreage—land left fallow—and the birds rebounded. On April 4, 1996, Congress reauthorized the Conservation Reserve Program (CRP) set-aside program for an additional seven years at 36.4 million acres as part of the farm bill. This proves once again that habitat—not predators or hunting—is the limiting factor on game populations.

Pheasant hunting is practiced by groups of a dozen or more shooters who walk crop fields to drive the birds to waiting gunners. They also can be hunted by one or two hunters with good dogs, and they are the object of adoration by those who can afford a driven shoot in England or Europe.

The pheasant is also adaptable enough that it is the mainstay on shooting preserves all across the country. Once released, it immediately becomes wild and therefore a worthy adversary, even at a low-rent game farm. Many beginning shooters cut their shooting teeth on shooting-preserve pheasants. They are a great way to start.

Pheasant Dogs

If you don't hunt pheasants with a dog, you won't get many pheasants. The bird provides some of the best dog work imaginable. Virtually any breed, from a farm collie to a blooded English setter, is better than no dog at all, but the flushing and retrieving breeds are the most popular: springer spaniels, Labrador retrievers, golden retrievers, and the like. Pointing breeds that handle pheasants well include Brittanys, German shorthairs, pointers, English setters, and any of the versatile breeds such as wirehairs, griffons, and pudelpointers.

The dog that can hunt pheasants effectively is usually a little long in the tooth, an experienced campaigner with a half-dozen seasons under its belt. A pointing dog hunts by locating game with its nose, then stiffening into a point, that same nose indicating to the hunter the location of the bird. The hunter then walks in and flushes the bird, which theoretically offers a clear shot.

In practice, however, pheasants haven't read the same play book. A

The flushing and retrieving breeds are the most popular for pheasant hunting. Steve Smith's daughter, Amy Schultz, is pictured with one of each: a springer spaniel at left, and Amy's Lab, K.D.

(STEVE SCHULTZ)

rooster pheasant (the brightly colored male, which is the only sex legal to hunt except on some shooting preserves) will let the dog point, then will skulk away, even in very thin cover where you wouldn't think they could find concealment. The hunter walks in to flush, but the bird has left already, and the dog must find it again.

The flushing breeds, on the other hand, have no predisposition toward pointing. If they had their way, they'd catch the bird on the ground, and that's what they try to do. They pursue the bird by its foot scent relentlessly until the bird realizes that staying on the ground is pointless and uses its last-ditch defense—its wings—to get away from what it sees as a ground-based predator.

I love both the retrieving/flushing breeds and the pointing breeds. Speaking purely personally, I can tell you for sheer beauty, nothing rivals a pointer or a setter locked up on a solid pheasant point. For sheer effectiveness, nothing rivals a juggernaut Lab, its nose to the ground, tail whipping, coursing a running pheasant as you jog along trying to stay within gun range.

A pheasant is a tough bird to bring to hand, even after it has been hit. A good retriever is about the best conservation agent there is, because if the bird stays on the ground, eventually a good dog will corral it and bring it back to you.

Pheasant Guns

A pheasant is the toughest upland bird to hunt. (Turkeys are considered big game.) This is not the place for small gauges and open chokes firing fine shot. Instead, this is 12-gauge country.

The upside of this is that the shots will be few because the limits range across the country from one to four rooster pheasants a day. The downside is that there is a lot of walking between shots, and the 12-gauge recoil with a big load is formidable. A pheasant has to be hit in a vital area—the head, neck, and upper chest—with *at least one ounce* of #6 or larger (#5 or #4) shot.

One ounce of shot can be fired from a 20-gauge, but the same amount of shot is more effective coming out a bigger hole, such as a 16- or 12-gauge. A number of light 12-gauge guns are available on the market, mostly Over and Under doubles, and a 1⅛-ounce load of #6 shot with 3 drams of powder is not a heavy-recoiling combination in a 6½-pound gun.

Barrels should be fairly long, no shorter than 26 inches on a repeating gun, and preferably 28 inches on a double. Pheasants, for the most part, are not fast-moving birds, so if there is no intervening cover, speed is not of the essence as it is with grouse or quail in the brush.

The typical pheasant shot is most likely to be of a steeply rising bird, making this bird the exception to the rule that most birds are missed by shooting over the top. In effect, these shots are commonly missed by being behind the bird, but in this case "behind" translates into "under."

A pheasant's life is forward of its wings; it isn't in that long tail. When a pheasant flushes, it looks big (it is) and slow (it's not). If you get lazy with your swing and hit beneath the bird or, worse yet, into the rear of the bird, it's able to run off and escape unless you have a good dog that gets on the bird quickly.

A pheasant passing by overhead with the wind behind it is as fast as a mallard duck, and you must swing through sometimes as much as two bird lengths *and keep swinging* to hit it up front. But its flight is usually pretty level, it doesn't zig and zag like a woodcock, dove, or snipe, and it gets started fairly slowly. Just concentrate on the head or the white ring around the neck. That's your target. *Keep swinging.*

Hunting Methods

Pheasants, as mentioned above, are hunted in a variety of habitats and places. Hunting methods also vary by weather and by season. The later season is more taxing because the cover is down, the birds are reduced in number and wary from hunting pressure, and the weather is usually worse.

The early season has its difficulties in that the birds, although young and inexperienced, also are scattered across thousands of acres of habitat not yet flattened by weather.

But there are opportunities here as well, and the well-versed pheasant hunter takes advantage of them. Let's take a look at the first outing of the year—opening day.

Usually, opening day across pheasant range comes in late October or early November. The crops pheasants depend upon for food—primarily corn—have not been harvested, and the birds use the cornfields for feeding, loafing during the middle of the day, and hiding from predators. Pheasants run from trouble, and corn rows offer virtual highways for their sprints.

In the early season, the birds follow a general pattern of behavior unless greatly disturbed by hunters or the harvest. They roost in the annual grass fields—land set aside through the Conservation Reserve Program—until sunrise, when they head for feed in corn or milo or whatever hasn't been harvested yet. They fill up fairly quickly, their crops bulging with feed that will be digested later with the help of a little grit they'll pick up alongside the road or in the field. (Gallinaceous birds such as pheasants have a crop so they can fill it quickly and head back for cover, thus reducing their exposure to predators.)

Pheasants will head for water if it's available, then lie in thick cover—at least thick overhead cover that foils hawks—until the afternoon, at which point they'll feed again, visit water if it's available, then head back to roost in the thick grass fields.

A good early-season strategy is to try to follow the birds on this daily pattern. The exception to this is the big crop fields, especially corn. Unless you are part of a party of ten or more hunters and a number of dogs, forget about going into the corn. The fields these days are so huge—many in the Midwest cover a full square mile—that they could contain hundreds of birds but you may never see one, at least within shotgun range.

A big-field drive consists of a number of hunters and their dogs lining up abreast of one another, and walking the cover toward a line of "blockers." A "blocker" is a person who blocks by his very presence, that is, prevents the birds from distancing themselves farther away from the approaching hunters. As the drivers approach the blockers, the theory is that the presence of the blockers will force any pheasants running ahead of the drivers into the air. It works, but many people dislike the civilized atmosphere that comes with a dozen people and a half-dozen dogs, each intent upon the same thing. For a beginning pheasant hunter, this is a daunting operation.

More productive hunting is available in smaller pockets of cover and with smaller parties. Many people like to hunt in pairs with a dog or two. A team such as this finds its best chances in the thick pockets where the birds gather during the middle of the day in the early season.

Such places are most productively hunted in bad weather—wind, rain, snow—the kind of weather when it would be best to be indoors looking at it through a window. But the truth is, early season or late, the best pheasant hunting takes place in the lousiest weather because the birds don't want to move; they want to stay put down in the thick stuff where it's warm and snug. If you hunt into the wind, which you should do so your dog can catch the scent of the birds more readily, the birds won't hear you coming. Your sounds will be muffled by the wind and the wet ground. As a result, the shots are likely to be at close range, resulting in more clean kills.

As the season progresses, a few things happen to turn early-season pheasant hunting into something entirely different. First, the young, foolish birds have been either shot or educated. Game officials estimate that, in the big pheasant states, 50 to 80 percent of all the birds bagged in a season are taken during the first hour of the first day of the season. These are young birds caught unaware. They smarten up, *pronto*.

When the fields of crops are harvested, the birds tend to gravitate toward the remaining cover: fencerows, weedy ditches, the banks alongside creeks and rivers, cattail sloughs, coulees and washes in the West, and the grassy, terraced hillsides between crop fields where it's too steep for the farmer to plow. Old, deserted homesteads—"house places"—in Iowa, Nebraska, and the Dakotas also are fine, out-of-the-weather spots the birds will head for once the corn is knocked down and the milo stubs plowed under.

So, the late-season pheasant hunter faces a peculiar situation: There are fewer birds, but there is also less cover for them. The birds will head for what's available—and so should you.

These birds should be hunted quietly. *Any* upland bird is spooked by the sound of the human voice, and pheasants are perhaps the worst for hearing you and running or flushing out of range. Avoid talking to the dog, to your companion, or even coughing if you can help it. Take regular breaks, get together and visit if you must, but remember that talking as you're working cover spooks even the least-wary bird.

Driven Shooting

A long-held tradition in the British Isles and on the European continent, and one catching on in the United States, is the driven shoot. Pheasants in such shoots are the bird most likely shot.

A driven shoot consists of a line of shooters, called "guns," who wait as drivers called "beaters" work a woodlot or a field to flush pheasants, which will then fly over the guns. The guns fire at the birds, which are picked up by dogs under the control of handlers waiting behind the line. The shooting takes place from numbered "pegs" or "butts," and after each "drive," the guns rotate so each gets a chance at the best location.

In Britain, this type of shoot is steeped in tradition, tracing its origin back to King Edward VI (1537–1553) and the royal family. Even today, the royal family maintains a shooting estate, Sandringham, in England.

Such shoots spawned an entire social infrastructure and gave rise to an industry, which was all based upon the fact that the courtiers, each currying favor with the reigning monarch, wanted everything to be just right. The boots came from Bond Street, the clothing from Saville Row, and the guns from makers such as Purdey, Holland & Holland, Boss, Woodward, and others, London makers exclusively. In fact, the guns were more often than not made in pairs for the gentlemen, and ladies—for many did shoot and shot quite well—spurned the new repeating guns and chose instead the traditional side-by-side, double-barrel side-lock shotgun.

But the birds were many—a daily bag of one thousand birds for eight guns was quite common—and the Brits craved firepower, for each pheasant on the ground was worth quite a few shillings when the game dealer's wagon trundled in and the birds were sold to restaurants and exclusive clubs in London. There was an economic reason to bring the largest number possible to earth. By using a pair of guns—identical in every detail, a "matched pair"—and employing a loader, the shooter would fire two shots at passing birds, hand over his empty gun to his loader, and have it instantly replaced by an identical, loaded shotgun. With a good loader and a matched pair, a good shooter could keep up a steady hail of shot at the incoming birds. Even today, shooting etiquette prohibits repeating shotguns—only doubles are allowed, including the Over and Under. This is for safety, of course. When the gun is broken open, it is harmless and everyone around you knows it.

The shooting party would be entertained by shoots in the morning, a lunch in the field complete with fine linen and servants, a shoot in the afternoon, and then a formal dance or other gala in the evening in the country house of their host. It was an era that ended when The War to End All Wars took an entire generation of men.

Or did it? Today many of those same estates feature driven shoots and all the hoopla that goes with them. But instead of entertaining for status or to reciprocate others for their invitations, today it is done for money, and Americans are the most likely to attend.

It is possible to go to England or Scotland for a shoot, be entertained in the finest tradition of British hospitality, and travel back in time to manor houses, butlers, gamekeepers, and shooters in ties and tweeds—if you've got the money.

For three days of such shooting, expect to spend several thousand dollars per person, less for nonshooting guests who just want to watch. The cost usually covers transportation from the airport, all lodging, meals, shotshells (and you can shoot a bunch in three days), and in some cases gratuities.

The shooting itself is highly regulated, and a predetermined number of birds are taken off shooting estates every year. The breeding stock that is left intact after the season ends in the winter is supplemented by young birds released and allowed to go wild the following spring and summer. The gamekeeper usually has a perfect idea of how many birds his estate carries, and how many can be safely taken by shooters. The shooting days are then planned and sold, usually through booking agents in the United Kingdom and the United States.

Driven shooting is tricky, and you have to develop a knack for it. The birds are coming toward you instead of going away, as we're used to in the States. Birds are much easier to kill when the head and neck are exposed, coupled with the bird's incoming speed and the shot charge's velocity. The collision of the two is almost always fatal, and if it's not, the fall from 25 to 30 yards will usually do the bird in immediately.

As the birds appear, often a dozen to twenty at a time, the shooter has to determine if any are going to pass over her stand, which is a rough 45-degree slice. This ensures safety and also ensures that each gun is taking only her fair share of the birds. Dangerous shooters or those not observing proper codes of etiquette are asked to leave the field.

The gauge of choice has long been the 12, and remains so today. But as mentioned, the Brits use light-recoiling loads with much less shot than standard U.S. loads. In some locales, shooters are limited to 20-gauge guns, and still others use this bore as a matter of choice, especially if the birds are not especially "tall" (high) by driven-bird standards. An incoming pheasant at 25 yards is easily killed with a 20-gauge load of an ounce of shot or a bit under.

The typical shot is an incomer that will pass a bit right or left. This shot is made by swinging through from behind and firing when the muzzle passes the bird's head. As always, *keep swinging.*

That's the pheasant in a nutshell: chased by farm boys and kings, it means something different to everyone who hunts it. Give it a try.

Quail Hunting

There are several species of quail in North America, but the most common is the bobwhite, named for its song, which every schoolkid learns to whistle.

It is found throughout the South, where tradition surrounds it, but its real homeland is America's Breadbasket: Iowa, Missouri, Nebraska, Oklahoma, and Kansas. Most quail in these states are taken as an adjunct to pheasant hunting, although a huge number of shooters head out for them on purpose.

Quail
(CHRISTOPHER SMITH)

In the South, there is not much of a stable population of quail outside of private lands managed especially for them. Some of these private lands are commercial operations that exist only for quail hunting on a per-day basis.

Quail also are a mainstay of shooting preserves across the country, along with pheasants and chukars. They are fabulous on the table, and are considered by many to be one of the three finest white-meat game birds; the other two are ruffed grouse and pheasant.

Quail live in family and extended family groups called "coveys." Each night, and when alerted, they form a circle with their bottoms facing inward, their heads outward. When they flush, they take off like a fragmentation grenade, each bird seemingly headed in a different direction. It is daunting to the uninitiated and the initiated alike.

Quail Dogs

Quail were made for pointing dogs, and it is no secret that the bloodlines of fine quail dogs are much more closely guarded than our own. Of the traditional quail dogs, the pointer is king because its nose, style, and ability to handle the heat make it ideally suited for the bird and the country in which it lives. Each year, field trials all over the country pit dog against dog to determine which is the best that day, culminating in the National Bird Dog Championship held on the grounds of the Ames Plantation in Grand Junction, Tennessee. The bird these champions of champions pursue? The bobwhite quail.

A quail dog is a hard-driving, fast-running animal that hits scent and slams to a halt, tail up (the better to be seen in tall grass). The dogs usually hunt in pairs ("braces"), and also are trained to be competent retrievers of downed birds.

With the possible exception of woodcock shooting, no bird-hunting pastime is more closely tied to the dogs. This is partly because the bird-dog culture runs deep in traditional quail country, and partly because the bobwhite acts like a real gentleman, holding quite well for the dog (although not as well as woodcock) in coveys, and very well as scattered singles.

Because of this, there is an etiquette, a form and function in hunting quail over pointing dogs. The dogs go on point. One shooter, or at most two, approaches the dogs, coming in from the side so the dogs can see them, and flush the birds. The shots are taken and the scattered birds from the covey, the "singles," are either pursued or not, depending upon the whim of the host and the availability of birds.

One shooter, at the most two, approaches the dogs, coming in from the side so the dogs can see them.

(LAURIE MORROW)

Since the covey arrangement is a protective the birds employ, it takes eight to ten birds to make it work. To shoot enough birds to drop the covey's number below this threshold is to doom the birds, especially late in the season when cover is down and weather and predators conspire to make life tough for six-ounce birds who whistle up their scattered mates before evening.

The etiquette also calls for no shooting late in the afternoon, because the birds may not be able to gather back together before darkness. In some states, hunting quail after 4:30 P.M. is forbidden for this reason.

On the fine plantations in the South, the dogs are often run in braces for no more than an hour, then fresh dogs are sent out. The dogs, knowing this, go all-out for their hour, like kids at lunchtime recess from school.

Dogs that can handle quail with the appropriate drive and fire are as valuable to their owners as the long-legged thoroughbreds at Churchill Downs. The offspring of these dogs command very dear prices, as do the services of the males as studs. Whoever coined the term "a dog's life" didn't have one of these old boys in mind.

Quail Guns

The bobwhite quail was invented for the 20-gauge shotgun. Or maybe it was the other way around. In any event, the 20 has both the fast handling and the ballistic efficiency for these small birds. The average quail is not hard to kill on the wing; only a few shot will bring a bird to bag. (By the way, the individual little round things in a shotgun shell are called shot or "pellets.")

There is an old saying among shotgunners that "pattern fails before penetration," meaning a bird that is out of range or beyond clean (effective) killing range is really beyond the sure killing range of the pattern. The pattern falls apart long before the individual shot loses its ability to penetrate the skin and bone of the bird—or someone standing in the line of fire 100 yards away. With quail, pattern is everything. An ounce of No. #7½ or #8 shot in a barrel bored Improved Cylinder, or Improved Cylinder/Modified in a double, is about right because the patterns are wide enough to allow for a little imprecise pointing, and dense enough so that the small birds cannot slip through unscathed.

A quail gun should be light enough that it can be carried easily, yet heavy enough (or gas-operated) so that recoil is not a factor. Of course, this is true of any gun used to hunt any upland bird; carrying it all day is part of the game.

In quail hunting, especially in the Old South, a repeating gun is frowned upon, and only doubles are socially acceptable. In fact, often some of the most expensive shotguns in the world are ordered and used by quail hunters. It is not uncommon to find guns from the finest British custom makers in the gun rack at a quail plantation in the South.

Although the 20-gauge is the bore of choice, fine gun dealers usually have on hand a smattering of very light 12-gauges, some 28-gauges, and quite a number of 16-gauge guns as well, usually older guns that have seen five or more decades of service. At one time, the 16 was *the* wingshooter's gun, especially in the South and in New England. As a result, the guns in this gauge are mostly doubles and nearly all of fine old American vintage, sporting names like Parker, A. H. Fox, and L. C. Smith. The quail is a fragile fellow, and so any of these gauges will do quite well. It's a matter of taste.

Hunting Methods

Quail are hunted in several ways, but most are brought to bag by two or three hunters following dogs on foot.

Quail inhabit the edge places where crop fields join thickets of resting cover, or where farmers have left areas too close to ponds and creeks to grow up wild. The wide shelterbelts between crop fields also offer the bird the year-round cover it needs. Quail have a number of predators—hawks, owls, foxes, coyotes, feral house cats, raccoons, skunks—and so hiding from these occupies a good portion of the birds' time. In cover that will shield them from all of those hungry eyes is where you will find them.

But the main predator of quail is weather. Unlike pheasants, these small birds cannot scratch through deep snow to get food, so where snow piles up deep for long periods of time, or where ice storms are common, you'll find no birds. Ice kills birds by stopping up their nostrils (which contain no heat-producing blood vessels) and suffocating them. The thick cover they seek protects them from the onslaught of wind, cold rain, and snow.

Quail carry out a daily activity schedule nearly identical to that of pheasants: rise early, feed quickly to minimize exposure to predators and weather, return to thick cover to hide and while away the day, feed again in the late afternoon, pick up a little grit and water somewhere both morning and evening if available, then return to the thick roosting cover. They are most vulnerable to you and your hunting party in the morning and evening, because they are more in the open, making shooting easier.

However, the real sporting shooting is in the resting cover during the middle of the day. Here, the coveys burst out and fly through the maze of branches and limbs and vines, twisting and turning, a dozen targets each more difficult than the next, and all of them getting farther away. A bird taken in this stuff is a prize indeed.

When you find one quail, you'll find more, and some of the most heart-stopping upland gunning in the world comes during a covey rise of bobwhite quail. Essentially, your dog is on point, you walk in, and the birds flush—all at once—and head in different directions, it seems. You'll spot a bird and mount your gun, concentrating on that one bird. But another swings across your line of vision and that one looks slower or closer or easier, so you switch to that bird. Then another does the same thing, so you switch again. By that time, the birds are getting out of range, so you panic and pop off a shot or two to no effect.

Or the birds get up all in a rush and you point at the biggest knot of them and blaze away, feeling that there's no way you can miss. But you do, because the sky is a big place, only a tiny portion of which is ever occupied by a quail. Bird switching and covey shooting are the best ways to miss quail; they're also the easiest.

Instead, the proper way to shoot a covey rise of bobwhites is to walk in past the dog—briskly, as when approaching any point—and when the birds flush, to pick one out and shoot at it. If it falls, pick another if there is time. If you should miss, stay with the same bird and shoot again. It isn't nearly as easy as it sounds.

When the birds are scattered comes the bread and butter of quail shooting: singles. Try to keep an eye on where they're going, and go after them. But wait a few minutes until the birds relax, move about, and give off scent for the dog. When they are pointed and flushed, single quail generally travel straight away from the shooter, and there's only one, so there's no bird switching and no covey shooting. And one quail sounds much less like a swarm of killer bees compared with the covey.

Whether in coveys or as singles, quail generally will fly toward cover. If you approach the dog with this in mind, the birds will fly away from you more often than not, thus offering the easiest shot in wing-shooting—the straightaway. If you place yourself between them and the cover, they're likely to fly right at you, and then you'll get no shot at all. You'll not encounter many of the crossing shots you get with doves and pheasants; quail shooting is a sport of gentle angles.

The thing to remember is that a quail, for all its bravado and sound and rush of wings, really isn't moving that fast. You have time to see the bird, raise your gun as you recite, "My, what a fine little bird you are," and fire. Most folks get into trouble because they are determined to make doubles—that is, two birds taken with two shots from the same covey rise. They are thinking about the second shot before they complete the first, and generally end up missing both.

Instead, concentrate on taking one bird, and be content. The time will come when you'll be able to make doubles if that's what you want. In any event, when the number of birds in the covey is ten or fewer, leave them alone—there are no excess birds to be cropped.

Plantation Quail

Shooting preserves exist for the purpose of presenting game before hunters who then harvest them in exchange for money. Although there has been a widespread proliferation of such establishments in the last several decades in the United States, their history is firmly rooted in Europe and England, where birds have been propagated and released for sportsmen—and sportswomen—for nearly two centuries. Even today, the best shooting estates in England shoot released birds, which have been reared and released for the purpose of being hunted. Although shooting preserves or "game farms" have drawn some criticism, the critics generally are against all hunting in any form.

Most shooting preserves release birds on an as-needed basis; some of the private clubs release birds as juveniles, allowing the survivors of weather and predators to become quite wild and sporting. Others, especially the commercial, open-to-the-public places, release birds for the shooting party hours or a day before the hunters take the field.

Shooting preserves offer a number of advantages. First, the visitor is virtually assured of shooting because the birds are there and normally not as wily as wild birds. Second, preserves are great places to start a shooting career, because the shooter can stay and hunt as long as her wallet holds out. Third, guides and preserve dogs are available to make the hunt easier and more enjoyable. Many preserves have luxurious overnight accommodations and fine cuisine to make the experience exceptionally civilized. Finally, they offer ready hunting and a wild experience close to metropolitan areas.

The staple preserve bird is the pheasant, followed by the chukar and the bobwhite. Of these, the quail is normally the least expensive to rear and release. Shooting preserves, at their best, can simulate almost any shooting condition you can imagine from driven, Scottish-style pheasant shoots to Midwest-type milo field hunting. But of the places that specialize in released shooting, none is better known and more enjoyable than the southern quail plantation.

The quail plantations of the South—northern Florida, Georgia, the Carolina Low Country, Alabama, Mississippi—got their start not as an antebellum planters' diversion, but instead as an interesting corollary to post–Civil War Reconstruction. With much of the southern gentry killed off in the War Between the States, the end of the war raised pressing questions about who owned what and who was left to pick up the pieces. Emancipation ended the days of cheap cotton and untold riches. Northern carpetbaggers forced harsh occupation rule upon the citizenry, and the fallout resulted in wealthy northern industrialists buying southern plantations as winter homes for themselves and their families.

About this time, pine was introduced as a low-maintenance crop, and landowners found that bobwhites were attracted to the high grasses that grew in piney woods. The crop was timber (and peanuts and some cotton), and the diversion was quail.

Some of these original plantations still survive, but many were parceled off and sold during the Depression when it wasn't necessarily a good thing to be a northern industrialist. Besides, a lot of wild quail hunting was available for the asking in the South.

It did not remain so. As human population centers increased in size and number, and clean-farming practices developed in the middle of this century, the habitat for bobwhites disappeared, and with it, the birds.

But as civilization spread and the number of hunting licenses sold each year began to rise, so did the era of the shooting preserve, and none is more elegant than those that have set out to re-create the old-style quail plantation.

They all have things in common: a big house, very often a rescued and restored plantation house; horseback-mounted guides and dog handlers; and a mule-drawn wagon (to give you an idea of the cost, here, at last report, a pair of matched mules was going for $16,000) that serves as dog wagon, chuck wagon, shooter conveyance, and social center for a day afield.

A day on such a plantation goes something like this: You arise from your sleep to a rap on the door, on the other side of which a fine, liquid-sounding southern voice drawls the time and says, "Breakfast in one hour, ma'am." You awake and shower and dress for the day's shoot. Breakfast is something southern and always features biscuits and redeye gravy.

After the meal, you wander back to your room for your shotgun and coat and hat, and assemble with the other members of your party—no more than four altogether—in front of the big house where the rubber-tired quail wagon awaits, drawn by matched mules or draft horses. Your gun is stored in a padded compartment. The dogs are already loaded in their kennels in the rear of the wagon, whining with eagerness. The guide and dog handler are mounted on Tennessee walkers—you can ride, too, if you wish, but today you'll take the wagon.

You step up into the wagon and slide onto the leather-covered seat, comfortable with the old-fashioned springs that will cushion your ride. A Labrador retriever watches you from his seat next to the driver, his tail flicking a friendly hello to these new friends whom he has not yet met, for that's the way Labs are. The driver clucks to the team, and you're off, soundlessly, except for the clip-clop of shod hooves on the gravel and the comfortable, easy creaks of the wagon—and of course, the whining of the pointing dogs in their kennels.

At the first likely-looking area, the dogs—a brace of pointers—are released and told to "Hi on" by the dog handler. Coursing the field, the dogs seek scent while your wagon moves easily and slowly along a sand trail, paralleling the dogs' hunting pattern into the wind. Suddenly, one dog slams to a halt, body rigid, tail thrust straight up. His bracemate, seeing the point, staunches into a point himself, pointing the dog that is pointing the birds—"honoring."

You are told to come down from the wagon. Your gun is handed to you and you load it, moving with your shooting partner and the dog handler (now afoot) toward the dogs. Only two shooters go out from the wagon at any one time for the sake of safety. You approach the dogs from the sides, the dog handler in the middle. He coos and steadies the dogs, then thrashes the weeds in front of the lead dog with his leather flushing whip.

The birds erupt—a dozen or more, darting and twisting. You pick out one, follow its path, swing through, and fire. The bird puffs in a halo of feathers. You track another, vaguely aware that your partner is firing as well. Choosing a bird on your side, you find a high straight-away that will not endanger the dogs. You fire, and that bird drops—a clean double.

The handler congratulates you and motions for the Lab, who has been watching from his perch on the wagon. At the signal, the dog leaps down from the wagon and moves expertly to retrieve each bird. He saw one but not the others—your partner got one bird—and so he is di-rected to the downed birds by the handler, who uses his whistle and hands. The pointers are already off again, looking for another covey or the scattered singles. On the next point, the other two shooters will get their chance.

At lunchtime, you'll either head back to the big house for a huge, southern-style lunch or one will be brought out to you in the field. The afternoon shoot goes like the morning's, and then it's back to get cleaned up for a dinner with all the trimmings: southern-fried chicken, maybe some collard greens or golden breast of quail—topped off with pecan pie.

And when you consider this can be done when the snows of Janu-ary and February have locked the northern states up tight, well, life can be very, very good.

Ruffed Grouse and Woodcock Hunting

Just as bobwhites are the bird of tradition in the South, ruffed grouse and woodcock are the storied quarry of New England and the Great Lakes states. Yet it is hard to imagine two birds, so closely linked in the minds of those who seek them, that are more different from each other.

While the daylight-loving grouse thrives in the deep snows of win-ter, the nocturnal woodcock migrates south before the temperatures freeze the ground. Where the grouse hammers through cover, seem-ingly unfazed by the branches and limbs in front of it as it rushes for thick cover, the woodcock acrobats its way through the canopy of leaves, scarcely brushing a wingtip as he heads for open sky. Where the grouse feeds on the aspen buds, berries, and seeds of the uplands, the woodcock bores for worms in the wet, boggy places along streams and in alder swamps. Where the grouse's breast is some of the finest white meat you'll ever taste, and his legs dark meat (like others of his chickenlike family), the woodcock has a dark breast carried about by white legs and thighs.

Why, then, are these two so often mentioned in the same breath? Grouse and woodcock. Scotch and soda. Burger and fries. Ruth and

Ruffed Grouse (*top*) and Woodcock
(CHRISTOPHER SMITH)

Gehrig. Perhaps because they are hunted using the same methods and dogs, in many places they inhabit the same covers, and the choice of guns is identical for both. Therein, as they say, lies the tale.

There are many excellent books on both of these birds, should you want to know more, so for the purposes of this section, I'll discuss grouse and woodcock pretty much as a single entity, noting their differences as we go, but only if those differences significantly affect your hunting.

Grouse and Woodcock Dogs

Although the English cocker spaniel, a flushing dog, was originally a "woodcocker," woodcock and grouse are traditionally and most effectively hunted with pointing dogs—the English setter, Brittany, German shorthair, pointer, Gordon setter, and so forth.

The dogs quarter the upland covers, freezing on scent until the shooters arrive to flush. The woodcock will not normally run (although he does sprint short distances on occasion), but the grouse will. Compared with pheasants, however, these birds lie quite well for the dogs. Dogs of a predominantly white coloration are preferred by experienced hunters because they show up better in the woods.

Dogs are belled or are run with a beeper collar that signals their whereabouts, and tell you when they are on point. The beeper collar beeps in a rhythmic cadence, the bell falls silent. The hunters should approach quickly, as they should any pointed bird, and walk briskly past the dog to flush the bird, taking the shot when the bird is well clear of the ground.

Well-trained grouse and woodcock dogs are also fine retrievers because these birds' coloration makes them difficult to find when down, especially the woodcock.

Grouse and Woodcock Guns

Most experienced shooters of grouse and woodcock use a 20-gauge, and usually a double, either the Over and Under or side-by-side.

The 20 is light and ballistically efficient for these birds, both of which are easy to kill with a few well-placed #7½ or #8 shot. The double is better balanced and therefore faster to get into action. The 28-gauge is often used, and increasingly so are light 16-gauges and even some very light 12-gauge guns, usually imported models. The gun should not weigh much more than 6 pounds, and for a woman of average height (about 5 feet 4 inches), 5½ pounds is better.

The grouse and woodcock gun should be well fitted because the shooting is very quick, perhaps the quickest of all upland gunning. There is little time to do anything except mount and shoot, especially for grouse, who add a heart-stopping, thunderous flush to their lightning speed to confound pursuers. A single ruffed grouse in thick cover can sound like an entire covey of quail when it takes off.

Barrel lengths vary, but a double of 26 to 28 inches is fine, and a repeating gun of no more than 26 inches is a good second choice. Recoil is not a normal consideration because you'll be using light loads, and the average grouse and woodcock hunt involves fewer shots than does dove hunting, for example.

Hunting Methods

Ruffed grouse and woodcock are birds of second-growth, young forest, and as such inhabit some of the thickest cover found in the uplands: aspen clearcuts that are regenerating, alder thickets, and patches of young forest with briars and berry bushes that pull at your clothing and wrap around your legs. Sounds delightful, doesn't it?

But because of their habitat, these birds are a true prize when fairly taken. Hunting with a dog that will find and point them for you is not only the classic way to go, it's also the *only* way to go. Even when pointed, these birds are tough targets. Grouse tend to be much more difficult than woodcock for the average shooter, although there are rare individuals who find the opposite to be true.

Windy days make the birds skittish and likely to flush before your dog gets close enough to point; cool, clear, crisp days in October, when the maples and aspens are aflame with color, are the best weather to hunt the birds.

As the season progresses, woodcock hunters start to anticipate the "flights"—the migration of the woodcock. North winds anytime after the days have equal amounts daylight and darkness will often set these birds on the move, following north/south valleys and river bottoms. They travel only twenty-five miles or so a night, and the winds that take the birds from nearby covers will bring others from farther north into those same covers in a few days. The woodcock male is 25 percent smaller than the female, and if you are seeing only males, the migration is about done. The birds usually are far south long before the legal shooting season ends in the northern states.

Grouse, on the other hand, are year-round, nonmigratory residents. As the season progresses and the cover is thinned by wind and weather, the birds will shift their habitat to the remaining cover. They'll move from the briar tangles and aspen thickets to the more substantial cover of swamps, preferring cover near mature aspens because the buds of these trees provide their staple winter food.

Unlike pheasants and quail, which are killed by prolonged deep snow, ruffed grouse require it; they roost in it, burrowing into it to form a little igloo that protects them from avian predators and the bitter cold winter nights, which burn calories and sap them of their strength. Many hunters, this one included, stop hunting ruffed grouse when the snows come and the birds have moved to their winter quarters. They are too vulnerable there, and birds shot at this time of year are most often birds that would have survived to breed the following spring. After all, we want them around next year.

Prairie Bird Hunting

The birds of the open places are a mixture of native and introduced species, and include the western quail species (native, and more like the other prairie birds in their habits and habitats than they are like the bobwhite, hence their inclusion here), sharp-tailed grouse (native), sage grouse (native), Hungarian partridge (import), prairie chicken (native), and chukar (import).

Although these birds collectively inhabit a huge portion of the American West and the western Canadian provinces, they live in the portion of the continent least inhabited by humans, and so are hunted by relatively few people every year, compared with the other birds discussed.

For this reason, we'll take a cursory look at the methods used to hunt them, bearing in mind that each of these fascinating species is worthy of several books—and, in fact, more than a few volumes have been written about them already.

There are, however, a few general statements that can be made about all of them.

Prairie Guns

The shooting in the great expanses of the West, for the most part, involves long ranges. This translates into larger-gauge guns and/or tighter chokes. If I were forced to hunt all of the birds named above with a single shotgun, it would be a light 12-gauge bored tight Improved Cylinder and the second barrel nearly Full. I probably would do no worse with a 16-gauge bored the same way, and I would save a lot of foot-pounds hauling the thing up every hither and down the next yon.

If your choice is a 20-gauge, consider one-ounce loads of fairly big shot: #7½ for the quail and Hungarian partridge, and #6 for all the rest. In a single-barreled shotgun, a tight Modified in a 20-gauge will be your best bet, but resist the temptation to take long shots—certainly nothing beyond 40 yards.

Familiarity with certain other sports can make it easier to judge shooting range. Forty yards is about as far as I can throw a football, for example, and is the normal baseball throw from the shortstop position to first base. With these distances imprinted in my mind, plus a lot of experience actually pacing off the distances at which I've shot birds, my guesses are pretty close.

Use your own frame of reference. Try pacing off the distances at which you shoot birds. As you gain experience, you'll find that birds you *hope* are in range are not; those you *think* are in range usually aren't; and those you *know* are in range really are. You're better off passing up a few shots that are at the edge of good range and taking only the for-sure, in-range opportunities. Beginning hunters who bang away at everything they see quickly find themselves hunting alone. If you have an experienced mentor who is showing you the ropes, listen to that person. Nowhere is the ability to judge range more vital than on the open prairies, where there are few trees or landmarks nearby to help you judge distance.

Prairie bird hunting involves a lot of walking, climbing (chukars), and sometimes running (western quail) in order to get the birds in the air. But once up and in range, these birds are not nearly as difficult to hit as a ruffed grouse or bobwhite. Usually, when you've found one bird, you've found them all, and covey living is the norm for these birds, even if they are loosely scattered as sage grouse often are.

The best bet for these birds is to read a good book on the specific species (see the Directory for suggestions), buy some good boots, and make a lot of tracks.

Chapter 7

—

Waterfowl Hunting

*Hunting ducks and geese is a sport unique
unto itself. Smith tells you why, and
explains what you need—and
what you need to do—to
enter this aspect of
shotgun hunting
properly.*

W aterfowl hunting is the other form of wingshooting, separate
from "upland" hunting in that it takes places in the lowlands—
swamps, marshes, lakes, rivers, and other wetlands. Only not all of it
does. Some of the finest waterfowling takes place in crop fields, right
where you would expect to hunt pheasants or quail.

Waterfowling has a long and storied tradition in North America,
and in fact predates upland hunting by a number of years. As opposed
to upland hunting, where a number of new species have been introduced into the North American ecosystems from Europe, China, India,
and other places, waterfowl are native North Americans.

The birds—ducks and geese—are migratory in nature, meaning that they must be hunted essentially as they pass through from the north to the south. The vast majority of our waterfowl nest in Canada or the northern tier of states in this country, and many end up overwintering in Mexico. Because of this, their hunting and management are controlled through international treaty, and the seasons and bag limits are set by the federal government. The U.S. Department of the Interior, through the Fish and Wildlife Service, gives states parameters within which each may establish its own opening and closing dates and bag limits. The system works well, provided there are birds.

Over the last couple of years, there have been birds. A series of wet springs and summers on the nesting grounds ended a decade-long drought that had severely crippled waterfowl nesting success. In 1995, duck numbers were at a thirty-year high.

Waterfowl hunting, for the most part, is a sport of waiting and deception; you try to conceal yourself and wait until the birds come to you, as opposed to going after them as you do with upland birds.

Waterfowl hunting also has several legal and practical demands placed upon the shotshell/shotgun combinations necessary to bring these big, tough birds to hand.

Finally, waterfowl hunting uses specific breeds of dogs bred, devel-

Duck hunting is the subject of this nineteenth-century watercolor.

oped, and trained for the express purpose of bringing back the game after it's been shot, unlike upland dogs which help you find the game in the first place.

Puddle Ducks

The largest ducks, in general, are the puddle ducks, or "dabblers." They are also the most recognizable, counting the ubiquitous mallard or "greenhead" as a member of their clan.

The dabblers get their name from their habit of feeding or "dabbling" in shallow water, ducking their heads, necks, and upper bodies under water to feed on vegetation that grows in shallow water. Their legs, centrally located on their body, allow this tipping motion, and also allow the ducks to walk on land, albeit neither gracefully nor quickly. Their habit of feeding in fairly shallow water accounts for the "puddle" designation.

Puddle ducks are gregarious creatures, and as such are attracted by a spread of decoys and the sound of a well-blown duck call. They are not suckers, however, and are quick to spot movement or anything that does not appear quite right to them.

The most popular dabblers after the mallard, which is first on everyone's hit parade, are pintails, widgeons, gadwalls, blue-wing and green-wing teal, wood ducks, and black ducks. They vary in their intelligence just as they vary in their habits, but they are all generally hunted on water using decoys and calls. Even when hunters get a chance to go after them in harvested crop fields, the techniques of blind, decoys, and calling are about the same.

Hunting Methods and Gear

Inlets of large bodies of water, ponds, and rivers offer the best opportunities for bagging these ducks. The decoys are set up so that an opening is available for the incoming birds to land. The wind should be at the hunters' backs, because ducks land into the wind. This means they will be coming toward you when they decoy in, flying or "flighting" in to join what they perceive as other ducks but are actually your decoys.

Experienced callers can imitate the "highball" and "feeding chuckle," as well as the "come-back" call, enticing the birds close enough to prepare to land, at which point the hunters stand from concealment in the blind and shoot; a blind is an enclosure built in the marshes or low waters of a pond or lake, which is screened with reeds and marsh grass so shooters are hidden from view of incoming ducks and geese. Ducks are not to be shot on the water unless a cripple has to be quickly and humanely dispatched.

Those who hunt ducks make sizable investments in equipment. Among the gear cluttering up the garage at my house are waders, hip boots, camouflage parkas, waxed cotton gunning coats, boot dryers (I fall in a lot), warm-weather hats, cool-weather hats, cold-weather hats, ditto for gloves, about eight-dozen decoys in decoy bags, each with line and anchor attached, and enough duck calls and dog whistles so there's at least one of each in every coat. There's also a 17-foot freight canoe, a 14-foot aluminum boat, trailers, two pickup trucks to haul all this stuff . . . did I mention the two Labrador retrievers? Well, I need all this stuff—even as I write this, it's duck season.

Cindy Marlenee waits in a duck blind for a flight of mallards.
(PHOTO COURTESY OF U.S. FISH AND WILDLIFE SERVICE)

Diver Ducks

Diver ducks are birds that never set foot on land. Their feet are located toward the rear of their bodies, making walking on land virtually impossible.

They are birds of big water: impoundments, big river systems, the Great Lakes, and the ocean coasts. They travel in sometimes huge flocks of several hundred birds. On the average, they are smaller than the puddlers, and feed differently, diving to great depths to feed on submerged weed beds. Their tiny eyes—small to allay the pressure of the depths—aren't quite as sharp as the puddlers, but they can spot a phony set-up nonetheless.

The most common popular species of divers include greater scaup (broadbills), and lesser scaup (bluebills, redheads, canvasbacks, buffle-heads, scoters, eiders, goldeneyes, ringnecks, and old-squaws). Of these, the redheads and canvasbacks were once nearly wiped out when their feeding grounds were spoiled by pollution, but they've been making a comeback in the last two decades thanks to improved water quality. Today, these great birds are again legal targets, although the limit is just one per day.

Hunting Methods and Gear

Divers are hunted on big water, using big blinds, big boats, big guns, big dogs, and great big strings of decoys. Diver hunting is cold, hard work. Diver hunting can be, at times, incredibly dangerous. I love it.

Why? Because in all the world of wingshooting, nothing is more elemental, more visceral, than being in a small boat in deep water that is often only a few degrees from freezing. You have ventured about as far as you can into the habitat and domain of a wild creature in order to hunt it. There are no guarantees of success or your safe return. This is the bird-hunting equivalent of going after Dall sheep in the Yukon—wild, dangerous, the quarry a free spirit that regards the hunter as merely a momentary intrusion into its world of wind and cloud and sky.

The typical diver hunt takes place in a boat in the open, and regardless of how it's disguised and camouflaged, the boat still looks like a billboard. No matter; the birds pay it no mind. Compared to the puddle ducks, the divers are capricious, unreliable, unpredictable, and irresponsible. And they're not overly bright. If things look right, they'll drop in, or at least zoom by within gun range, offering you a chance at trying to catch up and pass with your gun barrel what looks like a small Tomahawk missile.

You'll hunt with a *lot* of decoys; some of the big rigs use several hundred, all tied together on a "mother line" for ease of pickup and layout. "Ease" here is a relative term; putting the decoys out and picking them up at the end of the hunt can often take several hours in the cold.

One of the most exciting ways to hunt divers, especially for those who enjoy risk, is in a layout boat. If there is a heaven and I go to it, it will be layout shooting for broadbills. You have to be nuts to try it, and once you do, you have to be crazy if you don't want to do it again many times.

In layout shooting, the shooter rides alone in a very shallow-draft, low-gunwale boat that rides *very low* in the water. It looks like a bump on the water. The decoys are spread around the boat, normally in lines to the rear of the boat, which faces into the wind. The lines of decoys in-

Ducks are hunted with many decoys.
(LAURIE MORROW)

fluence the divers to approach into the wind—toward the boat—and land as they get very close.

In most cases, a "tender" boat is moored nearby to watch the proceedings. This boat holds the dog, food, hot coffee, and other hunters who will take their turns in this "coffin," as it's been called (not always in jest). They switch places about every hour in deference to the cold. Hypothermia, a condition in which the body temperature dips dangerously low, is a real concern in conditions such as these.

It's your turn: The tender boat drops you off into the layout boat, anchored fore and aft. The decoys bob on their lines in the gentle, rolling three-foot waves. You sit down on the bottom of the boat on *your* bottom, your feet in front of you. You load your gun and lie flat on your back, the gun across your chest. The boat rolls and pitches and yaws, the sky blank and gray above you. You raise your head periodically to sneak a look at the decoys, watching for the ducks you hope will come while your fingers still work, before the cold saps your strength and your will.

Suddenly, the ducks are just *there,* blazing toward you, a dozen small, round bodies on wings that move so fast they are blurs. Bluebills! You sit bolt upright, your gloved finger finding the safety. The birds see your motion and peel to the left, lighting the afterburners. You try to pick one toward the front of the knot of twisting, sideslipping birds. You pass the bird—poke ahead of it, really, for a smooth swing is impossible from such a position. *Crack.* The wind steals the sound of the big magnum load; your 12-gauge sounds like a 28 in the huge expanse of sky and the endless swells. For a brief second, nothing else matters— not the mortgage payment, your boss's temper tantrums, your teenager's grades, nor your car's balky transmission. There is only you and the bird, now a limp form arcing toward the water.

Splash. It hits and bounces, skipping like a flat stone in the trough of a wave. And then it is still. In the distance, you see the tender boat move from its moorings toward you, the eager Chesapeake Bay retriever standing in the bow, its tail waving in anticipation. Seventy-five yards from the last decoy, the tender boat stops and the dog hits the water. Its strong, steady strokes quickly cover the distance to the bird. Its huge, gentle mouth encloses the black-and-white bird, and it turns on a dime and swims back to its waiting owner. It's hard to tell which one of them is having the most fun.

Then the tender boat is gone, and you are again painting mind pictures on the sky as the waves lap below you a fraction of an inch away.

Divers are hunted in ways other than in layout boats. Many hunters prefer huge, permanent blinds with amenities such as stoves and heaters, benches, gun racks, portable barbecue grills, and tables for gin rummy games to pass the time. Layout boats most often are taken as an adjunct to big water-puddle duck hunts.

But there is something special about diver hunting, for the birds speak to us of wild places, of a land to the north of snow and ice and desolation, and when they pass through on their migration south, it reminds us that there is still a lot of wilderness out there.

Canada Geese

Duck numbers in North America have swollen thanks to wise land use and abundant rain. These birds are at a three-decade high at the time of writing. And that's good.

But a real management success story involves geese, particularly the Canada goose. ("Canadian" is a misnomer; the proper term for the big black-and-white-and-gray bird is "Canada goose.") Canada geese saw their numbers shrink until they became a rarity in the 1950s. In the following decades, the establishment of the refuge system along the birds' migratory route gave them places to rest and nest and feed, and enlightened legislation that protected at least a portion of their nesting grounds brought a comeback to the point that, in some parts of the country, the birds are a downright nuisance.

Because Canada geese interfere with farmers' newly sprouted wheat and can foul beaches and golf courses, a number of states have special early "nuisance-goose" seasons. These are fun, but have no impact on lowering the goose population to a manageable level. Hunting never does that; that's nature's job.

Hunting Methods

Canada geese often are shot as a by-product of duck hunting, both diver and puddler, but most often, goose hunting is done on purpose.

While there are good opportunities over water, where the birds rest during the day, the best chances come over land in the birds' feeding fields, for they are grazers and love the roots and seeds of tender plants. The best way to hunt is to determine what fields the birds are using to feed; pick one, and then be there when the birds show up.

Canadas are fairly civilized about getting up in the morning. Ducks

Sue King, Dial Dunkin, and Laurie Morrow hunt
waterfowl in Mexico.

are likely to pay you a visit a few minutes before sunrise; geese like to
sleep in, usually dropping by a half-hour or so later.

One way to hunt geese is to dig a pit in a harvested cornfield (with
permission from the farmer) and scatter silhouette or full-bodied decoys to look as if the birds are walking into the wind to feed. Geese land
and take off into the wind, so decoys that show this pattern look fairly
natural. If you can't dig a pit, hunkering down in any standing corn or
lying flat and covering with camouflage cloth and a few corn or grain
stalks will do the trick *if the birds want to use that field anyway*.

In fact, this is a good method for any kind of waterfowling: The
birds will be where they want to be, and no amount of decoys, expert
calling, or perfect blind placement and concealment will entice them to
come very far from where they want to go.

For this reason, and especially with geese, it is imperative that you do your scouting ahead of time to know where the birds are feeding and what time they show up. The daily pattern calls for them to feed in the morning, retire to water during the middle of the day, feed again later in the afternoon, and then head for water for the night. All waterfowl spend their nights on the water, far from shore and the reach of land-lubber predators.

Okay, you've got a field, the birds are using it, you're there well before daylight (gad!), and you're concealed. You hear the geese before you see them, honking to one another. They see your spread of decoys, and start to drop toward you. You lie on the call, telling them the following in goose language: *Good eats, no danger, we've missed you, come join us.*

The birds drop lower and lower, their talk quieting to a few little grunts, a way of keeping track of one another as they choose a landing spot on the ground—all those wings and necks could get tangled without this in-air traffic-control system. You wait. And wait. And wait. Suddenly, when they are over the decoys, you rise and pick a bird's *head.* The head is your target. If you can see the eye, so much the better. A winged goose at 50 yards is a crippled goose; a head-shot goose at 15 yards is Christmas dinner.

You fire and the bird drops. If state game laws permit, you can choose another if the flock is still in range. A flock of geese can vanish quickly once shooting starts, however, and at the very least they will have turned away so that their heavy primary feathers and heavier bones shield their vital organs. Be content with one. (The U.S. Fish and Wildlife Service and your state fish and game department publish hunters' rules and regulations every August. Copies are available at your local sporting goods store and local fish and game clubs, and are issued in every hunters' safety course.)

A dog is convenient but unnecessary, especially if the ground is frozen. A goose dropping from 30 yards onto a frozen field may as well be dropping onto a parking lot. Even wing-tipped, it will be dead when you go to retrieve it.

If you find wounded waterfowl, however, keep the dog under control so it's out of danger, and then quickly dispatch the bird with another shot, on water or on land. Crippled birds are a fact of life although there are not nearly as many as some people would have you think. Do what it is you've come to do, but do it humanely, quickly, and efficiently. The best way to prevent crippled birds is to make telling, killing shots at the outset. With *all* birds, that means the head and neck. These are your targets, *always.* This way, death is instant and painless, like turning out a light.

Snow Geese

The other common geese are the snow geese, and their color counterpart, blue geese. These birds nest farther north than any other hunted waterfowl, and can be found from the Hudson Bay to Mexico. They are fascinating animals.

During the migration, they normally travel in huge flocks, and few people who see them get a chance to hunt them because their migration flights are long and high. Some flocks reportedly leave the far north and do not set their wings to land until they are over the Gulf Coast.

Snow geese are hunted over land, in wheat stubble and in rice fields, where they, too, graze the roots and waste grain. Sometimes they invade the unharvested grain, making them incredibly unpopular with farmers, who may see one hundred bushels of wheat a day disappear down the gullets of a flock of birds.

On such hunts, the number of decoys can number from 500 to 1,000, and in such cases, almost anything white will work: old cloth diapers are the best. Some companies make and sell cloth snow goose decoys that look like old cloth diapers. Snow geese travel in huge flocks; you need a bunch of decoys to toll them in. In fact, another good rule of thumb for waterfowl (duck or goose) is that you must have more decoys out than the size of the flock you expect to come in. In the early duck season, for example, the flocks of ducks are small—maybe a half-dozen mallards. A dozen decoys may do it, and three dozen would look odd to the birds. Later on, as the birds congregate for migration, the decoy numbers must increase. Simply put, you won't get 500 snow geese to sit down among 50 snow goose decoys—unless they were going to that field anyway.

Geese are often hunted by a method called "pass shooting." After figuring where the birds are coming from and where they want to go, shooters position themselves below the line of flight and shoot at birds that come within range. You'll often see folks gathered around refuge areas, waiting for the birds to flap by to or from feeding fields. These "firing lines" usually are not productive, because invariably someone thinks he's shooting a rifle with a 100-yard range, and shoots at everything he sees, thus flaring the birds higher for everyone. I don't like pass shooting ducks or geese. You should have to work for them. But if that's all your area offers, well, work you must.

Waterfowl Guns and Shooting

Ducks and geese are protected under a special rule that dates from the 1980s and has since become the law of the land: non-toxic shot.

Studies found that ducks and geese ingest spent lead shot thinking it's grit, and die from lead poisoning. Since hunting is done from blinds that are used year after year, the lead buildup can be incredible. So, the U.S. Fish and Wildlife Service banned lead shot for waterfowl. This meant a nontoxic substitute had to be found, and it was steel shot.

Actually, it's really iron shot, and it has several not-so-good side effects. First, it is very hard, in many cases harder than the steel used to make existing shotgun barrels. Early steel shot had a tendency to damage the barrels of fine guns.

Second, steel shot lacks the specific gravity of lead shot, so it has less energy when it strikes a bird, making it less efficient—spell that: It doesn't kill as well.

However, three things have worked to at least mitigate these effects. First, it was found that using more open chokes kept the shot and the barrels out of contact with each other, and the shot was placed in thick polyethelyne cups to act as a buffer between shot and barrel. Second, it was found that using bigger steel shot made up a good portion of that lost effectiveness—#2 steel is about the equivalent of #4 lead, for example. Third, another recently developed new shot is nontoxic, approved by the USF&WS, and is denser than steel, although still not like lead: bismuth shot, actually a bismuth/tin alloy. This shot is expensive, but it won't harm gun barrels, and it kills better than steel.

One thing that this movement to less-efficient loads has done almost across the board is eliminate the small-gauge guns for waterfowl. I know some women who use 20-gauges; my daughter, a slight woman, uses a 20. But she lets the birds come right in on top of her before she shoots, and she is backed up by her husband and his 12-gauge and their crackerjack black Lab should she hit a bird too lightly. If she could handle a 12 for ducks and geese, she'd shoot one. I suggest the same for you.

From the standpoint of preparing game for the table (and avoiding biting on a pellet and cracking a tooth), steel shot has made food wildfowlers even more head-conscious of their targets than ever before. Steel shot fired into the head and neck of a duck or goose at good ranges, say inside 40 yards, is deadly. *Nothing* is deadly that hits too far back or passes harmlessly behind.

Waterfowl hunting also offers chances to miss in other, more imaginative ways. The birds are fast and require a lot of forward allowance. But most often, there are no reference points by which to at least gauge speed, so the inexperienced tend to shoot behind. It's always fun to watch new shooters fire at a diver skimming the surface of the water. They mount, swing, and shoot, and the shot charge smacks the water sometimes 12 feet behind. Seeing this, they instantly double the lead and swing faster, and the bird drops. Or several birds pass by, and someone fires at the lead bird, but the third or fourth one drops. This can get dangerous if the bird you're aiming at is legal to shoot but the trailing bird is not, or if the bag limit is one and you've already got your one.

Last season, for example, I was hunting wood duck and shot my two legal woodies very early. I decided to hang around for a chance at some of the fat mallards that fly by. Finally, a drake whizzed over the top of the trees, followed by a hen wood duck who happened to be going in the same direction. I didn't shoot for fear I would hit the woodie by mistake, and be in violation.

Another challenge offered by waterfowl gunning is the weather and the conditions. In most blinds and boats, footwork and stance are cruel jokes. You'll shoot most often from your knees or your keister. You should practice this on clay targets in the off-season. Even with practice, you probably won't shoot your best. The weather makes wearing everything you own pretty inviting. Long underwear, turtlenecks, heavy shirts, thick hunting coats, big hats with ear flaps—these do not make you a quick, deadly little shooting machine. The guns used for this type of shooting are usually heavier to soak up recoil, and they are often tough to get moving, especially if you've been sitting all day, getting colder and stiffer by the minute.

Gun fit, especially the length of the stock, should compensate for the many layers of clothing you will wear. You may find your duck gun ends up a full inch shorter in the stock than your quail gun. If you plan to use the same gun for both, commercially available rubber slip-on pads will lengthen the stock for when you aren't dressed up like Santa.

Actions

Duck and goose guns come in a variety of actions, but the pump or slide action is the favorite. Autoloaders are handy, but the grit and sand that seem to permeate everything about waterfowling have a way of working their way into the mechanism of these guns and turning them into single-shots. Pumps are a little more rugged and easier to unjam if this happens.

A double, especially an Over and Under, is a good choice, but if you get too much grit in one barrel, you may have a very big problem. Any firearm will fire less accurately if its barrel is "fouled" with powder residue and may misfire if the action is caked with hardened oil. The pump offers the undeniable advantage of a third shot (only three shots in the guns are legal in all waterfowling everywhere, and in most upland hunting—check your local laws) for dispatching a cripple. Try not to use a third shot on a bird that has not been hit; third shots from repeating guns used this way are cripplers because the birds are really putting distance between you and them by the time you fire the last shell.

Most waterfowl guns are not expensive. If I were starting out right now, I'd go to a gun store and buy a used Remington Model 870 pump gun in 12-gauge with a Modified choke. That would be my duck gun, and it would cost maybe $300 if the gun were in top shape; a new one doesn't cost much more.

Speaking of chokes, if you do all your hunting over decoys, use an Improved Cylinder choke; Improved Cylinder and Modified in a double. If you plan to do much big-water hunting for divers, go for the Modified choke. For geese, Modified is tough to beat. Don't use Full choke with steel shot; it's okay with bismuth.

Waterfowling Collectibles and Traditions

Waterfowling is tied closely with the history of early America. Waterfowl were among the first and hardest-hunted game crop chased into near oblivion by market hunters. The destruction of habitat, however, affected them most adversely.

In any event, the coastal areas of the East and the South have a long waterfowling tradition, and the memorabilia present there have, for the last twenty years or more, been highly prized. Old, original working decoys, the market hunters' guns and boats, old calls, brass shotshells— these are items to be prized, collected, traded, bought, and sold.

Since these became popular, newer forms of art and craft also have become popular: waterfowl stamps, limited-edition waterfowl prints by known artists, hand-carved working and decorative decoys, custom duck and goose calls by celebrated artisans.

Annual festivals in such places as Easton, Maryland, on the Eastern

Shore, and Stuttgart, Arkansas—the Duck Capital of the World, according to its Chamber of Commerce—celebrate the art, the history, and the waterfowling life. Art shows, auctions, duck-calling contests, retriever seminars and demonstrations, and a whole lot of folks in casual camouflage clothing make you feel right at home. If you get a chance, take in one of these, or the lesser-known but every bit as interesting, festivals that take place each year.

Field Dogs:
Where Would We Be
Without Them?

*As Smith explains, part of the pleasure of wingshooting
is watching a good field dog do what it does best.
The breeds, and what each is bred to do, are
discussed in this chapter.*

This chapter is probably going to sound biased, but can't be any other way with me: Dogs are the reason most of us who hunt birds, hunt birds.

Take my daughter, for example. She grew up in a family where hunting is acceptable and, in fact, to a certain extent is the way the family makes its living. Her father (me) writes hunting books and edits hunting magazines; her brothers, who grew up hunting, earned college degrees in fish and wildlife management. We always had dogs who doubled as bird dogs and family pets; my English setter slept at the foot of Amy's bed every night until Amy left for college. She learned to shoot, but never went hunting with us, even though the invitation was open and standing.

Amy graduated from college and her medical training, and eventually went to work in a fair-sized clinic. She married a mechanical engineer who is also a duck hunter.

They decided it was time to get a Labrador retriever pup. The training and the socialization, and the fact that the Lab was Amy's dog, not her dad's or brothers' hunting dog, forged a bond with the Lab she'd never had with other dogs.

When the dog's hunting training got intense, Amy signed on to try hunting herself. She took hunters' safety classes, practiced her shooting, bought all the upland and waterfowl gear, and started to hunt with her husband, her brothers, and, after all these years, with me—all on account of a big, black dog that begs at the table and licks any skin that happens to be exposed. Go figure.

I have found that many women enter the shooting sports exactly this way. The family pet also happens to be the family hunting dog. Attachment to these animals being what it is among those of us who love dogs, it's only natural that there is an urge to watch the dog perform those tasks it was bred and trained for—to watch pointers point, flushers flush, and retrievers fetch. During the course of the observation, the hunting and shooting part of it starts to look fascinating. The next thing you know, the dog's mistress is tagging along, gun in hand, and a whole new world has opened up.

Today, some of the finest breeders and trainers are women who are patient teachers of young pups, tending to be less heavy-handed and more willing to not quit on a slow-developing pup than many men.

Dogs and Their Uses

Canis familiaris was one of the first animals domesticated by humans as a helpmate—a fellow hunter with better senses, and a courageous protector of the family cave. Since that time, through selective (and sometimes accidental) breeding, they have been shaped and molded into all sorts of configurations and sizes. Today, you can buy a dog that weighs a couple of hundred pounds, or one that weighs less than five.

Dogs are reshaped wolves (Canis lupus); all dogs are of the species Canis familiaris and are further divided into breeds and strains. All dogs hunt—or would like to. A toy poodle would hunt and kill if it had to; it is its nature.

In hunting dogs, the natural instincts to stalk, pounce, chomp down on, and devour prey have been refined through selective breeding into what we think of as worthwhile traits to help us hunt. Some breeds of dogs do one thing exceptionally well; others do several things pretty well, and others do everything sort of okay. It is the rare dog that does everything required of a hunting dog exceptionally well.

Hunting dogs fall into several categories, according to what they are used for and how they have been bred.

Hounds

The hounds hunt by smell. There are a variety of breeds, but the most popular and widespread is the happy little beagle, used to hunt rabbits.

Other hounds, such as Walkers, blueticks, and redbones, are used to hunt larger game: fox, raccoon, bear, cougar, and where hunting them with dogs is legal in some southern states, deer.

Hounds find a track, follow it, and yowl their heads off. This trait allows the hunter to know where the dog is and get ahead of the game the hound is chasing in order to bring it to bag. Some people who run hounds simply enjoy listening to the dogs and never shoot the game.

Hounds are fairly noisy because of their breeding for the "voice," and as such are not always welcome additions to the neighborhood. However, with their long ears and soulful expressions, the puppies have a way of melting a dog lover's heart, and they often become valued members of the family.

Flushing Breeds

The flushing breeds are bred to hunt birds. Their job is to crisscross bird cover until they catch scent, then follow that scent unerringly until they get close enough to the bird so that it uses its last-ditch defense against ground-based predators—its wings.

The flushing breeds include the springer spaniel, cocker spaniel, clumber spaniel, and a few rare breeds such as the boykin spaniel and the Sussex spaniel. They all hunt essentially the same way and have fairly good noses, although nothing as acute as the hounds'.

Spaniels are also more-than-adequate retrievers, bringing back shot game to the owner in exchange for a pat on the head. A good retriever—and all the sporting breeds can be taught to retrieve, some of them enjoying it more than others—neither munches nor devours the bird.

The flushers are happy little warriors, even-tempered and friendly to a fault, making them excellent house dogs and pets. This trait, however, has led to their diminished abilities in the field in some circles. They have been bred with temperament and looks in mind, rather than for hunting ability. As a result, a vast number of "show" springers and cockers couldn't smell a pheasant if the bird moved in with them. These dogs are bred for and sold to people who want an intelligent and loving pet.

If you have a dog that is a crackerjack hunter, you should want to perpetuate those traits by breeding to another crackerjack hunter. If you have a dog with a nice disposition who doesn't hunt well, and you want cute, friendly puppies, you're likely to breed to another nice-dispositioned dog. It's all in what you're after.

Springer Spaniel
(CHRISTOPHER SMITH)

Fortunately for hunting dog fanciers, many breeders have bred for looks ("conformation"), disposition, trainability, *and* hunting ability, so the average hunting dog is a *very* cooperative animal. It has to be; it is a partnership with a human; it cannot do what its genes and its training teach without its human "half." Most hunting dogs, because of this, make better pets than many "pet" breeds.

The flushing breeds, compared with some other breeds, are slightly limited in what they can do, and therefore their popularity is correspondingly limited. For example, even though the flushing breeds hunt upland birds very nicely, certain upland birds—most of them, as a matter of fact—are more efficiently and traditionally hunted with pointing breeds. For example, quail, ruffed grouse, and woodcock are better hunted with pointing dogs, although some folks will disagree.

As far as retrieving goes, the retrieving breeds are better equipped to handle the cold, rugged water of late season, even though a springer makes a fine early-season, small-water duck fetcher.

Nevertheless, hunting behind a flushing dog is indeed exciting. The dog crisscrosses a field, pheasants the quarry. It hits scent and suddenly becomes incredibly animated, its stubby, docked tail whipping, its nose snuffling, its eyes glowing. As the birds cut left and right, unseen in the high grass, the liver-and-white dog mirrors those moves, closing in. You, not to be left behind, start walking fast, then trotting as bird and dog make tracks. You may break into a run. Suddenly, with a last surge of speed, the dog springs (hence the name) at the bird, which rockets skyward. You slide to a stop, fumble for the safety, your heart racing. The rooster pheasant cackles his disdain at orange-clad hunters and all little spotted dogs. The muzzle of your gun passes the bird and *you keep swinging*. . . .

Retrievers

The single most popular breed of dog in the United States is the Labrador retriever, according to registration records of the American Kennel Club (AKC); the fourth most popular is the golden retriever.

While these dogs don't do it all, they do enough of it to account for their popularity: they are hunting companions for both upland game and waterfowl, phenomenally smart (the breeds chosen for guide dogs, search and rescue dogs, and drug inspection dogs are mostly retrievers), loving, affectionate pets at home, cold-hearted, ruthless protectors of the home should the need arise, and a kid's dog without peer.

If I sound prejudiced, I am. I've got a couple of black Labs at my house who spend the time between hunting seasons shedding on the good furniture, begging from the table, and thinking up ways to get me to throw things for them to fetch.

Retrievers seem to bond with humans more closely than the other hunting breeds, and again, this goes back to their purpose. While hounds, flushers, and the pointing dogs do their thing "out there," the retrievers stick close, going into action *after* a bird is shot, usually. They can't hunt without us, so they *need* us, hence the bond.

Besides the Lab, which comes in three colors—black, chocolate, and yellow—and the golden retriever, other breeds include the Chesapeake Bay retriever, a big, rugged dog bred for the harshest, roughest water conditions; the American water spaniel; the curly-coat; the flat-coat; the giant poodle (no kidding); the Irish water spaniel; and a few other obscure breeds.

Retrievers are not just duck hunters, though. They also function very admirably as flushing dogs when the game in question can be hunted effectively with flushing dogs—especially pheasants. These birds are very hardy. Very often when you knock a pheasant down, it has enough life left to go hundreds of yards. Though springers are fine retrievers, it takes one of the retrieving breeds, in the opinion of many, to track it down and bring it to bag.

As mentioned previously in discussion about quail, often the pointing dogs are used to locate the game, and the retrievers then are called

Labrador Retriever
(CHRISTOPHER SMITH)

upon to round up the downed game. A half-dozen years ago, before my English setter, Jess, retired, my sons and I worked her with our older Lab, Maggie, for grouse and woodcock. Jess would locate a bird down in the thick stuff. If one of us had to walk in to flush the bird, we would have no chance for a shot, so we'd send Maggie in, who quickly came to associate Jess's points with the opportunity to go to work. Maggie would steam in and flush the bird. We'd wait out in the open, surrounding the spot, and more often than not we'd get a good, clear shot. Then, Maggie would make the retrieve.

The retrieving breeds, of course, are on their home turf when it

Retrievers were bred for waterfowling. Given the signal to retrieve, a yellow Lab springs and (1) crashes into the water, where it (2) retrieves a duck, and (3) brings it to hand for Nancy Scholz of Manora Labradors.
(LAURIE MORROW)

comes to waterfowling. They are bred as water dogs, and thus are inherently tougher when it comes to lousy weather conditions. Although few of them take the heat well—especially black Labs—they all handle the cold, and happily stay out in almost any weather conditions that drive other breeds (and often their owners) indoors.

I live in northern Michigan. Friend, it gets cold here in November. The wind was 25 mph from the north, the temperature was 18 degrees, and we got the to island at about half an hour before daybreak. The goldeneyes were flying, the dogs were retrieving in big waves—whitecaps. The decoys wouldn't hold in the heavy seas, and we finally turned tail and headed for shore about noon. My nine-month old Lab pup, Roxie, looked like a seventy-five-pound Labsicle: ice on her whiskers, ice on her paws, ice chunks forming under her fur, lifting it in all sorts of weird cowlicks. When we quit, she was genuinely peeved. She liked it out there. Next week, I'll take her to South Dakota to chase some of those tough, long-legged December ringnecks. The weather doesn't promise to be any better. She'll answer the bell; retrievers *always* answer the bell.

Pointers

It has been said that wingshooting did not become a popular sport among the upper crust of society until the dogs got involved. If the flushers are happy warriors, the hounds aloof workmen, and the retrievers solid citizens, then the pointing breeds are the aristocracy of the sporting dog world.

There are a few reasons for this. The pointing breeds can show you the *exact* location of game—within a few feet. When the flushing breeds and the retrievers work upland game, you get to know when a flush is imminent. But when a pointing dog locks up, you know where the bird is, and the timing of the flush—in most cases—is up to you. Because of this, most people shoot better when they shoot over pointing dogs; they

Three pointing breeds of upland field dog, shown here with their masters, are (*from left*) Weimaraner, English pointer, and English setter.

(LAURIE MORROW)

know almost to the second when the bird will come out and where, making footwork and stance so much better.

The pointing dogs also have a certain carriage about them. They're not indifferent; they just always seem more detached. They certainly have loads of enthusiasm, and like every hunting dog worth its salt, when the time comes to hunt, they don't want any petting or messing around. They want to *go*. But they are out, away from the hunters, who follow on foot and at times on horseback.

Hunting, with these pointing dogs, consists of their ability to find the bird and pointing it. To them, the job is then over (although many are natural retrievers as well). Because of this physical separation, the pointing dogs don't *need* hunters the way the retrievers do, who really cannot go into action until a bird is down.

The pointing instinct is present, to a certain extent, in all breeds of dogs. It goes back to the hunting techniques of the *Canis* genus, including wolves and coyotes. These animals stalk their prey, get close, hesitate in order to gather themselves, and then pounce or make an all-out dash toward their quarry, their genes screaming, "Lunch!" The point is simply that hesitation, through selective breeding and training, channeled into a *very long* hesitation—as long as it takes the hunter to get there. That's why one of the toughest parts of early training with a

Pointer

(CHRISTOPHER SMITH)

English Setter
(CHRISTOPHER SMITH)

pointing dog puppy is to get it to understand that it *has to wait,* that it can't go charging in to try to catch the bird for himself.

The pointing breeds consist of the pointer (sometimes incorrectly called the "English pointer"), the English setter, the Brittany (sometimes archaically called the "Brittany spaniel"; spaniels flush, not point), the German shorthair, the Gordon setter, the Weimaraner, the Vizsla, and a huge variety of lesser-known breeds.

A breed has certain characteristics that make it perform the way it does because of selective breeding and subsequent training. Within that breed, there are variations and individuals. Because of this, there are great dogs in each breed, and bad actors. Dogs are more individual than we think they are. There are close-working pointers—normally a breed bred for running big and far in search of birds. There are dumb Labs, a breed known for its brains. There are aggressive golden retrievers, who are known for their sweet dispositions. And there are big-running German shorthairs, who can depart from their close, foot-hunting reputation as often as they don't.

In other words, there are good hunting dogs, average hunting dogs, and lousy hunting dogs. True, you should buy the best bloodline you can from a strain of dogs that has, on average, the traits you're looking for, but in the end, the dog as an individual will turn out pretty much the way it wants, with your training establishing the parameters.

There is a certain amount of pomposity, at least to the uninitiated, associated with hunting with pointing dogs. But all of the traditions got their starts with good reason. For starters, two pointing dogs working together observe a decorum—after the proper training—of having the dog who is not pointing "honor" or "back" the dog that is pointing, as mentioned in the quail section. This is not done for courtesy alone. First, very often the hunters do not see the dog that made the initial find, but they can see the other one pointing his bracemate in the field. In addition, a backing dog is not running around and thus is less likely to startle the birds into a flush before the hunters are in position.

Tradition has it that not more than two shooters will approach a dog on point; the reason is safety. If two hunters walk in past a dog on point, they divide the shooting zone in half—you take'em left, I'll take 'em right. Dividing it into thirds and quarters is not only unsporting, it's also dangerous.

A dog must remain staunch on point until the shot is taken; very well-trained dogs remain steady to wing (the flush), shot (the gun going off), and fall (the bird dropping), moving only when they are released by the owner or handler to retrieve. This, again, is for safety's sake, this time the dogs'. Some dogs swear they can fly, and will leap up when a bird flushes, trying to catch it in the air. If the hunter happens to be shooting at that bird, well . . .

The pointing breeds make fine house pets, becoming valued members of the family and fine guard dogs and protectors. The long-haired breeds shed more noticeably, but all dogs shed, so that's why they make vacuum cleaners, right?

Versatile Breeds

The versatile gun dogs, growing in popularity every year, are a great piece of work and, for the most part, German engineering: the German wirehair, the wirehaired pointing griffon, and the pudelpointer.

These dogs are bred and trained to do everything all the other breeds can do. In Europe, tradition has it that a hunter sallies forth for a day afield. He may carry a drilling, a gun that is part shotgun, part rifle. He will hunt birds, hare, deer, boar—basically, anything that happens by. He needs a dog that will point birds, trail ground game, and retrieve downed game. His dog may chase down and capture a wounded buck deer, or point a pheasant. In short, he does it all.

There are those who say that these dogs do everything well, but don't do *anything* as well as the specialists—they don't point like a field trial champion pointer; they don't retrieve like a national champion Lab; and don't trail like a first-class hound. But so what? They do all of it very, very well.

These dogs are carefully bred and tested, and only the very best dogs are allowed to breed. Pups are in high demand because they are great hunters, especially for the person who hunts a variety of game and doesn't want to keep a kennel full of dogs. They are immensely loyal and courageous; the wirehairs especially are among the most skilled fighters of all the sporting breeds, and the most powerful—with the *possible* exception of a big Chesapeake Bay retriever—and they know it. A big male wirehair waiting at your front door or watching over things at night while you sleep is not to be taken lightly by someone who shouldn't be there. Life being what it is in the 1990s, a dog's courage and ability to stand effectively between you and danger are no small part of the equation you should consider when choosing a breed.

Training

There are a zillion books, half-a-zillion videos, and a bunch of magazines devoted to the topic of dog training. They're all good. Shop around when you get a pup and subscribe to the magazines (I selfishly recommend *The Retriever Journal* and *The Pointing Dog Journal*), buy some books, and look at a few videos.

What you'll find is that the basis for all dog training is patience and repetition. Dogs, especially the sporting breeds, want to please; they just have to be shown what you want them to do in a manner they can understand with a minimum of talking. Once they know, they have to repeat it until it's part of them. This can get tedious, but did you learn your multiplication tables the first whack at them? Me neither. And we're supposed to be the planet's smart folks.

One decision that comes up early on, after you've got the breed of your choice picked out, is whether to buy a started dog or a puppy. A started dog is more expensive, but it has most of the necessary medical care out of the way, and has started formal training, leaving it to you to finish up. A puppy is a blank canvas, waiting for your personal brushstrokes. There are pluses both ways, but most people pick a puppy, looking for companionship and loyalty as well as hunting skills.

At some point, you might consider the services of a professional trainer, who will take your dog at a young age after it's been with you for a while and teach it the basics. The dog will live in a kennel with its fellow students, and will probably get more exposure to proper technique and birds in a month than it will with you in a year. The pros aren't cheap, because they board and feed your dog as well as train it. Figure on several hundred dollars a month. If you are worried that Fido will forget you, don't; the dog will rebond with you overnight. This is a good alternative for busy professionals who have more money than time (or space) to train a dog, but want one of their own.

Of course, as mentioned in the preceding section about shooting preserves, many hunters frequent these places because of the guaranteed shooting opportunities close to home, and also because of the dogs. Preserve dogs are kindly souls used to putting up with a variety of hunters who may or may not know the wingshooting drill too well. Many preserves realize the lure of well-trained dogs and have a variety of breeds available, so you can pick and choose. Some members of clubs get the same dog every time; they like to think of the dog as "theirs," and will bring juicy treats and bones to Old Fang, who gets to recognize their cars when they pull into the clubhouse driveway.

The long and short of it is that most experienced wingshooters would rather hunt without their gun than without their dog.

Testing and Trialing

Eventually, humans being what they are, we'll want to find out how our dogs stack up against other people's dogs. Hence, the "field trial."

The field trial traces its roots to England, but it's a well-established institution here in the Colonies. Field trials are held for pointing, flushing, and retrieving breeds, and pit dog against dog in field-hunting conditions. Actually, that's not strictly true anymore; the dogs have become so proficient that it takes more than an average day in the field to separate the winners from the losers.

At the National Bird Dog Championship for pointing dogs, held annually at the Ames Plantation in Grand Junction, Tennessee, only the best of the best dogs that have won elsewhere are allowed in. They run grueling three-hour braces over narrow, twisting courses, attempting to find coveys of wild quail. Each is paired with another dog, and if one dog makes a find, the other must honor. The dogs have to be steady to wing and shot (although not fall, because the birds are not shot). Their speed and range are at the outermost limits of canine ability, so much so that the handlers, judges, and spectators, or "gallery," must follow on horseback.

A few years ago, I rode the first brace of the National in a driving rain with three hundred other equestrians. We looked like Jeb Stuart's cavalry after a bad day. The dogs didn't even notice.

Springers have their trials, as do retrievers, in order to determine a winner. Just as very few people even want a huge-running dog that must be followed on horseback, there are also very few times a retriever will have to do what these athlete dogs are called upon to do in a field trial. Imagine a duck-shunting scenario that calls for your dog to locate four ducks, none of which he has seen fall and the closest of which is 250 yards away. Never happen, you say, but the dogs have gotten so good that the trials have to be made harder and harder in order to find the best of the best. A good corollary here is professional golf. The golfers have become so big and strong, and the equipment so high-tech, that in order to make things competitive, tournaments are held on insanely long, narrow courses with rough like a Cambodian jungle and greens as fast and undulating as lumpy billiard tables stood on their sides.

This field trialing, like golf, is a big-money sport, the progeny of the champions being worth thousands of dollars. Professional handlers often campaign dogs for wealthy owners who love the game and pay handsomely to play it. A top-drawer dog handler who wins on the big circuit may never get rich, but he's gotta love it.

Tests are a fairly new wrinkle, and so far are most often associated with retrievers and the versatile breeds.

Unlike a field trial, where a field of competitors will be reduced to one winner, a test pits a dog against a standard for its breed and age. Every dog, on a given day, can meet that standard and earn an award. In the case of retrievers, it can earn a Master Hunter or Started Retriever, or any of the other, and often confusing, levels of award. It is asked to do certain things in terms of retrieving, "handling" (taking hand and whistle directions from his handler), and obedience. If it does these things within the predetermined parameters for the test, it has won.

It's the same with versatile dogs, the earliest test being one in which the dog's natural abilities are assessed in a Utility Test. The versatile people are so conscious of the purity of their breeds that only dogs who have passed this test are allowed to be bred and registered. It's a good way of maintaining the merits of the breed.

A variety of organizations have these tests, the North American Versatile Hunting Dog Association (NAVHDA) being the grandfather for the continental breeds; the North American Hunting Retriever Association (NAHRA), the United Kennel Club (UKC) and the American Kennel Club (AKC) hold tests of various levels for retrievers. People who compete in tests are a friendly lot, because they aren't competing against one another but against a standard for the breed. They are helpful and more casual than the field trialers, who are doing this for a living.

While field trials are fun to watch, giving you insight into the dog as athlete, the tests are where the participatory fun is; tests are a great way to spend a weekend in the off-season, and a great way to train your dog. If you train so that your dog can pass the tests for his breed, you'll have a stellar hunting companion for years—and a lot of folks on a waiting list for puppies.

—

The Shooting Games

*Non-hunting shotgun sports are the fastest growth segment in
shooting sports today. Next to golf and tennis, clays shooting
has been cited as the third-largest year-round outdoor
sport in America. Smith tells you what they are,
how they developed, and how to get
involved in clays shooting.*

I f dog field trials and tests aren't really hunting, neither are skeet, trap, and sporting clays. But like the dog side of things, they sure are fun.

The fact is, more shells are fired at clay targets every year than in a couple of decades of field shooting for live targets. Some people take up shooting with the idea of cracking clay exclusively—never intending to shoot at birds, just at disks the size of ashtrays whipping across the landscape at odd angles.

Trap

The progenitor of all the shotgun target shooting games is trap. It got its roots in England, starting with live pigeon shooting. When the pigeon supply dwindled, shotgunners developed and experimented with a variety of targets to try to duplicate the flight of the bird.

The most interesting of these, to me, has always been the glass balls filled with feathers, though I'm not quite sure where the feathers came from. The glass balls were launched by mechanical "traps" for the amusement of top-hatted Englishmen.

The search for the ultimate target did not take long, and eventually the modern form of the clay target came to be. It is used as the basis for

Shotgun target shooting games are the fastest-growing segment of the shooting sports.

(DON HOFFMAN/WSSF)

all of the clay target games, and comes in an increasing array of shapes, sizes, and colors.

Trap is shot from prescribed distances, beginning at 16 yards. There are five stations, or shooting stands, in a semicircle, all facing a hidden trap in a trap house. The trap oscillates back and forth in an unpredictable pattern, and when the shooter is ready, she mounts her gun, calls "Pull," and the target is released electronically by a scorer with a remote control. One shot is then taken at the target. When five shots have been taken by each of the five people on the "squad," the shooters move one position to the right, the person on the far right goes to the far left, and the process is repeated until each shooter has fired at 25 targets. A system of classifications allows handicapping that places highly skilled shooters at extreme ranges. This "handicap" shooting at distances up to 27 yards from the trap house places a premium on gun and load combinations as well as quickness, for the target is out of effective range in a twinkling.

Trap at the international level is fired from long distances at targets emerging at crazy angles from a series of traps concealed in a trench. This is a tough game, an Olympic event, in fact, and those who win at it are among the finest athletes in the world, their eye-hand coordination second to none.

The stations shown here are used in five-stand sporting clays.
(DON HOFFMAN/WSSF)

Trap Guns

Trap guns are commercially made and sold by virtually all major manufacturers. They are universally 12-gauge, the largest gauge allowed by the game's rules. The shot load is limited to 1⅛ ounces of shot as a standard in American trap. The choke is almost always Full, perhaps Improved Modified or Modified for 16-yard shooting.

The trap gun itself can be any action, but these days it is mostly the Over and Under or a specially made single-barrel gun designed for this game alone. The typical gun for trapshooting is a 12-gauge with Full or Improved Modified choke and ventilated rib barrel 30 to 32 inches long. Although many top trap shooters favor Over and Under shotguns, single-barrel, pump, and autoloading shotguns are also common. Registered trap is always shot with a 12-gauge shotgun. Trap guns really have no other use, because they are usually quite heavy—more than eight pounds—to reduce recoil in a long match (a match almost always made up of at least 100 targets). The barrels are also very long, anywhere from 30 to 34 inches, for smooth swing and precise pointing. Since the trap target comes rising out of the oscillating trap, the comb of the stock is very high, making the gun shoot high, placing its pattern well above the point of aim, perhaps a foot high at 40 yards. Trap shooting has been called the closest thing to rifle shooting with a shotgun, and it is. The distances are long, the target small, the pattern spread very tight.

Those who shoot a lot of trap—or any clay target game, for that matter—are home reloaders of shotgun shells. At first they do this to save money; later on, they realize that it allows them more shooting for the same money. When you figure in range fees (minimum of $3 for a 25-target "round," usually a lot more), guns, shells, trapshooting vests, trapshooting shoes, trapshooting pants, trapshooting glasses (in about 30,000 colors for the different light conditions), trapshooting gloves, trapshooting hats and visors, bags and boxes, and sometimes special vehicles to haul all this stuff, you'll find out that it may be cheaper to save up for your own space shuttle.

But trapshooting is addictive. A good shot will break 22 out of 25 targets, on the average, within a few times of trying the game. It may take a hundred more rounds of trap before she breaks 25 × 25. It may take years—if ever—until she can shatter 100 × 100. This is what's maddening and addictive. The angles the target takes are varied, but not infinite. In one round of trap, watching all 125 targets thrown for the squad, you'll see every angle the trap is capable of throwing, or nearly so. Why, then, can't we break them all? If we can break 5 in a row, why not the next 5 or 50 or 500?

That's what brings the trapshooter back—the quest for perfection. That's what makes her buy more guns and vests and gloves, and all the other gear. But when you think of it, how many times in our workaday world do we get a clear chance at perfection, with only ourselves to blame if we don't achieve it? Not many . . . not many.

In the original version of trapshooting, live birds were released from holes in the ground that were covered with silk top hats. The first mention of trapshooting as a sport was in an English publication called *Sporting Magazine* in 1793. The practice of shooting live birds from traps was first introduced in the United States in 1831 by the Sportsmen's Club of Cincinnati, Ohio. Targets first replaced live birds about the time of the Civil War.

There are three basic types of trapshooting: the 16-yard event, handicap, and doubles.

> *The 16-Yard Event:* In the 16-yard event, the shooters stand "on the 16-yard line," which is 16 yards behind the trap house. The trap throws targets that will fly 48 to 52 yards from the shooter. Targets are thrown at varying angles within a range of 45 degrees to left or right of straightaway.
>
> *Handicap:* The shooter stands 17 to 27 yards behind the trap house, depending upon her previous scores. The better the previous scores, the farther back she is "pushed."
>
> *Doubles:* This event is also shot from the 16-yard line. Unlike in the regulation 16-yard and handicap events, a pair of targets are released simultanesouly. Double targets follow a set course, usually 35 degrees to left and right of straightaway. The shooter has one shot for each target. A standard round of doubles is 25 "pair"—50 targets.

The shotshells used in trapshooting may vary slightly with shooter's preference and wind conditions. The standard load contains 3 drams of powder and $1\frac{1}{8}$ ounces of #7½, #8, or #8½ shot. Loads with only 1 ounce of shot are also popular.

Regulation targets measure not more than $4\frac{5}{16}$ inches in diameter and $1\frac{1}{8}$ inches in height, and weigh 3½ ounces. They are composed of pitch and clay or limestone, are saucer shaped, and are painted black with bright orange or white crowns.

Many trap enthusiasts shoot "registered trap." In registered trap, your scores are recorded by the Amateur Trapshooting Association (ATA), and your previous scores determine the classification in which you are placed for competition. In addition, your "average" is published each year in the official ATA Average Book. To shoot registered targets, you must be a member of the ATA. Top trapshooters gather in Vandalia, Ohio, each year to participate in the Grand American Handicap, first held in 1900 in Long Island. In 1924, Vandalia, Ohio, became the permanent home of the Grand. Today, almost six thousand participants travel to Vandalia each August to participate in the ten-day tournament. More than 4½ million targets are thrown.

For more information on trapshooting, contact the Amateur Trapshooting Association, 601 West National Road, Vandalia, Ohio 45377. To find a club where you can shoot trap in your area, send $2 for a copy of the National Shooting Sports Foundation *Directory of Public Shooting Ranges,* which offers information on more than 900 clubs nationwide, to NSSF, 11 Mile Hill Road, Newtown, Connecticut 06450-2350.

Skeet

In the early 1920s, William Harnden Foster, a magazine editor, New England ruffed grouse hunter, artist, and the future author of *New England Grouse Shooting,* invented a shooting game he called "shooting around the clock." He and his friends used the game to brush up for the angles and chances their cherished grouse gave them in the fall coverts.

The story, according to his son, the late Bill Foster Jr., whom I knew late in his life, was that the game as it was originally devised called for the participants to put a target-throwing trap at one point of a circle, and then rotate around the circle, shooting at targets from various points on the circle. Bill said that a neighboring pig farmer worried about stray shot sprinkling his hogs, so the game was amended, calling for two traps, one opposite the other on the circumference of the circle, and the shooters moving only in a semicircle. They still got all the left-to-right and right-to-left shots, but the neighbor's porkers could swill away in peace.

Still later, Foster asked his magazine's readers to think up a name for the new game, which was catching on like free beer. A female reader came up with the name "skeet," which is Scandinavian for "shoot." She won the contest, and the name stuck. Many people use the term *skeet* interchangeably with *clay target,* as in, "Let's go out in the field behind the house and shoot some skeet." That's correct only if they have a skeet field back there. They probably don't.

The game as it is played today in the United States has a high house on the left and a low house on the right. There are seven stations, starting under the high house, moving counterclockwise around the circumference of the field, and ending right beside the low house. The last station, station eight, is shot from the center of the field. There are four shots taken at station one: a high-house target, a low-house, then the two thrown simultaneously (you have to shoot them with separate shots—you lose a target in your score if you break them both with one shot). Station two is the same; then station three, four, and five have only the single high and single low—no doubles. Station six and seven have the two singles and a double again, and station eight has one high-house, then one low-house target. That makes 24. The 25th target is either a repeat of the first miss you have, no matter where you miss it from, or—if you haven't missed—a second station-eight low-house target. Compared to trap, skeet is pretty complicated the first couple of times.

As a shooting game originally devised by bird hunters, skeet was great practice. You couldn't mount the gun until the target was in flight, and the short ranges (the center point of a skeet field is 21 yards from each of the shooting stations except the last one, station eight, which is in the center of the field) and open-choked guns closely approximated the chances encountered in the uplands. But, being Americans, we got too competitive, and pretty soon the rules became rigidly structured. Those who had a hard time with gun mounting eventually relaxed the rule so that the gun can be mounted to the face before the target is called for. Since so much of proper wingshooting starts with a proper mount, this doesn't help. But you don't *have* to shoot it that way. Tournament shooters do, of course, because there's cash and silver on the line.

The game is shot with four gauges: the 12, 20, 28, and the .410 (which is a caliber, not a true gauge). The 16-gauge was eliminated because the record showed that identical scores were being shot with this gauge and the 12, making the 16-gauge redundant. Actually, today the same reasoning could be used to eliminate the 20—nearly the same scores are being shot with the 28-gauge—but that's unlikely to happen. Skeet as it is has become an institution. Dropping the 16 was one of the reasons the gauge fell into disfavor for so many years; thankfully, it's coming back.

Few people fanatically shoot both trap and skeet; most gravitate to one or the other. One reason for this is that few people can afford a gun for each gauge, plus shoes, vests, gloves, glasses, bags, and boxes you need for skeet.

Like trap, skeet is also an international sport played in the Olympics. But international skeet is played from the gun-down position (no mounting until the target is visible), and the target is harder and goes faster. Also, there can be up to a three-second delay from the time you call for the target and the time the target is released.

Skeet shooting today has more than twenty thousand registered shooters—that is, shooters who regularly shoot in competition. They are classified according to ability and compete for money and prizes in their classes.

Although the genesis of skeet as a bird-hunter's off-season practice game has been somewhat forgotten, it is still a great way for hunters to get to know their guns and tune up before the season. Since a skeet gun—although heavier than an upland gun—approximates a shotgun you'd choose for hunting quail, ruffed grouse, or woodcock, your bird gun will work just fine as long as it will hold two shells. In fact, some of the older shotguns made for skeet make fine upland guns such as a 16-gauge Parker skeet gun from the 1930s, when that gauge was still part of the full card of guns in shooting.

Skeet has contributed a choke to the shotgunner—called, aptly enough, Skeet. It is more open than Improved Cylinder, and has wider shot dispersal than true Cylinder, which is no choke at all. Skeet is a good early-season grouse or woodcock choke. For years, when I was younger, quicker, and shot way too fast, I had a little 20-gauge double choked Skeet and Improved Cylinder.

Both skeet and trap have also been responsible for fine advances in shotgun shells. Competitors want the best available, and this means shot-protecting wads and extra-hard shot for the best patterns. These are manufactured and fired by the millions each year. A box of #9 skeet loads in any gauge makes a fine early-season load for grouse, woodcock, quail, and dove, before the birds have put on heavy feathers and fat for the coming winter.

Trap and skeet started out as off-season practice for bird hunting and evolved into disciplines all their own, and there's nothing inherently wrong with this.

By the way, did I mention that the best way to hit a crossing skeet target is to swing through *and keep swinging?*

In skeet shooting, squads of five shooters fire from each of eight shooting stations arranged around a semicircle. There is no guesswork as to which house the target will come from and what path it will take. The high-house target starts from a point 10 feet above the ground and the low-house target from a point up to 3 feet above the ground.

Skeet shooting is done with 12-, 20-, and 28-gauge and .410-bore shotguns. Avid skeet shooters favor short-barreled guns with open chokes. Virtually all skeet is done with shotshells loaded with #9 shot. For 12-gauge events, shotshells carry 3 drams equivalent of powder and 1⅛ ounce of shot.

The following target sequence is standard in a round of skeet:

Stations 1 and 2: High-house single; low-house single; high-house/low-house pair.

Stations 3, 4, and 5: High-house single; low-house single.

Stations 6 and 7: High-house single; low-house single; low-house/high-house pair.

Station 8: High-house single; low-house single.

The 25th shot, completing the round, is taken at the time of the first miss, or with 24 consecutive broken targets, the 25th shot may be taken from any position on the field. New shooters tend to rush themselves on doubles and get confused as to which target to break first. Always shoot the target moving away from you first, then break the incoming target.

The four categories of competitive skeet are as follows:

All-Bore Event: Open to 12-gauge or smaller.

20-Gauge Event: Open to 20-gauge or smaller.

Small-Gauge Event: Open to 28-gauge or smaller.

Sub-Small-Gauge Event: Open only to .410 bore.

First Ladies' Skeet Tournament*

A southwest wind, a perfect sky line, and a general holiday atmosphere favored the first Ladies' Skeet Tournament, held at the Everett Gun Club, West Everett, Massachusetts. Mrs. Sidney R. Small of Detroit won the match with fifty straight. Mrs. Anna Mary Vance of Waban, Massachu-

*Previously published in *National Sportsman*, August 1932.

setts, and Mrs. Gertrude Wheeler of Brewster, Massachusetts, tied for second place with forty-three. But, to us, the point of the match was brought home sharply: Ladies can, and ladies do, shoot shoulder-to-shoulder and enjoy it. We saw them do it at Everett—with as much enthusiasm as the members of the opposite sex. We were properly thrilled to see the first official Ladies' Skeet Tournament, to see the five leading lady skeeters compete in such a colorful event—and turn in scores which would reflect credit on many a five-man team.

Here are the scores: Mrs. Small of Detroit, fifty straight; Mrs. Gertrude Wheeler, Brewster, Massachusetts, forty-three; Mrs. Anna Mary Vance, Waban, forty-three; Mrs. Walworth Pierce, Brookline, thirty-four; Miss Gertrude Travis, Boston, thirty-four.

Mrs. Small and Miss Travis shot 20-gauge doubles; Mrs. Pierce and Mrs. Vance, 16-gauge autoloaders; Mrs. Wheeler both a 12-gauge and a 20-gauge autoloader.

Spectators sat on the clubhouse porch or under the High Wide umbrella on a settee and, while this squad stepped up and smacked 'em, they held their breath and forgot that the mosquitoes were biting. Referee Bill Powers, who has seen and refereed many a great match, called dead-and-lost for the ladies and got himself another layer of sunburn, and was heard to remark, "That's shooting," which is the same as laurels for the ladies.

For eighteen months we have marveled from long range at the high scoring of Mrs. Sidney R. Small, Detroit, Michigan. We thought of her more or less as one thinks of Diana—just a mythical goddess of the skeet fields, but without reality. Someone you talked about, but never saw.

On Wednesday afternoon, June 29, at the Everett Gun Club, West Everett, Massachusetts, the myth became real. We saw—actually saw—Mrs. Sidney R. Small step onto a totally strange skeet field, break an effortless fifty straight to win the first official Ladies' Skeet Tournament seven birds ahead of her nearest rival. Piling up treasure, she made a straight run of seventy-five in the attempt to beat her own record of eighty-one for the ladies. Her score sheet showed also a ninety-eight out of a hundred for four events. Next, she picked up a strange .410 and broke nineteen. The whole affair left us feeling that we had been everywhere and seen everything and that therefore we might as well go out behind the barn and end it all.

Shooters Appear Calm

So far as we could tell, this squad was cool, collected, and having as good a time as any five male veterans. But instead of plus fours and caps there were white skirts and hats. A lost target brought a grin or a pleasant growl from the loser; a snappy break a "Good shot!" from the other squad members. It was rather an inspiration, and we are tempted to say—again—that there is no reason why ladies can't enjoy skeet and shoot it as well as men.

Sporting Clays

Sporting clays is another game that started off with the bird hunter in mind, and has become more competitive over the years—but with some benefits that trap and skeet don't offer.

While trap and skeet are shot on strictly structured, regulated fields in the open, no two sporting clays courses are the same, and the more brush and trees thrown in, the better.

Sporting clays got its start in England as a teaching and off-season shooting game, and it's still immensely popular there—so popular that tournaments often are held on weekends, with courses laid out in a bare field.

In the United States, sporting clays got its first real introduction when the Orvis company opened a course as a teaching/shooting school in Houston, Texas, in the mid 1980s. It quickly became incredibly popular, thanks to a few of us who wrote some of the early magazine stories about it. It quickly spread via the efforts of, first, the United States Sporting Clays Association and, later, the National Sporting Clays Association.

Sporting clays has been a boon for sportswomen. Sue King of the Women's Shooting Sports Foundation, a registered shooter, certified instructor, and a crack shot, was one of the early proponents of sporting clays. The game is flourishing. It has become an almost-automatic sidelight of shooting preserves, which use it to tune up their hunters before they go afield or to generate some off-season revenue from the faithful.

On the downside, it has started to evolve into a competitive game, which—as with trap and skeet—has a tendency to scare off participants. But because the courses are what they are, which we'll get to shortly, there is still room for a few people to get together and work on their shooting.

The upside is immense. Sporting clays is shot on stations, each a self-contained "field" that closely resembles real bird-hunting conditions. There are stations called "springing teal," "towering woodcock," "driven pheasant," "the dove field," "bounding hares," and a virtual cornucopia of other setups. The land and vegetation are used to make each station as close to a natural bird-hunting situation as possible. I have shot at stations in which clay targets drop in from over the trees to a pond (complete with decoys) that for all the world looks like a duck-hunting setup. I have seen and shot stations in which targets are released overhead, incoming in pairs and threes and fours, that reminded me of driven red grouse in Scotland. I have been at stations that had five targets released at once, approximating a covey rise of quail. Still others have been in the thick brush, the target thrown straight up like a woodcock making for the canopy.

Sporting clays also features a special target that can be thrown along the ground without breaking (sometimes even when you swear you've hit it), bouncing like a rabbit in full flight. As soon as you shoot at the "hare," a "bird" target is released. I tell you, it's *fun*.

Speaking of targets, sporting clays come in several sizes. There are regulation skeet, trap target (which is harder and can be thrown faster and farther), the "midi," which is smaller, and the "mini," which is smaller still (about the size of a mustard jar lid, which looks like an aspirin at 30 yards). There is the rabbit target, and a special one that's my favorite, the "battue," a flat disk with no rim that turns sideways after the trap's impetus is gone. You can't see it once it's released until it turns; it's just *there*. It's tough.

The rules of sporting clays forbid mounting the gun until the target is in view, and the release comes anytime during a three-second period after the target is called for by the shooter. In addition, the traps used to throw the targets are manually operated, thus no two targets are exactly alike because of the variation caused by the target's placement on the arm of the trap by the "trapper" operating it. Whew!

Sporting clays rules prevent changing guns or chokes, if you have screw-in chokes, except between stations. As a result, there are times when the targets are high and fast and far, other times when they are close-in and floating. Experienced shooters know when it's best to change chokes before it's their turn; the rest of us use Improved Cylinder and Modified and let it go at that.

Sporting clays guns are proliferating, as are the other paraphernalia: shoes, vests, glasses, bags, and boxes. Because of this, part of the popularity of the sport has been manufacturer-driven. Still, after a few false starts while shooters tried to sort out the best gun for the sport, the Over and Under seems to have won. It is reliable, has a single sighting plane, and the handling dynamics are tough to beat. Some of us (including those of us who regularly finish dead last in tournaments) cling to side-by-side doubles. I'm quite sure we're wrong.

Although sporting clays can be shot with any gauge, most serious shooters use the 12-gauge. Lately, there have been special gauge tournaments, where all the competitors use the same, small-gauge guns—20 or 28, for example.

The slickest setup I ever saw was developed by my friend Mike Sommers at his Cascade, Wisconsin, Highland Hunt Club. He calls the game "Fieldsport." Mike has a wood-chip walkway that goes along the base of a hill, near a brushy fencerow, along the shore of a pond, and across an open field. The whole walk is about 200 yards long.

Periodically, as you stroll along, gun in hand, you'll step on a pressure plate, which electronically triggers first a recording—maybe a bobwhite whistling or a duck quacking—followed by one or more targets that approximate that bird. You'll hear a pheasant crowing, look up, and see a pair of high targets streaking toward you overhead—just like a pair of driven pheasants. A few more yards along, you hear *bobwhite, bobwhite,* and four targets are released: a real clay covey rises. It's a gas, and sure to catch on with other clubs.

Starting in the Clay Target Sports

It can be intimidating to start off shooting trap and skeet. The clubs are usually quite busy, the shooters apparently all experts, and it looks as though there is no room for a beginner who doesn't even know where to stand or how much it might cost. We see some of the real experts, their shooting vests covered with "100 straight" patches, and we decide it's easier and less embarrassing to just go home. Nothing could be further from the truth.

First, realize that all experts were once beginners, going through the same thing you are. I have never met anyone, from the club champion on down, who isn't eager to share his or her knowledge with a beginner. People tend to be flattered by the chance to show a neophyte what they know. Shooters are no different.

Second, realize that no matter how good a shot you are, you'll miss more targets than you expect in the beginning. Trap and skeet have certain tricks and optical illusions that, until you learn them, are sure misses. Finally, remember that even if you're missing more than you think you should, you are getting good, hands-on experience with your shotgun. The best teacher is a case of target loads.

But because the trap and skeet fields are out in the open, often in full view of the clubhouse where others await their turn to shoot, and because the huge majority of the club membership is male, this type of shooting can be intimidating for a woman, especially a beginning shooter. Although you'll find your fears groundless, they exist nonetheless.

The best way to beat this, then, is with sporting clays. Since each field is self-contained and out of the view of the other fields, it is much more comforting to try your hand here, at this game. With another beginner, or—better yet—with someone you trust who has experience, you can shoot any or all of the stations at a sporting clays course and gradually warm up to clay targets. In addition, many sporting clays facilities offer shotgunning instruction by certified instructors who can give you lessons in gun fit, mounting, footwork, and stance and swing; very few trap and skeet clubs offer this.

Sporting clays courses offer a much wider variety of shots and these shots, of course, are set up to replicate the types of shots you'll find in shooting wild birds. Finally, sporting clays, unlike the other clay-target games, seems to have been more readily embraced by women, perhaps because it is a relatively new sport without an "old boys'" network in place for decades. Women's tournaments, "women's days," and women instructors teaching other women—as well as men—have made it a decidedly democratic game.

Manufacturers have designed (with the help of some of the well-known women in the field, such as Sue King) shotguns for sporting clays made to a woman's dimensions and in weights women can handle easily. Vests, glasses, shoes, bags, and boxes are proliferating every year as the shooting industry seeks out female participation.

There is one final aspect of sporting clays that makes it attractive to beginners, regardless of their sex: Nobody gets them all. In trap and skeet shooting, especially in tournaments, there might be 20 shooters tied at 100 × 100 or even 200 × 200. In sporting clays, a world-class shooter will still break only 90 to 95 percent of the targets thrown. There is no shame in missing, because everybody does it—a lot.

Chapter   10

Shooting with
Sue King

Mrs. Sue King, considered the foremost authority on women's shooting today, is a former chief teaching instructor for the United States Sporting Clays Association and is currently serving her second consecutive term as a member of the Board of Directors of the National Rifle Association. She is the founder and executive director of the Women's Shooting Sports Foundation. An accomplished outdoorswoman, upland and waterfowl bird hunter, and big-game enthusiast, Sue is the mother of two adult sons and the wife of Houston lawyer Jerry King, who also is an avid outdoorsman.

You can never learn enough about shooting technique. Investing in lessons from a qualified shooting instructor is money well spent. To augment and underscore Steve Smith's instructional section on shotgunning technique, we've incorporated Sue's—affording you the woman's viewpoint and providing you with the best advice from two of the best in the world of shooting.

Reading the Target: Eye Function

Just in case you didn't already know it, you have been practicing shotgunning technique all your life. In fact, you've been doing it since you first began to focus your eyes in the cradle and reach out with your hands for the toys mommy and daddy bought you. It was in the cradle that we all began developing the ability that makes it possible for us to drive our cars, hit a tennis ball, stick the candy bar in our mouth instead of our ear, and successfully swing a shotgun. We call it eye/hand coordination. We all possess it and have been using it every waking moment every day of our lives. It is so much a part of us that we really don't appreciate what a wonderful ability it is or how good we are at it. Even those of us who bird-hunt and shoot the clay target games seldom focus on the wonder of it or the importance of it in shotgunning. It is, in fact, the essence of shotgunning. All of the techniques, from proper foot position to mounting to leading the bird, are predicated on our ability to visually focus on an object and to point at it.

The beauty of it is that we all possess sufficient eye/hand coordination to shoot well—provided that we also practice the correct basic shotgunning techniques. If we do not use correct basic technique, we actually make it difficult for our pointing skill, our eye/hand coordination, to work for us when we swing a shotgun. Since shotgunning techniques have evolved for the purpose of making it easy for the eye and hand to point the shotgun, perhaps we should spend some time considering what the eye does, and how it functions in the context of shotgunning.

One of the most basic rules in shotgunning is that the shooter must focus her eyes with great concentration on her target, whether it is a clay target or a living bird. This concentrated visual focus on the moving target makes it possible for the eyes to "read" the target and absorb all the essential information about the target that the shooter requires in order to know how much to lead the bird. By focusing solely on the moving target, the eyes instinctively determine the speed of the target, the size, shape, and color, the distance from the shooter to the bird, the angle at which the bird is flying in relation to the shooter. This visual information is passed to the motor center of the brain, which then causes the body to react appropriately. All this occurs without any conscious, deliberate thought on the part of the shooter. This is what would happen if I were to ask you to point at an object across the room. First, your eyes would move to the object, focus on it, "read" the necessary information, and the motor center would direct your finger to point at the object. The beauty of it is that you point perfectly every time. You would never miss, nor should you—you've been practicing this all your life. Furthermore, you can do the same thing with a moving object. This is pointing, not aiming. This is what we do with a shotgun.

If we were shooting a rifle or handgun at stationary targets, the process would be quite different. Our principle focus would be on the gunsights, and the target would be seen only in soft focus or peripherally. This is aiming, and since the target is not moving, it is not necessary for the eye to provide constant visual updates on its speed and movement.

Consider, though, what would happen if we were to try to use a shotgun as if it were a rifle. What would happen if we tried to shoot a moving target by aiming rather than by pointing—by focusing our eyes on the gunsight rather than on the moving target? The answer is simple: Our eyes would not be able to "read" the movement of the target effectively. We would not see changes in speed, angle, or movement clearly, and that information would not register with the motor center, so we would not know where to point the shotgun in relation to the bird. Only as long as the eyes are focused sharply on the moving target and providing a constant evaluation of speed, angle, and distance to the motor center, can we successfully point at a moving object or point to a spot ahead of a moving target—the spot that indicates the correct lead.

This, to me, has always been a truly wondrous thing, this ability that we all have to focus on a moving target and point ahead of that target to the spot where we must shoot in order to lead the bird correctly—without taking our eyes off the target, without ever looking or focusing on that spot. In other words, if an object is within your field of vision, you can point at it without focusing on it or looking at it. Try it and you'll see what I mean. Look around: pick out any two objects that are both within your field of vision. Focus your eyes sharply on one and, without taking your eyes off it, point at the other object. Now, look down your pointing hand and see if you're pointing at the object you weren't focusing on. You will be. This is how we point, not aim, a shotgun. This is the natural ability that we all have. This is the ability that enables us to fold up a high-crossing dove flying 200 mph at 40 yards, or smoke a pair of following doubles at sporting clays.

You might ask why, as I'm sure some will, if we all have such wondrous pointing ability, how can we miss so many birds, both feathered and clay? The fault, alas, rarely rests with our natural pointing ability but with one of the following: We did not use the eyes properly, i.e., we took our eyes off the target to look at the front bead; or we failed to observe proper mechanical techniques of mount, footwork, and so on; or we have a purely physical condition called cross-dominance.

Just as most of us are either right-handed or left-handed, so are we also right- or left-eyed. Normally, one of our eyes is dominant over the other eye. Dominance does not mean that the eye in question sees or focuses more clearly than the other. In that sense the dominant eye may well be the weaker of the two. The dominant eye is simply the one that relays visual stimuli to the brain approximately 14 milliseconds faster than the other. It is the eye that controls the parameters of perception understood by the brain and acted upon by the body. This eye controls our pointing ability, our eye/hand coordination, and our ability to point a shotgun precisely where we wish. As long as our dominant eye is on the same side as our dominant hand, no problems will occur in our shotgunning. But if the shooter is right-handed but left-eye dominant—if she mounts the gun to the right side of her face while the left eye controls the parameters of perception—then she will shoot to the left of her target. Imagine that the dominant eye functions like the rear sight of a rifle and you will see what I mean. In shotgunning, it is essential that the dominant eye be the one that lines up with the long axis of the barrels.

The shooter plagued with cross-dominance has three options available to her: 1) learn to shoot from the other side; 2) close the dominant eye when shooting; or 3) use lip balm.

I'm not kidding—use lip balm, or lipstick, or a piece of opaque tape on your shooting glasses. Simply place a smear of lip balm or something similar on the lens of your glasses so that it lies between the pupil of the dominant eye and the front bead of the shotgun when it is mounted. It is not necessary to completely block out the eye but just to interrupt it or slow it down so that the eye over the barrels becomes dominant. A little experimentation with the three different options should help you determine which works best for you.

In my personal experience as a bird hunter, clay target shooter, and shotgunning instructor, I would usually recommend that the bird hunter learn to close the off-dominant eye as she mounts the gun to take her shot. For those shotgunners interested primarily in the clay target games, I would recommend the use of tape or lip balm on the lens of the shooting glasses. If you are truly ambidextrous and use the right or left hand equally well, I would suggest you learn to shoot from the side of the dominant eye.

Remember, though, that we are all different, and what works well for one may not work well for another. Be that as it may, there is one universal absolute in shotgunning. The eyes control the way you shoot.

Mounting the Gun

The shotgun games, whether we're talking about skeet, trap, sporting clays, or whatever, are as subject to the whims of fad and fashion as women's clothing. One year no fashionable woman would be caught dead in short skirts and no shotgunner would use 30-inch barrels. A year later women will be wearing hemlines at midthigh and shooters will be standing in line to buy the longest barrels available. We all give far too much attention and money to following the latest fads. It's always easier to try to buy success or to think that by copying the equipment of the great shooters, we too can be great shooters. Not true.

If you want to be good at any sport, there's really only one way to get there, and that's by study and practice. Yes, having the correct basic equipment is important, but unless you've developed good technique, the equipment is not going to make you a good shot. A shooter with good technique and a secondhand, off-the-shelf Remington will always outshoot the shooter with a matched pair of custom Purdeys and lousy technique.

I have often said that all shotgunning techniques have evolved to make it easy and natural for the dominant eye and the pointing hand to kill the target. Unfortunately, one of the least understood, or least used, techniques is the one most crucial to this operation. I refer to the *gun mount.* If you don't mount the gun properly your chances of hitting the bird are about equal to those of a blind hog finding an acorn. More birds, both clay and feathered, are missed because the shooter has made a poor mount than have ever been missed because the lead was wrong. If the mount is wrong and the dominant eye is not properly lined up with the long axis of the barrel, the shooter will be practicing involuntary bird conservation—that is, lousy shooting.

There are two statements I hate to hear made about mounting a shotgun, and you'll hear them repeatedly at all gun clubs. One is,

"Mount the gun to your shoulder," and the other is, "Keep your head down." Both of these statements are tremendously misleading and yet have wide acceptance as obvious truths among shooters.

Consider the first comment, "Mount the gun to your shoulder." It is true that the butt of the gun comes to rest on the upper part of the body, but it's not that part of the body which most of us call the shoulder. The shoulder is the rounded joint that sits directly atop the upper arm. If you're placing the butt of the shotgun there, you're also going to have to cant and twist your head well over in order to line your eye up with the barrel. This is unnatural, uncomfortable, and almost guarantees that you will frequently raise your head off the stock so you can see better. Our eyes and face are structured so that we see best with our head erect and our eyes level and, when shooting, we need to take advantage of that. The butt of the shotgun should actually be on the clavicle well inside the shoulder joint. This way, because the stock is so much closer to the face, it will not be necessary to cant or twist the head over in order to line up with the barrels. You will see better and be less likely to lift your head for a better look at the bird.

Let's go one step further than that. Let's not mount the shotgun to your "shoulder" at all! Think about it. What's more important to hitting the target—your "shoulder" or your dominant eye? Which of the two do you need to line up with the long axis of the barrel? The eye, of course. So don't even think of mounting the gun to your "shoulder" or even your clavicle. Bring the gun to your face—in line with your dominant eye. If you do that, the gun will be in the right place on your "shoulder"/clavicle. Remember, though, that you need to keep your head reasonably erect and level as you mount the gun up to your face. With the gun brought *up* to your face instead of bringing your face *down* to the gun that has been mounted on your shoulder, you won't have to worry about keeping your head down on the stock. It was never down to begin with. The basic rule for mounting the shotgun is: Bring the gun up to the face instead of bringing the face down to the gun.

This rule is essential to consistent shooting. How you go about bringing the gun to the face is equally important. In sporting clays, the mount should begin each time with the stock on the same place on the body. The rules state that you may begin your mount from any stock position on the body so long as that place or "ready position" has the stock visibly positioned beneath the opening of the armpit. If you wish, you may call for the target with the stock at waist level, but less time and movement is required if your "ready position" places the stock just at and barely below the armpit. By starting your mount from the same place on the body each time, it is simpler to bring it to the same place

Sue King shows how to mount the gun.

(DON HOFFMAN/WSSF)

on the face each time. This will give you more economy of motion and reduce the tendency to wave the muzzle of the gun as though trying to swat an enraged African bee instead of moving the muzzle only along the line of the bird.

This process also can work quite well in the field on live birds. Whether you're sitting on a stool waiting for doves with the gun across your knees or quick-stepping into a dog on point, there is almost always time to bring the gun to that ready position before actually mounting the gun. With a little practice so the movement becomes habitual, this technique can add birds to your bag. Since your armpit has been in the same place all your life, you won't even have to look down to find it before bringing the gun into the ready position.

For some reason, most shooters want to mount and swing the gun in two distinct steps. First, they bring the gun to the face and then, second, they begin their swing along the line of the bird. This two-step mount is not only unnecessary, but also wastes time. The longer those barrels are sticking out in front of your nose, the more likely you are to take your eye off the bird and look at the barrels. It's simpler and more productive to mount in one movement that combines those two steps. Begin pointing the gun along the line of the bird as it is raised to the face. Be very careful, though, and be sure to let the left hand (for a right-handed shooter) begin the movement through the line of the bird while the right hand follows. Keep both hands in the same plane so that both hands raise the gun to the face. If you use the right hand to flip the stock up to the face, you will cause the muzzle to flip down and off the line of the bird. Combine the movement of the gun to the face with the movement of the gun along the line of the bird and you will have more X's on your scorecard and more birds in your bag.

The downside of learning any new technique is that you must practice, and practicing with a shotgun can run into big bucks with the price of shotshells these days. The upside of practicing the mount, however, is that you don't need to fire a single shot. You don't even have to stand out in the sweltering heat. Practice inside—with an unloaded gun, of course. A few minutes every night and you just might be amazed at the improvement in your shooting. Stand well away from the center of a long wall and, from the ready position, mount and point to the right and then to the left corner, pretending that the line where the ceiling and wall meet is the flight path of the bird. If you sense that you may not be lining up the eye properly with the long axis of the barrel, stand in front of a mirror and mount from the ready position, pointing at the reflection of your right eye. You should be able to see whether you're getting your eye lined up correctly.

This kind of concentrated, focused practice can do wonders for your performance in the field on clay or feathered birds and it doesn't cost a dime. Even if you're unable to find the time to tune up for opening day on the clay target courses, you can still practice the mount at home—no cost, no sweat, just four or five minutes a night. It has nothing to do with fashions or fads. It has nothing to do with long barrels, short barrels, barrels with holes, barrels without holes. Don't try to buy success—practice for it!

Body Position and Footwork

If you've done much bird hunting or clay target shooting you know that one of the most common mistakes shotgunners make is shooting behind the bird. Year-round at any clay target club and during live bird seasons, you'll hear the same phrase repeated time after time. "You're shooting behind that bird, point farther ahead," or "Tail feathers don't have much meat, get in front." It doesn't seem to make any difference whether the shooter is an experienced hand at competition shooting, an avid bird hunter, or just an occasional shooter. The most often repeated "miss" is that of shooting behind the bird.

Unfortunately, all the well-meant advice that fellow shooters offer each other, like "You're behind, get in front," doesn't seem to count for much because we all tend to keep repeating the same mistake over and over. Often as not, when we shoot behind we know we've done it without being told—but we continue to do it. The problem really is not where we've shot (behind), but *why* we shot there.

Understanding the *why* of a missed target is every bit as important as understanding the *where* of a missed target. In fact, if you're going to improve your shooting you must understand both the where and the why. In the case of the target missed behind, there is more than one possible explanation. First, there is the dumb mistake: The shooter wasn't really alert and ready when she called for the bird and just never caught up with the target, or she was simply caught by surprise when the covey busted. None of us can be eternally vigilant and ready. Second, perhaps our shooter simply lacks experience and hasn't had enough exposure to develop an understanding of the leads required. Another, and the principal culprit in missing behind, is poor body position and lousy footwork. This holds true not only for the skeet or sporting clays shooter but also for the bird hunter.

Shotgunning is a swinging sport. Our targets, whether clay or feathered, are moving and moving darn fast. If the shotgun is not moving,

Sue King demonstrates body position and footwork.

(DON HOFFMAN/WSSF)

swinging even faster than our target, then we will miss. Ask yourself, "What moves the shotgun?" Do our arms swing the shotgun or is the swing, the movement of the gun, done by the body? If you answered that the arms swing the gun, perhaps you'd better rethink the question. Once the shotgun has been mounted to the face, all of the gun movement is provided by the body, not the arms. Once mounted, the arms, head, and gun must become one and must remain locked together until the sequence of the shot is completed. It is the rotation of the body that swings the locked-together arms, gun, and head. The why of the miss behind the bird is failure of the shooter to properly position her body, failure to rotate the body properly, and failure to use the proper footwork.

First, let's consider *body position*. The body should be facing that point along the flight line of the bird where the shot will be taken. If, as many "miss behind" shooters do, the body faces that point where the target originates, then by the time the shot is taken, the body has already had to rotate so far that there is not enough flexibility left to permit good follow-through. Either the shooter stops the gun as she fires because she cannot turn or swing any farther, or the speed of her swing slows because her body begins to bind up. In both cases, the shot will be missed behind. By facing the body at that point where the shot will be taken, the shooter has plenty of body rotation left and can swing the gun on past the point of the shot, maintaining good barrel speed and follow-through. It's easy enough for the clay target shooter to adopt this body position in relation to the flight line of the bird. After all, she's seen the target before. She knows where the target is coming from, where it's going, and how it's going to get there. What about the bird hunter? She frequently doesn't know exactly where the bird is coming from until the instant it's suddenly there and she certainly cannot predict what the bird's line of flight will be. How in the devil can a bird hunter, in the field, position her body so that she faces the point at which the shot will be taken? How can she know where that point will be? The answer is, she can't know where that point will be. At least I've never been able to tell. On some occasions I've guessed right, but plenty of other times I've guessed wrong. Nonetheless the bird hunter must be ready and positioned to take her birds from any direction, speed, and angle. The question is, how?

The answer is *footwork*. Remember, the body swings the gun. How well or poorly the body swings the gun depends upon footwork. Using the proper footwork the bird hunter can rotate her body almost 300 degrees so that she can face her body toward that point where she will take the shot.

If you're not sure whether your footwork is correct, try this simple experiment. *With your shotgun unloaded,* stand in the middle of a room facing the center of a wall. Mount the gun and swing it as far as you comfortably can to the right and to the left. Make note of how far you were able to swing. If you couldn't comfortably rotate the gun and body close to 300 degrees, then you've either got lousy footwork or your arthritis is even worse than mine.

Try it again. This time when you face the wall place your feet closer together, certainly no farther apart than the width of your hips (my feet are about nine inches apart which, I'm sorry to say, is a lot narrower than the width of my hips). Be sure your stance feels comfortable, and do not place the right foot too far behind the left. Left-handed shooters need to reverse the foot position. Mount the gun and as you swing to the left, transfer your weight to the left foot, let the right heel come up off the floor, and pivot your body. Repeat the maneuver swinging to the right. This time, transfer your weight to the right foot as the left heel comes up off the floor and the body pivots to the right.

It might feel a bit awkward at first, but a little practice will smooth the movement out and soon you'll feel comfortable and able to swing that shotgun through nearly 300 degrees. You'll be able to follow through after the shot, and you'll be less likely to stop the gun when you shoot. Now, you won't miss behind!

A good swing is one of the keys to consistent shotgunning, whether in the field or at a clay target club. Just remember, it all begins with the correct foot position and footwork or pivot, which gives us the body rotation necessary to swing smoothly through a wide arc with good follow-through.

If you're going to make the best of your bird hunting this year, it's time right now to dust off that shotgun and sharpen up your skills. Get out to a clay target range this weekend and begin practicing. Do so at every possible opportunity. First, it's fun to shoot the clay target games. Second, with improved skills you'll enjoy your hunting much more. Third, improved skills mean fewer crippled and lost birds. There are many good sporting clays facilities all across the nation—use them.

Ear Protection

Family history has it that I've been shooting one sort of firearm or another since the mid-1940s, which works out to about forty-five years of exposure to potentially harmful levels of sound. The first twenty-five years of shooting was without any form of hearing protection. The last twenty years I have worn hearing protection religiously when on the range for a very good reason: I have a serious hearing loss.

With only 55 percent of my hearing remaining, a less than perfect phone connection leaves me straining to understand the other party. Cocktail receptions or noisy restaurants are torture because the background noise makes it impossible for me to distinguish words. I can't hear the doorbell ring from most rooms in the house, and running water in the kitchen sink means that I can't understand what my husband is saying from the table or hear the timer on the oven buzz. Riding in a car, it is extremely difficult for me to understand what a passenger is saying. I love the cashier display terminals that tell you how much you owe because I can't hear the salesclerk. If my gynecologist doesn't have his head above my knees I can hear the sound of his voice but I can't read his lips.

At best, a significant hearing loss is annoying. At worst, it can cause real domestic misunderstandings and, in a hunting situation, can even be dangerous.

Inside the inner ear are tiny nerve endings that receive the vibrations produced by sound and translate them into nerve impulses, which are relayed to the brain and interpreted as sound. These nerve endings can be permanently damaged either by repeated exposure to dangerous sound levels or by one single exposure to a loud sound. Both the cumulative exposure involved in years of shooting without hearing protection and single-event acoustic trauma are responsible for my deafness. Believe me, having a 10-gauge magnum go off five feet from your ear is acoustically traumatizing. It is literally painful. The damaged nerve endings will not "grow back" or heal themselves. No surgery or medication will correct the damage.

As shooters, we must primarily be concerned with the cumulative effects of repeated exposure. The questions are, how loud is too loud (at what degree of loudness should hearing protection be employed) and what is the best method of protecting our hearing (or what's left of it)?

The loudness of sound is measured in decibels, abbreviated as dB. The louder the sound, the higher the decibel rating. For example, normal conversation is rated 60 to 70 dB, a screaming child may hit 115 dB, a shotgun blast from the shooter's position is rated at 120 dB. Hearing specialists generally agree that hearing protection should be worn whenever we are repeatedly exposed to sound levels in excess of 80 to 85 dB. There are no ifs, ands, or buts about it: If you shoot, you'd better wear hearing protection. Can you hear me?

The question is, which of the different types of hearing devices is going to offer the best protection, and how do we tell how much protection each provides? Taking last things first, check the package labeling for an "NRR" rating. NRR means "noise reduction rating" and is expressed in decibels. A noise reduction rating of 31 decibels, NRR 31 dB, is superior to a rating of NRR 21 dB. If you are presently using a hearing protection device with a rating of NRR 21 dB while shooting a shotgun that puts out 120 dB of sound, you are still exposing yourself to approximately 99 dBs, which is well above the accepted standard of 80 to 85 dB. This exposure can damage your hearing if you are subjected to it repeatedly.

Hearing protection devices are available in several configurations. The least expensive are compressible foam plugs which you roll into a tight cylinder and stuff into the ear canal. These normally cost less than $1 and can be reused many times. Those made by E.A.R. have a noise reduction rating of 35 dB when properly inserted. This is the highest NRR of any of the various types of hearing protectors I know. Understand, though, that if you don't read and follow the instructions, you may not get optimum protection. One way of testing whether you've inserted these properly is to cover and uncover the ears alternately with tightly pressed hands in the presence of shooting. With properly inserted plugs the noise level should seem nearly the same whether the ears are covered or not.

Also available are preformed soft plastic plugs costing about $7, but these do not have as high a NRR rating and I do not find them at all comfortable. In fact, because we all have different size ear canals, I worry about relying on a "one size fits all" approach. If the device does not properly fit your ear canal, you are not going to obtain good protection. One of the most popular of these types is rated NRR 6 dB. Thanks, but no thanks.

My personal choice is the custom-fitted, molded plugs such as the "Insta-mold" type. With an NRR of 31 dB, I know that I'm well protected from dangerous sound levels on the range, and because they're custom-fitted, even I can't put them in wrong.

Another style of hearing protection that is popular with many shooters is the "earmuff" variety. Priced from $10 to $30 and offering NRR ratings from 19 to 30 dBs, these are a viable choice for the shooter. If you're shooting regularly with repeated exposure, opt for the more expensive, higher NRR rating. Don't risk permanent hearing loss. Also keep in mind that if not worn correctly, the earmuffs will not give you the advertised NRR protection. Wearing them over glasses or earrings or with a pencil stuck under the pad reduces their effectiveness. They also keep your ears warm in the winter and hot in the summer.

Several years ago, earmuff protection was introduced that contains built-in electronic circuitry to suppress any noises above 85 dB. Battery-operated, these styles allow any sounds—human conversation, animal sounds—to pass completely through the muff. By adjusting the unit, you can even amplify sounds, though not beyond 85 dB. One such unit currently being offered has a NRR of 21 dB. Prices for these range from $65 to well over $100. These are particularly nice if you like to talk to people when you're shooting. Unfortunately, they are somewhat bulky and interfere with my mount when I shoot sporting clays. I keep slapping the heel of the stock against the underside of the unit.

The best and the most expensive hearing protection are custom-molded inserts that fit inside the ear with electronic circuitry. One great advantage of this device for those of us who are avid bird hunters is the ability to wear it in the field. I have never recommended the use of hearing protection in the field because such use might have prevented the shooter from hearing a rattlesnake, another hunter calling an unsafe shot, or the instruction of a guide. Ten years ago I reasoned that my hearing really wasn't too bad, and besides, I didn't fire that many shots while bird hunting.

Hearing loss is not only cumulative but insidious. It sneaks up on you, and when you finally realize what has happened, it's too late to recover what you've lost. If you shoot regularly, wear the very best protection you can afford.

One of the more interesting aspects of hearing loss due to noise damage is that certain frequency ranges of sound are lost before others. High-frequency sounds are lost first. Indeed, this was my first clue that something was amiss. It happened in the early 1960s at a performance of Vivaldi violin concertos. When the violinist went for the really high notes, I couldn't hear them. But in my early twenties, I felt both immortal and bulletproof. Besides, I could still hear all of Fats Domino and Elvis.

We can still function well socially, without embarrassing ourselves, with a hearing loss in the high frequencies. When the loss dips down into the lower sound frequencies, it's a different story.

The English alphabet contains twenty-six letters. Of these, five are vowels and the remaining are consonants. Vowels fall within the lower sound frequencies, which are the last to be affected by shooter's hearing loss. Consonants, falling in the higher frequencies, are lost earlier. There are lots more consonants than vowels. If I can't see the movement of your lips, I can't tell whether you've said "now" or "cow."

With so many young shooters entering the game, a word about hearing protection for the little ones is in order. Because their ear canals are so much smaller than those of adults, and because their heads are smaller, muffs, foam plugs, and preshaped plastic plugs do not fit them properly. This means that they will not receive the rated NRR protection. Audiologists suggest that the foam plugs, cut in half lengthwise, will offer reasonably good protection, as will the ear putty used by swimmers.

The importance of protecting your hearing cannot be overemphasized. Take it from someone who learned the hard way.

Loud, Louder, Loudest

Quiet library	30 dB
Normal conversation	60–70 dB
Vacuum cleaner	70–90 dB
Lawn mower	90–105 dB
Chain saws	100 dB
Outboard motor	110 dB
Shotgun	120 dB
Jet plane at takeoff	130–150 dB

▬

Chapter 11

Lest We Lose
Our Edens

A hunting trip with Laurie Morrow.

My hunting partner was Sue King. Our host was Dial Dunkin, a south Texas banker and devoted outdoorsman, well known for developing several successful, superbly appointed hunting and fishing camps in Mexico. They were my partners on an adventure, and though they both knew much more of hunting than ever I will, and much of Mexico, a place I never had been to, we were pleasant company together. We hunted for a time; and time can weave a special bond between hunters, and take us to places only hunters dare to go.

It's a personal challenge, too—an exploration that goes far beyond the game and the gun. Search for the words! Shake open every hunting book ever written! See the prose tumble out from between the covers! Only a few were good enough to capture it on paper—Jim Corbett, John Hunter, Corey Ford, and "Papa" Hemingway. But it's illusive, that flinty spark that ignites deep inside the heart and sets the spirit ablaze. Hunting does that. You think you are the hunter. In fact, you are at the mercy of something far greater than mankind: the wildness of nature. In Mexico, in the hidden places where it is untamed . . . yes, in Mexico . . . that's where it happened to me.

So we arrived, Sue and I, in Harlingen, Texas, a town I had never heard of before, only minutes from the border. It was a stormy November Thursday, a week to the day after I had received an out-of-the-blue, whip-cracking invitation from Dial to hunt ducks and quail the opening week of Mexico's hunting season. He had a new quail camp, and we'd be the first guests. The birds would not be good, Dial promised; they'd be incredible. There wouldn't be a few coveys; there'd be countless ones, he assured us. The flights wouldn't come by the dozens but by the hundreds, he whispered. And they did. After all, Dial Dunkin is a man of his word.

Late November is the downside of bird-hunting season in New Hampshire, and all our geese and most of our ducks have pretty much migrated south. Besides, this year most of the Atlantic flyway was closed to Canada geese. November snow is good tracking for grouse, but somehow, busting a bird you can track and see through leafless limbs seems an unfair advantage to a lot of us who hunt. It's the time of year, after all, when grouse, like us New Englanders, are hunkering down for the winter. So Mexico beckoned, and I answered the call.

The Quail Camp

I don't remember crossing the border that Friday morning. It was four o'clock and dark as pitch, too early even for a thick cup of coffee to start the blood running. Our southbound journey took us over choppy, single-lane highways. Daybreak unveiled a land that was pancake flat, but in the distance gentle, old mountains rose, softened by eons. The villages were crumbling, their people incredibly poor. Time moves slowly in Mexico. The natives seem to be dragged down by its weight, struggling against monotony. And yet there is something tranquil about a way of life that, unlike ours, takes time at face value.

In sharp contrast, there was Dial. They broke the mold when Dial

Dunkin was born. Larger-than-life and lucky, he's able to wring more minutes out of a day than anybody. Pecos Bill could lasso twisters; Dial could lasso time. If I reach an exalted age when days and weeks melt into one, I will think of Pecos Bill and Dial Dunkin together, as legends. Have you ever met a legend? When you do, you'll know. A legend is someone who makes up his own rules and somehow manages to get away with it. Like Dial.

By nine o'clock, we had arrived at Dial's newly built quail camp, a charming hamlet of little thatched-roofed haciendas built along a pretty stream, and immediately set out for our morning's hunt. "We've leased hundreds of acres of fields and hedgerows that are chock-full of quail," Jim, the manager of the quail camp said, beaming. Unbelievably, he was wrong.

Just one thing was against us: the time of day. By ten o'clock it was hot and too late to start a quail hunt. Had the rains the night before not delayed us in Harlingen, then surely we'd have been afield at the crack of dawn. We felt sorry for Jim. After all, this was the first quail hunt of the season. Sue and I were hunting fields that had never been hunted before. Poor Jim had worked hard for so many months. He negotiated the hunting leases with a dozen landowners. He handpicked and trained a half-dozen local men to staff the hunt. He imported a kennel of excellent English pointers, directed the gun carriers, taught the beaters how to beat, and gave orders to the drivers of the two vehicles that accompanied Sue and me all the time. It was a full-blown operation, he was the boss, this was his hunt, and everything was in place—except the birds.

It was hot; a brisk breeze soon died and the morning and the pace heated up. Jim was anxious. We were anxious for Jim. The first field was choked with cactus, mostly prickly pear, and we were careful not to step in them or in wood piles, which is where rattlesnakes linger. We wore snake chaps and boots; like Indiana Jones, I hate snakes, I really do. New Hampshire, unlike Texas, has no poisonous snakes, and the thought of coming face to fang with a rattler was something new I was desperate not to live to tell about.

In the back of the Ford truck were eight kennels, stacked four on four, each holding a fine pointer. The oldest was six years, the youngest a year. Each was "birdy" with a good nose and an athletic, powerful build. None had been raised as a pet. These were working dogs, out to do a job. Even the best-trained dogs were set out with electronic collars. Twenty minutes tops was all a pair was good for in this heat. Then they'd be called in, watered, and replaced with a fresh pair. They were real athletes, these dogs; among the best I've ever seen.

We did a good deal of walking, which was swell until I unwittingly confronted a prickly pear and drove an iron-hard spine right through my chaps, jeans, and clear into my kneecap, painfully paralyzing the joint for days. That's when Sue and I took to riding in the pair of open-air seats that were welded to the front bumper of the truck. It was fun, but we both preferred to walk, stiff knee and all. Now the sun was high in a cornflower sky, the breeze diminished to a whisper. Fast approaching midday, the two or three coveys we broke held only a few birds and they scattered distant. By the time we went back to camp for lunch, our bag was thin—only three birds. Jim, by now, was disconsolate.

Sue was shooting the official gun of the Women's Shooting Sports Foundation, a Browning Over and Under 12-gauge with 27½-inch ported barrels, serial number 1. Browning asked Sue to consult on this model, the first woman's shotgun to come out of recent production by the major firearms makers, and many of us refer to it as the "Sue King gun." It is turquoise-painted wood, real eye-catching, with a full pistol-grip stock and silver trim. The Mexicans loved it. "Please, Sue," I begged. "Won't you ask Browning for a stained wood stock without holes in the barrel?" You sorry traditionalist, I kicked myself. Looks were deceiving. That gun shot true. Or rather, the shooter who shouldered it was, simply, the finest woman shotgunner I have ever seen—and one of the two best shots I ever witnessed, the other being my writing partner, Steve Smith.

Dial joined us for the afternoon hunt, and boy, did those birds fly. We took several huge fields, mostly on foot, and scattered seventeen coveys, no less than a dozen birds in each covey. The birds exploded from a patch or a hedgerow like fireworks, scattering in all directions. They were good, plump little birds, too. The dogs performed their canine ballet, a joy to watch. Sue, Dial, Jim, and I spent that idyllic Friday

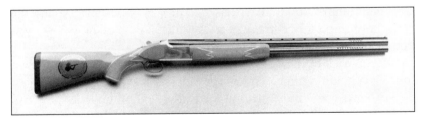

Browning created this women's Over and Under shotgun by consulting with Sue King. It is the official gun of the Women's Shooting Sports Foundation, and available through WSSF or Browning.

(DON HOFFMAN/WSSF)

afternoon in virgin hunting fields, busting covey after covey of quail that knew nothing of our kind.

By the end of the day, as the sun set, the sky was clouded dark with flight after flight of geese that had come home for the winter from the cold north. As we made our way home in the twilight, we could hear them talking to one another, a resounding chorus that, in its way, was as spiritual and beautiful as any sung in a cathedral. For the out-of-doors is nature's cathedral, and the choir are the birds and wild creatures that are, quite simply, the lesser children of God.

It was Saturday morning, and once again Dial made sure we were up to greet the dawn—well before the dawn itself was ready to rise. Sleep was a limited commodity, not a necessity, and Dial did not believe in investing much time in it. So there we were, once again, waiting on the sun in a fresh field that promised to be splendid with quail. Again we had five Mexicans to field the dogs and act as beaters; and we had Jim, our guide. When it was light, we walked.

We walked and we walked. A pair of dogs laced across the field, zigzagging in tangents, this way then that, working hard, but they could find no scent. Suddenly, like a stuck frame in a movie reel, they both froze on point near a mound of high grass. When a dog is birdy and gets serious about it, that's a sure signal to speed up and get to where your canine guides are summoning you. We slowed our pace as we came upon the knoll. The dogs were quivering, anxious to lurch, and we saw why: not six feet in front of us were two, three, four quail running through the grass at a breakneck speed. Then they exploded, twenty at least, helter-skelter into the sky with such force that for a moment we could feel their wings whip the air. When it was all over we had six birds, four by Sue and two by me. Ten minutes later and fifty yards farther there was a repeat performance. Again and again we came upon cover rich in quail. By midday we had busted sixteen coveys and had our limit. Jim's face beamed brilliant as we set back for the camp. It was a fitting end to a magnificent hunt.

But soon we were off again, off to the duck camp.

The Duck Camp

Down in Old Mexico,
Near the Rio Grande,
Spanish daggers, coyotes, vaqueros
And the San Bartolo Ranch.

Snow geese float on silent wings
Across the misty coastal branch;
And when they call their lonely call,
On scented breezes it drifts,
To all the music that is, the magic of the hunt

And if you are a hunter,
And if you are ever down in Old Mexico, near the Rio Grande;
And hear the Snow geese calling across the misty coastal branch,
Your heart and soul will be forever locked
On the San Bartolo Ranch.

And if you seek my counsel
In years long gone by,
You will find my heart and soul
Where Snow geese fly.

So listen to their lonely call,
For it will tell you all . . .
On the misty coastal branch
Of the San Bartolo Ranch,
Down in Old Mexico
Near the Rio Grande.

DIAL DUNKIN, *"The San Bartolo Ranch"*

"I have often thought that the best way to define a man's character would be to seek out the particular mental or moral attitude in which, when it came upon him, he felt himself most deeply and intensely active and alive. At such moments there is a voice inside which speaks and says: 'This is the real me!'" So wrote William James to his wife in 1878. I, too, came alive, once I saw the delta.

We wended our way along a ribbon of rain-beaten road to reach the delta region that lay four miles inland from the Gulf of Mexico and Dial's duck camp. Dial drove Sue and me, sometimes sideways, through miles of mud in his four-wheel-drive Suburban; past a few pitiful farmhouses where poor, cheerful families shared their dirt-floor lodgings with goats and pigs and cows. Once a coyote crossed our path— a blur, the tip of its tail a mere streak. Millions of tiny crabs like miniature soldiers marched along the ribbon trail that would lead us, eventually, to our destination. There were clusters of cows grazing in the marshes, sometimes a horse. The horses in Mexico are elegant animals; their line harkens to the days of Balboa when Arabians were brought on Spanish galleons to gallop, to carry Conquistadores, to conquer the New World.

We drove for a long time until we reached a canal. Waiting for us were three Mexicans and a johnboat. They unloaded all of our gear, and Dial's footlockers full of mechanical things that kept his fleet of extraordinary vehicles in working order. The duck camp was a self-sufficient community because it had to be. We crossed the canal.

On the other side stood a monstrous tractor: I had never seen one so big. Behind it was a Dial-designed pneumatic platform with bars. Dial drove, as always. Sue looked like a figurehead on a schooner, majestically watching over the horizon. I held on for dear life. The mechanical megalith roared, the platform rose high over the wheel base, and we lurched forward on rough terrain, mud splattering mercilessly. The ribbon road became a mere thread.

Suddenly, there it was. A vast silvery delta unfolded before my eyes, an immense wetland that looked as though a giant, gray silk scarf had tenderly been laid aground to cover the earth. It shimmered. Above was a blanket of gray and graying sky, because it was now late in the afternoon. The grunt and grind of the tractor engine grew louder and louder, and I knew that Dial was challenging time, anxious to get to the camp, frantic to get to the duck blind before the light of day was altogether sapped by dusk. Suddenly the roar of the engine was eclipsed by the thunder of not hundreds but thousands of birds flying overhead— honking, cackling, chirping, talking to one another in a clattering chatter and whipping the temperate air with their wings. There were geese and cormorants, widgeons, pintails, teals, and birds the likes of which I had never seen. We were trespassers.

Up and up the tractor climbed, high along a bank that skirted the delta. There stood a bunch of large, roomy trailers circling a makeshift courtyard. Down below, built on a ledge, was a rough patio that overlooked the expansive delta plain below. There was no time to admire the view. We each went to our own trailer, changed into waders, and departed for the duck blind.

It wasn't far. We were handed down from the tractor platform onto a much smaller one that was hooked up to an ATV. The wheels were almost entirely covered by water but we managed to get out to the blinds. And what blinds they were.

Like bunkers, of cast cement. There were two, adjacent to each other and swathed with grass and reeds. There was a bench inside with plenty of room for two plus our boxes of shells, and a footrest under a couple of feet of water. Sue and I were led to one bunker; Mike, a personable, supremely capable young Texan who was Dial's duck camp manager, shared the other with his boss. The vehicles departed. We waited. Cormorants flew high overhead, and geese. But the ducks, when they came, were out of range, busily settling in for the night on a farther bank. Only one small flock came close enough, and we took a couple of ducks, that's all. Once again, it really didn't matter.

My gun was a first-year production Fabrique Nationale Browning automatic shotgun—the original Model A-5—in 12-gauge that I bought for the trip. I'd been told it was not unusual for a gun to be confiscated in Mexico. I didn't want to risk my fine side-by-sides. I found the little automatic in my hometown gun shop, and traditionalist or not, that gun's now my favorite. It's not only pretty to look at—fully engraved on the action *and* the barrel—but it has no recoil.

In the United States, a gun must be plugged to three-shell capacity for duck hunting, so my professional gunsmith husband plugged mine just in case the same rule applied in Mexico. There is no law in Mexico, however, that requires steel shot for ducks. With steel shot, a gun should be open choke or Improved Cylinder for minimal constriction at the muzzle so the hard steel pellets can pass without causing pressure that could damage the barrels. Had steel shot been law, I could not have used my gun on duck. Tom had no opportunity to alter the choke, which was really Full. Upon reflection, this 1905 vintage gun probably shot the equivalent of Modified, since shotgun charges back then were not as potent as cartridges are today. The gun had proved far too tight for quail, which fly close up, and most effective on duck at distances exceeding 35 yards. Close range, it was a veritable rifle, patterning like a fist. I am used to a side-by-side, and I had to adapt to the long-forearmed automatic. I failed to pivot for overhead shots, didn't lean into the gun, but instead pushed the buttstock into my shoulder. Despite the choke and my poor technique, it was still impossible to miss birds.

We'd been out a little over an hour and had to get back before night pulled its pitch blanket too snugly over us. The sky was fast turning gray-black except for a wild streak of red that shot across it. It was too painful to look at, it was so intense. The birds crooned softly now. The tractor's headlights were all we had to guide us home. Cottontail rabbits skirted through the beams. Coyotes howled not far off. It's time to sleep, they called.

But not for us, not yet. We had dinner, a feast of duck and tortillas. Then we sat in front of a blazing fire in a pit built into the patio that overlooked the delta. It was cold now. The fire felt good. The red streak that cut the sky had turned to dull crimson. We talked about things that make friends out of strangers: our mutual love for the out-of-doors, how difficult it is to enjoy life and take time to hunt in a day and age when everything is work, work, work. We talked about our plans for the next day, and Dial became enthused at the thought that his bullish tractor might get stuck in the mud, and we'd have to get out and push it. His men guests just loved that, he said. Said that once the tractor got so deeply rutted in the mud that he went to the local bar and hired a hundred men for a buck apiece to lift that massive vehicle out of the mire. Sue and I demured, and allowed how lifting and pushing tractors—well, that was a guy's thing. We talked more dreams, and then we went to bed and I dreamed some, too.

And when I awoke I realized I wasn't dreaming, I was still on the

Sue King and Jim pose with the Mexican "bird boys" who worked
the pointers and gathered the quail.

(LAURIE MORROW)

delta. During the night the boys had repositioned the blinds at the throat of a waterway into the big lake. We heard geese and ducks before we saw them, and fired our first shots with the dawn. Waves of ducks descended three, five, eight at a time. Some circled three or four times before they were within range. Flashes of white-yellow from the muzzles of our guns punctured the steel gray sky. The ducks kept coming. Behind us, from the right, to the left, circling like a corkscrew from above.

From time to time we'd pause, break open our guns, and give the bird boys and Babe, Mike's year-old yellow Lab, time to collect the fallen ducks. The Lab was young, willing, unafraid of gunfire. Once or twice she'd come back with two birds in her soft mouth. It was nice not to fire steel shot. We had so many clean kills, so few cripples. But then, we had the luxury of taking many birds close, sometimes only fifteen feet away.

By eight it was over for us, we had to leave, to trek back through the isolated marshes to rejoin civilization and go home. We didn't want to go. The night before, when we returned from the blind, that red streak across the horizon? It overwhelmed me, and I wept. Everything suddenly was overpoweringly beautiful—where we were, what we had done—and I couldn't take it in: the immense expanses of unadulterated land and water, the birds, the wildlife. Sometimes we have to get far away from the lives we lead before we can discover what really counts. So when nature surrounds us, and the companionship of loved ones and friends embrace us well, it's a shining thing. I guess that's it.

An Indian named Crowfoot whispered these words just before he died in 1890: "What is life? It is the flash of a firefly in the night. It is the breath of a buffalo in the wintertime. It is the little shadow which runs across the grass and loses itself in the sunset."

I have seen flights of birds flash across the night sky. I have felt the breath of a cormorant close to my cheek, and seen the coyote dance in the shadows. And I have lost myself in the sunset. I have been to Mexico to the secret places. And there I found my Eden.

Chapter 12

—

Basic Riflery

*Laurie Morrow provides a comprehensive introduction to
rifle hunting and discusses suitable guns, appropriate
ammunition, and other elements that must be
understood before entering this great and
highly varied segment of the
shooting sports.*

The subject of hunting and shooting with a rifle is extensive and
complex. The purpose of this section is solely to introduce you to
basic riflery. It is neither comprehensive nor definitive. That would (and
may) take another book for us to write. Listed in the Directory (see
pages 217–218) are shooting sports associations that can provide you
with further information on rifle target shooting and small- and big-
game hunting. Countless books have been written on the subject—rifle
hunting in particular—and we urge you to read all you can about the
sport. We have recommended several books in the Directory under
Suggested Reading (see pages 246–251). Talk to experienced outdoors-

men and outdoorswomen. Join your local fish and game club and attend lectures. Practice at your local range. Enter tournaments. We cannot stress enough how important it is to be knowledgeable, capable, and comfortable with a rifle in any circumstance, but most important before you even entertain the notion of going after wild game.

The late Jack Connor, *Outdoor Life's* arms and ammunition editor for over twenty years and an international big-game hunter, provides an excellent layman's definition of a rifle: *A rifle is a firearm with a rifled barrel, designed to fire one projectile at a time and to be operated by one man (or woman) from the shoulder and with the use of both hands.* No matter what type of action, a rifle is a shoulder arm with spiral grooves cut inside the bore of the barrel that forces a single projectile to rotate, or spin, in flight. The seven steps of operation listed for a shotgun (pages 44–46) apply to rifles as well.

This definition excludes shotguns, even those with rifled muzzles (those designed to fire a single ball), or rifled slugs, which are called *slug guns.* They are intended for short-range use and are required for deer hunting in many eastern states due to dense human populations. These include Maryland, Delaware, New Jersey, Connecticut, Massachusetts, parts of New York, and some townships in southern New Hampshire, because their ranges are considerably shorter than a rifle's. (Be sure to

Ann Hallowell aims a Gene Simillion custom rifle in .270 Winchester. This gun is built on a streamlined Winchester pre-1964 model 70 action, considered one of the classic bolt actions.

(MORRIS HALLOWELL)

check your local game regulations.) The range of a slug-loaded shotgun is up to a half-mile; a true rifle has a random range of well over two miles. Nor does this definition apply to shotguns, since these fire anything from a few large buckshot to several hundred small birdshot at a time—not a single projectile, like a rifle. And handguns are designed as one-hand firearms.

Two popular types of rifles are currently in use in the American hunting fields. These are the modern breech-loading rifle and the muzzleloader.

The Muzzleloader

The first truly American rifle was called the Kentucky rifle, a muzzle-loading longarm that originally was developed in Pennsylvania by any one of a dozen makers in the early 1700s. We do know it was designed and built by gunsmiths of German extraction because the style of the Kentucky rifle is very similar to German arms of the period.

Obviously there were no factories in these early days, so the Ken-

The first truly American rifle was called the Kentucky rifle. This Hawkin-style percussion rifle in .50 caliber was made by Tom Morrow.

(LAURIE MORROW)

tucky rifle was made by individual gunsmiths, usually in one- or two-man shops located as far west as Missouri, as far south as Tennessee, and as far north as Ohio. This was the first rifled longarm specifically designed for American conditions. Its barrel was much longer than that of its European counterpart (40 to 45 inches as opposed to 30 to 34 inches), which had the effect of placing the front sight far from the eye, making shooting more precise in dark woods or at dawn and dusk when deer are apt to move. Its caliber was smaller (40- to 50-caliber as opposed to European 60- to 70-bore—bore is the European term for caliber) because lead was scarce, expensive, and heavy: A man could carry a great deal more ammunition for a smaller bore on his long treks into the wilderness.

Though not widely used during the Revolution (the musket—a smoothbore gun that can fire either shot or ball—was the standard weapon of the day, a kind of general-purpose gun that corresponds to today's shotgun), the Kentucky rifle was used by elite units such as Morgan's Riflemen, and to great effect in the Battle of Saratoga, where American riflemen succeeded in picking off a number of important British officers.

These early guns were all flintlocks. A flintlock is a lock mechanism whose charge is ignited by flint and steel—just as fires have been started since the dawn of man. As time went on, the ignition system of muzzleloaders changed from flintlock to percussion. A percussion lock is a mechanism in which fulminates (substances that explode when struck) are placed in small copper caps and struck by an external hammer to jet fire into the powder charge. This is essentially what most people use today for muzzleloading hunting rifles.

The muzzleloader can be a viable and accurate hunting (and target) gun. It needs to be reloaded, using separate powder and bullet, after each shot. To load it is a time-consuming procedure. In hunting, it is used for special deer seasons scheduled exclusively for muzzleloaders, and these vary with each state (check the state fish and game regulations). Some states require special muzzleloading licenses.

Firing a muzzleloader is a test of skill and a foothold in the past. Rarely does a hunter have a second chance with a muzzleloader at a fleeing deer if she misses with her first shot, so the level of skill is far greater than that required with a modern breech-loading rifle. In some states, a hunting license allows you to take one or more (depending upon the state) deer during muzzleloading season and one or more (again, depending upon the state) in regular rifle season. Hunting during both muzzleloading and rifle seasons increases the hunter's chances for a deer and extends the time she or he can enjoy the woods each year.

Some years, certain states limit rifle season to antlered deer only. This is because state fish and game departments, which monitor regional wildlife populations, determine that doe should be protected in order to increase the size of the resident herd. Under these circumstances, some states permit both sexes to be taken during muzzleloading season, further providing the skilled hunter with an opportunity to take a deer.

How accurate is a muzzleloader? That depends upon the gun, the load, the caliber and, most important, the marksman. Here's a good example. In 1921, Captain John G. W. Dillin, a noted collector and authority on Kentucky rifles, took a famous flintlock, appropriately called "Old Killdeer," to a local man who was acclaimed for his skill at off-hand shooting. Off-hand shooting is to fire a gun from the shoulder from a standing position without a gunrest of any kind—by far the most difficult position in shooting. The marksman's first targets were live pigeons sitting on a barn roof 35 yards away. Two birds were killed in three shots. His next targets were much smaller and farther away—sparrows at 40 yards—and he took six with eight shots. Dillin then took "Old Killdeer" to Ontario, where he killed one duck out of three at 150 yards—pretty impressive when you consider that duck today are legally shot with steel shot that contains 100 to 200 pellets per shell at an effective range of 50 yards. Dillin then fired ten shots at 300 yards and took five ducks.

This is a fascinating field, providing a unique challenge for the modern hunter. There are hundreds of books and many organizations devoted exclusively to the use of muzzleloaders, and we've listed some in the Directory in the back of the book. Contact them if you are interested in learning more about the muzzleloading rifle.

Light Calibers

The .25/20, first developed by Winchester for the Model 1892, is a light-rifle cartridge that, along with the .32/20, was one of the original modern, smokeless powder loads specifically made for varmint hunting. It has a good velocity and a flat trajectory that enables a capable marksman to group into ¾ to 1½ inches at 100 yards. The earliest version of the .25/20 was an 86-grain bullet with an approximate velocity of 1,450 foot-seconds, and had the desirable attribute of disintegrating when it hit the ground. The .22 Hornet and other subsequent .22-caliber center and rimfire cartridges have greater speed—but beware of the little .22 rimfire! It does *not* disintegrate upon impact, and can travel and ricochet for more than a mile. If fired in uncontrolled conditions, the bullet can be dangerous or even fatal to anything or anyone that crosses its path.

No modern production rifles are being made in .25/20; however, ammunition is obtainable since many guns chambered for that

Dated 1906, this American postcard depicts an outdoorswoman returning from a solitary afternoon's hunt with her English setter. She is carrying a deluxe-grade Winchester Model 1892 rifle, probably in .25/20 caliber.

cartridge continue to see use. When models or guns in certain calibers are discontinuted, ammunition eventually becomes obsolete.

Varmint Hunting

Varmints are birds and animals that are classified as small game and, in many cases, considered pests or nuisances. These include woodchuck; red and gray squirrel; rock chuck; prairie dog; marmot; coyote; red and gray fox; cottontail rabbit; fisher; raccoon; skunk; weasel; snowshoe hare; white-tailed, black-tailed, and antelope jack rabbit; and crows. Check the hunting and trapping regulations of the state *and county* you plan to hunt in. In New Hampshire, for example, certain game have no closed season at all, such as coyote; others have limits, such as cottontail rabbit, or no limit, such as crow; and it's unlawful in some counties to take gray squirrels, which until recently suffered precariously low numbers in certain regions. It truly depends upon what you're hunting and what neck of the woods you're in.

The Modern Rifle: How to Get Started

This book focuses on the modern breech-loading repeat rifle. First, let's take a look at general information about rifles. There are several things you must determine before you select a rifle:

1. What is the game animal you plan to hunt?

2. What are the rifle and caliber best suited for the purpose?

3. What is the type of gun that's best for you?

The most powerful rifle in the world is useless if the person shooting it can't handle it—the same holds true for a man or a women, and for men it's far more common to get "too much" gun than it is to get too little. On the other hand, you have to be careful to get a gun powerful enough for the purpose. That's where calibers are very important. For the purpose of our discussion, we'll discuss lever-action, bolt-action, and single-shot rifles.

Lever-Action Rifle

The lever-action rifle is the most common deer rifle in America. It's generally light, handy, and comes in cartridge sizes adequate for other similar sized game. You'll recognize it as the "gun that won the West"—the rifle that John Wayne and other celluloid cowboys made famous. Be that as it may, the lever-action rifle truly was the gun that won the West and was the longarm of the pioneer, cowhand, and cattle rustler alike, the law and the lawless. It remains extremely popular today and is the only distinctively American style of rifle. Today, Winchester, Marlin, and Browning pretty much corral the domestic market.

There are several modern types of high-power lever-action rifles that descend from three early designs. They are the Marlin 1893 (today's model is the Marlin 336), the Winchester 1894 (today the Winchester Model 94), and the Savage 1899 (shortened to the Savage 99). Most of these guns have been chambered in .30/30.

How the Lever-Action Operates

The lever-action rifle is operated by a finger lever (hence its name) and carries cartridges (four to seven or more, depending upon the caliber and the length of the tube) in a tube held underneath the barrel called a *magazine*. A standard lever-action rifle, in most cases, has a magazine that equals the length of the barrel. This is called a full magazine. Some older guns have shorter magazines that, obviously, hold fewer cartridges, such as the half magazine and the button magazine. The Savage and the Browning BLR rifle have a box magazine, or clip, underneath the receiver that generally holds four to five rounds.

You load the gun by pushing the cartridges into the loading gate at the side of the action (side-loader) or from the top (top-loader). The gun is operated by moving the lever forward and then back. This takes a cartridge from the magazine and moves it into the chamber. Most lever-actions have an exposed hammer which is now fully cocked when the lever is closed, and the hammer must be carefully lowered to the half-cock position (which is the only safety that most of these guns have). To do this, put the thumb on the hammer, pull the trigger with your forefinger, and lower the hammer until it reaches the half-cock notch (you'll feel a click). Great care must be taken when lowering the hammer to the half-cock position, because letting it fall could result in an accidental discharge. For this reason we repeat from our chapter on safety: *Always be sure where the muzzle of your gun is pointing!*

Some lever-actions, notably the Marlin, have a hammer-block safety designed to prevent accidental discharge when lowering the hammer. This should always be in the "on" position when putting the rifle on safety.

When you are sure of your target and are ready to fire, bring the gun to your shoulder, aim at your target, pull the hammer back to full-cock, and fire by squeezing the trigger. The gun is quickly reloaded by working the lever, which engages another round from the magazine into the chamber. If you're going to fire again, repeat the procedure.

Throughout the book we stress the importance of taking shooting lessons with an accredited instructor. Rifle shooting is no exception.

Bolt-Action Rifle

The bolt action is the most popular and generally useful of all the rifle actions. First designed in 1888 by Paul Mauser in Germany, essentially it is operated by turning a bolt at the rear of the action and drawing it backward. This unlocks the action and exposes the cartridges in the magazine. Pushing the bolt forward strips the cartridge from the magazine and feeds it into the chamber. At this point the rifle is ready to fire, and the manual safety must be engaged before carrying the rifle afield. Although a safety should never be trusted, there's much to be said for an exterior safety that you can see is engaged or not, as opposed to the kind of half-cock safety that you can't see, as on the lever-action rifles.

Despite my love of the Savage 99, on the whole I would prefer to take a good bolt-action afield. Bolt-actions are arguably the most accurate of all rifle actions. They are available in an incredible array of calibers. The same model rifle can sometimes be obtained in calibers suitable for everything from varmints to grizzly bear. Some of the lightest rifles made today are bolt-actions. If you get one with a composite stock, it may well weigh under six pounds. They all take a scope with great ease—today most rifles are drilled and tapped for scope mounts. Unlike the lever-action rifles, there are many makers of bolt-action rifles: Winchester, Savage, Ruger, Remington, Anschutz, Seiko, Colt, Browning, and many imports and American custom makers. The person who can't be satisfied with what's available in bolt-action rifles is mighty tough to satisfy. You can get modest, affordable workaday rifles or exquisitely beautiful works of art. Stocks are available in the plainest-grade woods to the most exotic, and synthetic stocks are growing rapidly in popularity. The reason for their popularity is that synthetic stocks can take far more abuse than wood. They don't ding or break, and are waterproof, which is no small advantage if you are hunting for several days at a stretch in wet weather. From a practical standpoint, they are an excellent choice. They cannot match the aesthetics or appeal of a nicely built wood-stock gun, however. And it's far too early to tell whether synthetic-stocked guns will bear any collectible value in the future. My guess is they won't; like the plain guns of the pioneers, these are solid working tools that do the job.

Single-Shot Rifle

The single-shot rifle is exactly that: a rifle that fires a single projectile. Firearms inventor John Browning's first successful gun became the Winchester Model 1885. The single-shot is considered a transition gun, between the muzzle-loader and the repeating rifle. Most single-shots have a falling block action. They come in small calibers such as the .22, which is the most popular single-shot, up to enormous buffalo and elephant guns from the black-powder days. Most target rifles are single-shots.

Traditional Hunting Techniques

There are three traditional ways of hunting: *still hunting, stand hunting, and driving.*

Still hunting is the technique most associated with hunting in New England and stories told in front of the fire on cold wintry nights. Many years of experience in the woods and woodscraft are behind a successful hunter who sets out in the forest after a whitetail. All the elements must be taken into consideration—the direction of the wind, where the sun is in the sky, the time of day. A woodscraftsman can tell where deer were feeding, where they bed at night, the buck's rut, when a deer was last in a certain place by the color of its droppings, and can determine the pattern of a deer. A deer generally moves in the early hours of dawn and at dusk, and rests during midday. As a result the hunter knows to look for the glint of an eye or the movement of horns, because in the thick woods, at least, it is unlikely she will see much more. A good still hunter knows she will cover only about 200 to 300 yards a day. Her pace is slow: two or three paces, then pause and look around. Her movements must be slow or she will attract a deer's attention. The hunter stays downwind. A deer's sense of smell is exceedingly good (for that reason, do not wear perfume). A deer is color-blind, and the glare of the sun as it descends in the sky at the end of the day can temporarily blind it, but it is extremely sensitive to movement and sound. Rain or snow gives the hunter a great advantage in that she can see fresh tracks and attempt to follow them. A deer generally lives its lifetime within one square mile of where it was born.

Stand hunting involves finding a place that overlooks the feeding area of active trails of deer. A stand can range from a makeshift wooden perch that you erect yourself, to a portable, collapsible metal tree stand available at most sporting goods stores, to a veritable treehouse or a man-made tower. A hunter sits in her tree stand and scouts the area. Usually it is best to take your position just before dawn and in the late afternoon, before dusk. This is when the deer are moving.

On a deer drive, two or more hunters (usually no more than six, depending upon the state law) stake out an area and split up, one group moving toward the other with the hope of pushing a deer toward one of the hunters. Blaze orange clothing is absolutely essential in a deer drive so that each hunter is in visual check with the other members of his or her party. Each member of the drive must know the plan. That way, he or she is certain where the others are, to minimize danger. Walkie-talkies or other radio-type devices are illegal to use in hunting. Hunters may set up a signal system of calls or whistles. Drives are often successful, and as with any type of hunting, a lot depends upon skill—but more depends upon luck.

Types of North American Big Game

White-tailed Deer

The white-tailed deer is the most popular, abundant, and varied of North American big-game animals. It can reach a height of 30 to 36 inches at the shoulder and 6 feet in length. A male can weigh between 75 and 400 pounds, and a female between 50 and 250 pounds. Deer prefer brushy, low-lying woodlands and forests.

Deer are believed to be color-blind, although recent studies indicate they may perceive some color slightly. However, deer are extremely sensitive to movement, and their senses of smell and hearing are second to none. As a result, they provide an extremely challenging hunt. They tend to be creatures of habit, and generally live in a remarkably small area—about a square mile—all their lives. That means they know their own territory better than the most skillful hunters do.

Deer tend to get bigger the farther north you go. They're bigger in New Hampshire than in Massachusetts; still bigger in Nova Scotia than in New Hampshire.

The best target on a deer for the vast majority of hunters is the heart and lung area. A shot directed immediately behind the shoulders and between a third and halfway up the body gives a lethal zone of almost a foot in diameter. In the center are the lungs, the largest lethal target on any game animal. A shot that goes a little low will hit the heart; a little high, the backbone; farther forward, you hit the shoulder; and farther back, you hit the liver. Any one of these hits will anchor the deer almost immediately. That's old-time advice—and it's good advice.

White-tailed Deer
(CHRISTOPHER SMITH)

If you wish to go deer hunting, you need to study the subject in great detail. Hunter safety courses specifically focus on deer hunting, and you will find that a good instructor can help you understand what is necessary before you even venture into the forest. Before that, it's a good idea to do a little field research by yourself. Take walks in the woods. Learn the habits of the animal that you are hunting. Practice naturecraft. Look for tracks. If there is new-fallen snow, or if the ground is damp and water is starting to fill the tracks, then they are fresh; if they're filled with water, they are not. Fresh deer droppings are soft and of a bright green color. They quickly turn brown with exposure to air— by which time, of course, your deer is long gone. Deer are "browsers." That means they don't eat hay or grass, as cattle do. What they do eat are the buds and tips of tree branches, berries, corn, acorns, and apples. Where deer have been actively feeding, careful inspection of low-growing shrubs will show that the branch tips have been neatly nibbled off by the animals' sharp front teeth. In a forest where the ground is covered with leaves, if you find leaves scuffed up with the dark side of the leaves turned up and still wet, that means a deer has recently passed through. It's extremely difficult to tell by a track whether a deer is a doe or a buck, size notwithstanding. During the rutting season, in the fall (the exact time varies with the locality), a sexually active buck will emit a powerful and unforgettable musky odor. This is an absolutely certain indication that a buck deer is in the immediate vicinity.

Recommended Calibers for Hunting Deer

Deer hunting is the most popular American big-game animal. The most popular cartridge for many years was the .30-30, first developed for the Winchester Model 1894 (in 1895), and deadly effective. It remains a favorite among many hunters to this day. Other popular and appropriate calibers are .35 Remington, .32 special, .300 Savage, .308 Winchester, .243 Winchester, .250 Savage, and many others. One of the favorite subjects of conversation among deer hunters is: Which caliber is best? There are many factors to consider.

First is the area you are hunting in and the average size of the deer there. It's estimated that there are thirty-eight subspecies of white-tailed deer, for example. A male can weigh 75 to 300 pounds or more. A Texas whitetail tends to run smaller than a Maine whitetail in weight (in the Southwest, even one-third smaller), but in Texas an average rack will run 8 points, and a nice trophy buck is 14 points; in Maine, a 200-pound buck, dressed weight, with an 8-point rack is considered very good indeed. (A point is exactly that—the tip of an antler. If a deer is an 8-point buck, that means it has 4 points stemming from each antler.) In the West, they only count the points on *one* antler ("Western count"), and in the East, *both* antlers ("Eastern count").

Texas land is largely privately owned and deer herds are carefully cultivated. Most managed leases won't allow hunters to take a buck with a rack that is less than 8 points, when mature bucks are in their prime breeding time and reproducing. The unwritten law is that you don't take a buck in Texas until it's older, say four to five years. The average life span of a whitetail is six to eight years. If they're taken before that age, good specimens don't have enough time to affect the gene pool. In the West and North, where the forests are on high ground and densely populated, it's difficult to monitor a herd closely and therefore control breeding.

A relatively light cartridge like the .25/06 is popular for smaller deer, as are similar high-velocity cartridges. The classic .30/30 and .30/06 are popular in New England for whitetails. The .270 is a good all-around caliber for most deer. Ask seasoned hunters, your local outdoor store, and your favorite gunsmith for their suggestions before you decide what caliber rifle to buy. And of course, read as much as you can on the subject in any number of good books (see the Directory for suggestions).

As a woman hunter, I want a deer rifle that is light and of sufficient power to make a clean and effective kill with one well-placed shot. My personal preference is a Savage 99, in .250 Savage, which is no longer made, but is widely available in the used gun market. I feel that the Savage 99, more than any rifle, has been shortchanged by the gun-buying public: It has a smooth-operating action with fewer internal parts than any other lever-action and therefore is not subject to breakage. This is important when you are deep in the woods and must depend upon a gun's reliablity. Next, it's relatively simple to mount a telescopic sight on it (earlier models need to be drilled and tapped to take a sight; later models are already set up to install a mount). It's extremely accurate— in the hands of good markswoman, it will put five shots within an inch at 100 yards. The .250 Savage has a very light recoil and is therefore easy and pleasant to shoot. It also has ample power to do the job. Other suitable calibers in Savage 99 are the .243 Winchester and the .300 Savage. Beware, though, of the .303 Savage as this caliber is on the brink of obsolescence and is increasingly difficult to obtain.

The Winchester Model 94 carbine is the most common lever-action rifle sold today, and is available in a wide range of calibers. A carbine is a short-barreled rifle, usually 20 inches, designed for brush hunting and short to moderate ranges. The most popular is the .30-30, but for the woman shooter I think another caliber is more suitable. The .30-30 in the Winchester carbine and other similar guns has a surprisingly sharp recoil, and for the beginning hunter, this can be a serious handicap. Many first-time women shooters are put off by any rifle that's painful to fire, and as a result aim and accuracy are jeopardized. It's a natural thing to flinch against pain; therefore, it's common sense to avoid it when you can.

The caliber I recommend for the Winchester 94 and other similar rifles is a relative newcomer called the .7-30 Waters. Its light, fast bullet makes it an astonishingly effective round on deer and keeps recoil to a minimum. It also tends to be somewhat more accurate than cartridges in the .30-30 category.

Your husband or companion might argue that he has been shooting all his life with the .30-30, and beware—most men have. But cartridge development has not stood still all these years. The .30-30 first came out, after all, in 1895. Some of the new developments are as good or better for the beginning woman shooter, and in the case of the .7-30 Waters, I say better. You may find that there is a tremendous lure attached to cartridges like the .30-30. This one in particular is probably the caliber that your husband's father and his father before him used. The test is to try both. Try several calibers, and get a sense of your personal preference. After all, the bottom line is that the gun you shoot has to suit you.

Moose

Moose are the largest of North American big-game animals and are hunted only by special license, usually obtained through a lottery or draw. They can reach a height of 7½ feet at the shoulder and measure 10 feet long. A male can weigh 1,400 pounds and a female between 600 and 800 pounds. Moose are not particularly intelligent, are relatively easy to stalk and shoot, and tend to be slow-moving. Their habitat is wilderness forest near wetlands, such as shallow lakes, marshes, and swamps. Heavy loads, such as cartridges in the .270 and .30/06 class, are popular for moose.

Elk

A bull elk can be as long as 9½ feet and 4 to 5 feet at the shoulder, and weigh up to 1,100 pounds. A female can weigh between 500 and 650 pounds. They favor open woodlands and forests at higher elevations,

Elk

(CHRISTOPHER SMITH)

such as mountain meadows and foothills, in the summer and early fall, and lower elevations such as plains and valleys in the summer. Although elk, on the whole, are somewhat smaller than moose, they're more difficult to kill. They seem to be tougher creatures altogether. Their bone structure is dense and heavy. If you're using a .270- or .30/06-class rifle, stick to lung shots (or the neck if you're close enough.) Don't try to break those heavy shoulder bones with a rifle of less than .338 class, because the bullet is likely to stop in the shoulder joints (which can be nine or ten inches deep) and not reach the vital organs. You'd need a heavy bullet of 250 grains and up to penetrate that heavy bone structure reliably. Elk can run off cheerfully with wounds that would drop a moose in its tracks.

Black Bear

A black bear can be 5 to 6 feet long and 2 to 3 feet at the shoulder, and weigh between 200 and 400 pounds or more. They live all over the continental United States, in forests, swamps, and mountains, and will adapt themselves to semisuburban life. You've heard stories of bears hanging around garbage dumps, and occasionally walking through a house and to scarf up a fresh-baked blueberry pie before walking out the kitchen door. For that reason, bear-hunting season has been lengthened in many states. Generally speaking, any rifle suitable for deer is also fine for black bear, with the possible exception of the .243. It's rare in hunting country—and more prevalent in national parks—for a bear to get ugly. In national parks, bears are protected, not hunted, and they lose their fear of people. They'll freeload at campsites, and can get violent if disturbed. In any case, stay away from bears with cubs. Female bears become very protective and can attack—and kill.

Mule Deer

The mule deer is a different species from white-tailed deer and tends to be a plains, or open-country, animal. It lives in such states as Colorado, Wyoming, and Montana. The mule deer is comparable to the whitetail in many ways, but differs in physical appearance primarily in its rack structure and the long ears that give it its name. The same class of rifles used on whitetails is appropriate for mule deer, but given the greater ranges typically involved in hunting mule deer, the higher-velocity, flatter-shooting calibers are generally preferred, such as the .270 and 7mm magnum.

Other North American big-game animals include barren ground caribou, pronghorn antelope, bighorn sheep, Dall sheep, desert sheep, mountain goat, bison, musk ox, brown bear (grizzly), coyote, and mountain lion. For the purposes of this book, however, we will focus on white-tailed deer hunting.

Hunting Bullets

This is an enormous subject and best explored with a seasoned hunter or someone at your local sporting goods store who is well versed in ammuntion. Factory loads come in a variety of weights and qualities, and again, these too should be discussed with someone with experience. There are several types of bullets: flat-pointed, round-nosed, soft-point, spitzer, and so on. You'll find that every major ammunition manufacturer offers a high-quality brand, such as Federal's Premium and Winchester's Supreme. By and large, the extra money does indeed buy you a better cartridge. Many hunters prefer to handload their ammunition. This requires special equipment that enables the handloader to make rifle bullets and even shotgun shells specifically for her firearm. It can result in an appreciable savings over time, and the hunter has the satisfaction of knowing her load is well made and will do the job she is after. Reloading is extremely popular in rifle target shooting and, in fact, is the preference of serious target shooters.

Popular Hunting Cartridges

These are some of the most common rifle cartridges used in hunting today:

Varmint: .17 Remington, .22 Hornet, .223 Remington, .22/250, .243 Winchester

Short-range: .30/30, .35 Remington, .358 Winchester, .444 Marlin, the classic .45/70

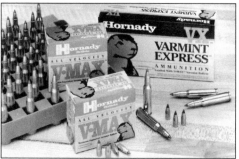

Rifle ammunition comes in a vast range of calibers.

(PHOTO COURTESY OF HORNADAY)

Long-range: .243 Winchester, .25/06 Remington, 270 Winchester, .270 Weatherby Magnum, .280 Remington, 7mm-08 Remington, 7mm Remington Magnum, .307 Winchester, .308 Winchester, .30/06, .300 Weatherby Magnum

Dangerous or large game (Cape buffalo, moose, elk, etc.): .338 Winchester Magnum, .340 Weatherby Magnum, .375 Holland & Holland, .416 Remington Magnum, .458 Winchester Magnum

Sights

There are two basic types of sights on a rifle: *open,* or *metal,* sights and *telescopic* sights called scopes. The telescopic sight is most popular today, because it can provide excellent magnification. In hunting, your primary goal is to effect a clean kill. A scope enables you to place your shot with accuracy that can be superior to what you'd have with open sights. Also, you can see better through a scope in dim light because of the lens's ability to gather light. Be careful not to choose a scope with too much magnification; this is a common mistake. For most hunting, 4X is good; in open country, 6X or a variable scope. Be sure to invest in good scope mounts. These will ensure that your scope is held securely to your rifle and won't shift.

Iron sights remain the preference of many hunters and are accurate and effective at close range, usually 100 yards or less. For greater distances, a scope is essential. The one time iron sights are preferable over telescopic sights is in the rain. There are many types of iron sights, and always two are mounted on one gun—one on or in front of the receiver (rear sight) and the other at the muzzle of the gun (front sight). The rear sight is usually adjustable for distance.

Telescopic sights are the most popular today, providing excellent magnification. Pictured here are (1) Leupold Varmint/Silhouette scope in 6.5X20-50mm, and (2) Leupold Vari-X III 1.75X6 E.

(PHOTO COURTESY OF LEUPOLD & STEVENS, INC.)

Rifle Target Shooting: "Shooting at the Mark"

*Rifle target shooting was America's first national pastime,
and continues to be a strong and growing segment of
the shooting sports. Morrow explains the game
and envisions the excitement generated by
the first international rifle match.*

Position Rifle Shooting

Position *rifle shooting* requires competitors to shoot from various positions during different match stages. Two governing bodies regulate this sport: the International Shooting Union (UIT), which specifies standing (off-hand), kneeling, and prone (lying down), and the National Rifle Associaiton (NRA), which uses the same positions, plus the sitting position.

A typical match will consist of several stages fired at different distances from each position. Targets are round bull's-eyes with numerical

This shooter demonstrates the standing, or off-hand, position.
(DON HOFFMAN/WSSF)

scoring rings radiating outward from a center (10-ring or X-ring). Both rimfire and center-fire rifles are used in position events. Small-bore shooters engage targets at ranges from 50 feet to 100 yards; high-power shooters deal with targets at ranges up to 1,000 yards.

Time limits vary with the stage and yardage. For example, high-power shooters firing at 600 yards are allotted 20 minutes for 20 shots; the rapid-fire stage, fired at 200 yards, allows 60 seconds for 10 shots.

The total number of points accumulated by a shooter, as indicated by hits in the scoring rings, determines a shooter's score. In the event of a tie, the number of X-ring or "bull's-eye" hits will determine the winner. Shooters are classified by skill level based upon previous scores and compete only against shooters within the same class.

Rifles are classed by division, by caliber (small bore, air rifle, high power) and subclasses by weight and stock configuration. Some matches—the NRA Service Rifle, for example—have rigid requirements for an individual rifle that specify even particular makes and models. Other classes are less demanding and offer a wider latitude of firearm types. Scopes are permitted in some matches under NRA rules, but are not allowed in international competition.

The oldest competitive sport in America was rifle target shooting, or "rifle frolics," which originated around 1700 and involved shooting flintlocks in the off-hand position at approximately 80 yards, or in the "rest" position at 100 yards. The winner walked away with a turkey or a "beef creature" (cow).

It wasn't until the Civil War, when recruits were virtually untrained in handling firearms for war, that Colonel William C. Church and Captain George W. Wingate of the New York National Guard undertook training programs that ultimately resulted in the establishment of the National Rifle Association in 1871.

The history of target shooting in America dates to Colonial times when *shooting at a mark* was a widely practiced sport. Its popularity increased with the meteoric expansion of our country, and by the 1850s it was universally acclaimed as America's national pastime. Only later, when leagues were organized for baseball (1903) and football (1921), was target shooting supplanted, but it was relegated to an undisputed niche as the father of national pastimes. Target shooting never retired from the public scene. It continues to provide enjoyment and personal challenge to thousands of marksmen and markswomen, from aspiring amateurs to celebrated professionals, nationally and around the world. No sport equals it in skilled accuracy. In order to appreciate rifle target shooting and introduce women's involvement in it, let's take a page from its illustrious history and relive the greatest tournament of them all—the First International Rifle Match in the United States for the Championship of the World.

Perhaps the following story will give you an idea of just how important and exciting rifle target shooting was, in its day, as America's original National Pastime.

The First International Target Match in America

The year was 1873. Ireland had just taken the coveted Elcho shield, the highest trophy awarded at the Wimbledon, England, target matches, in the 800-, 900-, and 1,000-yard competitions between the Lands of the Realm—England, Scotland, Canada, Australia, and Ireland. The Irish team's victory was unprecedented. Record scores were achieved. In the exhilaration of their triumph, the team's captain, Major Arthur B. Leach, sent word to the New York Herald that his unrivaled, unbeaten team hereby tendered a challenge to the finest marksmen in America for the Championship of the World. Let's step back in time . . .

Ireland's challenge ignites the headlines, and becomes the talk of the town. But it is not the staid National Rifle Association that bites the bullet, so to speak, for that dignified body refuses to entertain any challenge that is not directly and formally presented to them. It is the fiery, dauntless, fledgling Amateur Rifle Club of New York City that seizes the challenge without hesitation. It is simply too tempting to refuse—despite the fact that the club has no organized team. Nor have they the £100 stake . . . or the requisite match rifles with Vernier elevation and wind-gauge sights! In fact, only five matches have ever been held by the young Amateur Rifle Club of New York City, and not a single one of its seventy members have ever fired a shot over 600 yards! But they have spirit and embrace the challenge. They can do anything they set their mind to. After all, this is America.

Two major firearms makers of the day, E. Remington & Sons and Sharps Rifle Company, get involved. Each company puts up half of the team's stake, and sets about industriously developing state-of-the-art target rifles for the newly christened American Rifle Team. No longer is a tap of the hammer to adjust an iron sight enough to ensure accuracy, let alone distances up to 1,000 yards. Remington and Sharps propose outfitting the American team with an innovation in firearms: the machine-made, hand-finished breech-loader. Both firms guarantee this new development in firearms technology will be second to none in accuracy.

The breech-loader is unlike anything the Irish team ever saw, let alone competed against. The Irish Rifle Team's captain is John Rigby of Dublin—*the* Rigby, whose firm engineered and manufactured some of the finest rifles ever made. The team was outfitted with Rigby's entirely hand-crafted, muzzle-loading target rifles, calibrated to 1,000 yards. No longer was this a mere challenge between nations: it was a challenge between the muzzle-loader and the breech-loader, and the future and direction of firearms technology hung in the balance.

The tournament is scheduled for September 1874 at the Creedmore Range on Long Island. It becomes, for lack of any other place, the first official rifle range in America, but compared to the impeccably manicured Wimbledon Range outside of London, Creedmore, as one observer notes, is "little more than a cow pasture." It was designed by General George W. Wingate and built two years earlier, in 1871, on land purchased jointly by the State of New York, the National Rifle Association, the City of New York, and the City of Brooklyn, donated for the purpose of providing land for exclusive use as a public rifle range.

By May 1874, the innovative Sharps and Remington breech-loading rifles are presented to the American team by Remington's chief designer, L. L. Hepburn, who himself will earn a position on the American Rifle Team. These long, heavy-barreled, breech-loading rifles are chambered for .44 caliber and fire a 550-grain bullet, hardened 1:50 (one part to fifty parts), and backed by 90 to 100 grains of black powder.

Tryouts for the six positions available on the American Rifle Team are advertised, and men travel from far and wide with hopes of achieving scores that will earn them a place on what is acclaimed as the greatest sports team America has ever known. Finally the winners are announced: Lieutenant Henry Fulton, G. W. Yale of Sharps, Colonel John "Old Reliable" Bodine, Colonel H. A. Gildersleeve, General T. S. Dakin, and, last but not least, L. L. Hepburn.

On September 28, 1874, eight thousand spectators make their way on horse, in buggies, by special train, and on foot to Creedmore. The air is electric. Never before had so many fans gathered in one spot to watch a team sport. They line the course, which stretches more than one thousand yards, keeping a safe distance beyond the range. The six members of the Irish team shake hands with the six members of the American Rifle team and the tournament begins. The crowd roars, and the momentous occasion of the first World Championship begins. Even the hot, sultry Indian summer weather cannot dampen the exhilaration of the great event.

The toss—and the American team wins and chooses the favorable firing points 19 and 20, the positions at which Ireland had chosen to practice the entire previous week. Point 18 is thrown down to provide visual space between teams, and the Irish riflemen take points 16 and 17. The crowd waits in silence to see which team will fire the first shot in the first event, the 800 yard.

There's considerable delay. One man is concentrating on the final cleaning of his gun, another is permitted to test-fire his rifle one last time. Each team waits for the other to take the first shot. The tension heightens, you can cut it with a knife . . . and finally Captain Walker of the Irish team takes the initiative. The handsome, six-foot-tall military officer lowers himself to the ground and takes the *active service position,* lying face downwards with both elbows resting on the ground. He fires the first shot . . . and misses! The American supporters roar in discourteous approval, and Colonel Wingate, captain of the American team, pleads loudly for good conduct and sportsmanship, and succeeds in quieting the crowd.

Now the rotation begins. Next up is Dr. Hamilton of the Irish team, and he, too, assumes the *active service position* . . . and scores! Now the Irish contingent applauds and yells to such an extent that Major Leach, captain of the Irish Team, follows Colonel Wingate's example and demands silence. From that point, and throughout the tournament, the crowd refrains from impulsive outbursts. However, as the tournament progresses and the tension mounts, this becomes almost too much to ask. As each string is completed, the atmosphere intensifies, thick with excitement.

By the time the 800-yard match is completed, Dr. Hamilton achieves a final score of 13 bull's-eyes out of 15 shots. John Rigby shoots, realizing an equally brilliant score. It is his consistently flawless delivery that had earned him the reputation of the steadiest and most reliable shot on the Irish team.

J. K. Milner follows, with a stunning eleven consecutive bull's-eyes. The Irish team completes the first string to riotous applause. It is midday, and the sun on the treeless range is now beating down with a vengeance. Nonetheless, not one spectator even thinks of leaving in search of relief.

Now the American team takes position. Lieutenant Fulton, the team's finest marksman, walks forward as if oblivious to the attention marking his every move—and assumes a unique position: "Lying down on his back and crossing his legs, Mr. Fulton turns slightly to the right, placing the butt of his rifle over his right shoulder, resting against his cheek," the *New York Herald* reports in its evening edition. "The barrel rests in the V formed by his crossed legs, finding a remarkably solid support. The left hand is passed behind the neck, grasping the heel of the butt, holding it firmly against the cheek. In this way the rifle is held as in a vice, and the marksman proceeds to take aim coolly and with the greatest deliberation." Fulton has chosen a Remington, but, contrary to its breech-loading innovation, prefers to load it from the muzzle for absolute accuracy. Breech-loaders require meticulous cleaning after each and every shot. Accuracy can be compromised as a result of fulminate powder residue accruing in the breech, hindering the discharge of the projectile; whereas muzzle-loaders require little or no cleaning. Fulton fires again and again until he achieves a perfect score, 15 out of 15.

Next up is Colonel John Bodine, the oldest member of the team at almost sixty, who has chosen a Remington, loaded from the breech, and takes the *active service position*. Hepburn is next, also shouldering a Remington, and then follow the other three team members, each firing a Sharps. The sixth and final shooter on the American team, General Dakin, scores the lowest of any of the marksmen at the match. Nevertheless, the Americans take the 800-yard match with 326 points, to the Irish team's 317. More than ten minutes pass before the ardent cajoling of the course officials succeeds in silencing the wildly cheering supporters of the American Rifle Team.

The 900-yard match begins with J. K. Milner of the Irish team. He suffers a terrible blow by delivering a bull's-eye at the *Americans'* target, thus forfeiting his score. Worried about this unfortunate start—Milner made the same mistake at Wimbledon—the Irish heat up to overcome this early obstacle and perform brilliantly, edging forward, overtaking, and finally winning the 900-yard match by a hair: 312 points to the American team's 310.

Women spectators fan themselves under the now brutal sun, seeking paltry refuge under their parasols. Little did they know that one of their own sex would in just a few years take her place as the finest marksman the world has ever known—a petite young woman named Annie Oakley. Members of both teams now complain that the sweltering sun and steamy humidity is forming mirages across the green, compromising their skill. Nonetheless, the 1,000-yard match begins.

The Americans take an early lead, but soon the Irish close in on their opponents' 14-point advantage. Suddenly all eyes gaze heavenward. A sudden cold front blows in, and heavy gray clouds chase across the sky. Instantly the temperature cools and for the first time since they sailed from their motherland into New York Harbor, the Irish comment how this is just like the weather back home. Their shooting becomes inspired.

Lieutenant Fulton of the Irish team now takes his position for the team's final round in the tournament. If he succeeds in a flawless score, he would almost assuredly win not only the 1,000-yard match for Ireland, but the World Championship as well! Rapidly he fires . . . three centers! The Irish team has completed the 1,000-yard match with a staggering 302 points. Five points behind with 297 points, even if the American team took a bull's-eye with their last shot, that's only 4 points. They would still be 1 point behind and would lose not only the 1,000-yard match, but the championship.

There's only one chance, and it's as much a long shot as the 1,000 yards that the American team's final shooter, Colonel Bodine, positions himself to make. The Irish team was levied a 3-point penalty when Milner fired at the Americans' target. The penalty is a technicality that could, in fact, win the Americans the World Championship when the final results are tallied. . . .

One shot. Only one shot and the championship will be determined. It's been neck and neck all the way; the tension mounting in the crowd is unbearable. The members of both teams are anxious, some even noticeably agitated. Unbearable excitement shows on every one of the eight thousand faces lining the Creedmore Range. Everyone knows the chances for a perfect shot are almost nil. Bodine would not have been the choice, but the rotation pits him as the final shooter. He is the team's biggest risk. Not only is he its oldest member, but he is so severely farsighted that he must wear *two* pairs of glasses just to clean his gun. But that's the least of it. Moments before, Bodine severely cut his shooting hand on a broken bottle. Refusing offers of assistance, he wraps his jagged, bloody wound himself, reaches for his Remington, and loads it at the breech.

With the courage that earned him honor and respect as a Union soldier fighting bravely in the Civil War, and the heart that earned him the reputation of a devoted sportsman, Bodine takes position. The crowd is silent. The wind ceases. Bodine takes aim . . . and fires. A puff of white smoke hits the target, followed by the deafening explosion as the bullet erupts from the muzzle. Three interminable seconds pass, the time it takes for sound to report that the bullet has traversed 3,000 feet at 1,000 feet per second. And a cry: *"It's on! Bull's eye!"*

The crowd explodes. Cheers and cries reverberate over the thundering applause. Colonel Bodine is hoisted on the shoulders of his supporters and carried triumphantly around the field. The American Rifle Team has won!

Front-page headlines plaster every newspaper in the country and around the world! MAGNIFICENT SCORES AT HALF-MILE RANGES!, THE BATTLE OF THE RIFLES—MUZZLELOADERS V. BREECH-LOADERS!, HONOR REPEATED, EVEN IN DEFEAT! The *New York Herald* would report:

> When the challenge to a trial of skill was accepted it was possible that America could furnish a team of long-range riflemen capable of competing successfully with the victors of Wimbledon. And it must be confessed that to good luck as much as superior skill do we owe our success in the very close contest. The error of making a bull's eye on the wrong target made by one of the Irish team gave the victory to America. Had it not been for this mischance, our plucky visitors would have carried back their fame—scotched, in deed, but still secure. As it is they have the consolation of knowing that the points actually scored by their team exceed by one that made by

their opponents. But the ruling out of Mr. Milner's mis-directed shot deprived them of four points, and so decided the contest in favor of America by three points. With such a record, defeat loses all its sting, and the unsuccessful marksmen may console themselves with having merited victory, if they did not achieve it.

The final score was Ireland 317 points, America 326 points at 800 yards; Ireland 312 points, America 310 points at 900 yards; and Ireland 302, America 298 points in the 1,000-yard match; for a tournament total of Ireland 931 points and America—the World Champions—with 934 points.

The members of the Irish team embraced their opponents and rejoiced, at least outwardly, at their victory. For on that momentous September day on a green meadow in Long Island, the greatest shooting tournament of all time was held, and there was but one victor.

The victor was the breech-loading rifle, and from that time forward, the muzzle-loader became a thing of the past. Firearms technology took off and never looked back. There was a young man, named John Browning, waiting in the wings ready and raring to go, and others, too, would succeed in taking firearms design and technology to great heights.

As for the Irish Rifle Team and the American Rifle Team, this must be said of each team: Every man overcame personal bounds and, in some cases, handicaps. The six men on the American team came from all walks of life and pooled their skills to form the first team in the history of the young nation they proudly joined to represent. Their triumph was the first international sports victory of any kind in the history of the United States, predating even the first modern Olympic games, held in 1896, by twenty-two years. Likewise, a half-dozen seasoned competitors crossed an ocean from a far older land to defend their country and title—only to surrender it in one of the most noble and greathearted displays of sportsmanship ever witnessed on any playing field, anywhere. The Irish Rifle Team won a place in history as the first foreign team to land on our shores to compete in the first international sporting event ever held in America.

In the words of Winston Churchill, "In Victory: Magnanimity, In Peace: Good Will." *Magnanimity and good will.* That is the very essence of sportsmanship.

Achieving a high level of accuracy begins with the rifle. Most top competitors today use custom-built bolt-action rifles with synthetic stocks (such as Kevlar or Fiberglass), precision-rifled barrels, lightweight target triggers, and high-magnification scopes. Benchrest shooters also take meticulous care to assemble the finest loads available. Individual bullets are weighed and only those that are precisely equal are used. Cartridge cases are measured, weighed, and trimmed to exacting dimensions before being fire-formed to achieve the desired fit to the rifle's chamber. Powder charges are measured to within .1 grain for uniformity. The National Bench Rest Shooter's Association hasn't logged the perfect .000 group yet; but that's the goal of every benchrest shooter.

Rifle Silhouette Shooting

Originally developed in Mexico, *siluetas metalicas* (metal silhouettes) is a hunter's game with simple rules and equipment: The targets are life-sized steel-plate silhouettes of chickens, pigs, turkeys, and sheep. These are arranged in banks of five each with the chickens at 200 meters, pigs at 300, turkeys at 385, and sheep at 500. A shooter is given 2½ minutes to fire one round at each of the five targets.

If your bullet knocks the target completely off its stand, it counts as a hit. Anything else is a miss. Shooting is done from the off-hand standing position, without the aid of slings, padded shooting jackets, palm rests, or even shooting gloves. Shooters compete with scoped rifles that are appropriate for hunting. The most popular rifles are bolt-actions chambered for popular rounds, such as the 30/06 and .308.

By using scaled-down versions of the silhouettes, small-bore class matches are now being held for .22 rimfire rifles. In the small-bore game, downsized chickens are placed at 40 meters, pigs at 60, turkeys at 77, and sheep at 100. Regardless of the rifle used, a standard course consists of 10 shots each at the chickens, pigs, turkeys, and sheep. A full match may consist of 40, 80, or 120 rounds, requiring the course to be fired several times.

Summer Biathlon

Summer biathlon is a combination of running and shooting that requires physical endurance and mental concentration. After running a mile, the heart, lungs, and muscles are pumping in sync as the brain focuses on servicing the exerted body parts—controlling the heart rate, slowing down the breathing, steadying the muscles, and concentrating on shooting a rifle. Until a few years ago, the only people who had ever heard of summer biathlon were a few Olympic athletes who used this warm-weather version of the Olympic sport to train. Today, what began as a way for Olympic-caliber athletes to stay in top form without snow has blossomed into a full-blown sport.

In summer biathlon, competitors start the innovative 5-kilometer race by running a 1-mile course to the rifle range, where they pick up a .22 rimfire rifle and fire five shots from a prone (lying down) position at five special metallic "knockdown" targets positioned 3 to 25 yards away. After running another 1-mile loop that returns them to the range, racers fire another five shots from the standing position before running 1 mile to the finish line. Scores are based on the combination of race times and shooting scores. Every prone target toppled deducts 15 seconds from the runner's time. Targets hit from the standing position are worth 30-second deductions. The racer with the lowest net time within each category is the winner.

For information on participating in a summer biathlon event, contact Summer Biathlon Race Series, P.O. Box 997, Portland, Oregon 97207.

Chapter 14

—

The Hunter as Conservationist

*Conservation means replenishing our natural resources,
land, and wildlife to ensure it for our children and
future generations to come.*

In *A Sand County Almanac* (1949), American wildlife management pioneer Aldo Leopold wrote: "We face the questions whether a still higher 'standard of living' is worth its cost in things natural, wild, and free. For us of the minority, the opportunity to see geese is more important than television, and the chance to find a pasqueflower is a right as inalienable as free speech." It is pitiful that, almost a half-century later, his sentiment still applies today.

It is also pitiful that we who hunt must defend why we hunt, and stand up for our constitutional right to own the firearms we shoulder in order to pursue our sport. Again Leopold hit a nerve when he said:

"There are some who can live without wild things, and some who cannot." We who hunt cannot.

And yet when we hunt we kill the wild things we love. "Sport that involves killing has no more today to be honestly said for or against it than when primitive man cast the first stone at another animal not of his kind," wrote Edward Cave in 1931. "Let the humanitarians say their worst. Likewise the holy and the unholy among us who shoot. The whole incalculably vast subject, and all its world-mist of controversy, detonates of its own expansive gases when touched with the fire of one imperishable truth." The imperishable truth is that humans as hunters are a cog in the food chain wheel as old as mankind itself. Hunting is harvesting and maintains healthy wild game populations, crucial to keeping the nature in check.

Legislation has been passed over the years that is sensitive to the biological cycles of plants and animals, and how human infringement on the land has affected nature's balance. As an outdoorswoman, it is important to understand that wildlife is not just out there for the taking. It's like being invited over to someone's house for dinner; you bring a bottle of wine, a small housegift—something to reciprocate in kind. When you take an animal from its habitat, you need to do something to enhance that habitat to ensure healthy procreation of wildlife.

Acquaint yourself with the efforts of conservationists that have resulted in cornerstone legislation to ensure that what we have today will continue into tomorrow. You'll be shocked when you see that such efforts came into being a mere half-century after the Pilgrims set foot on Plymouth Rock:

1677 A law is enacted in Connecticut that prohibits taking game out of state. In 1900, the Lacey Act stipulates penalties against hunters who illegally take game and transport it over state lines.

1738 In order to maintain healthy herd populations it is made illegal to hunt does in Virginia.

1846 In Rhode Island waterfowl hunting is banned in the spring to protect nesting.

1878 Iowa imposes bag limits on game. By 1900, 13 more states do the same.
New Hampshire and California create Fish and Game Departments and the positions of state game wardens and conservation officers. By 1900, 31 other states follow suit.

1895 Michigan and North Dakota require hunting licenses for sportsmen; within 25 years, 33 states require licenses. The resultant revenue is directed into conservation efforts.

1930 The father of conservation, Aldo Leopold, presents his studies on the quality and quantity of habitat in direct relation to game populations, and asserts that wildlife biologists must be an integral part of monitoring the ecosystem. This results in the American Game Policy.

1937 The Pittman-Robertson Federal Aid in Wildlife Restoration Act imposes a 10 percent excise tax on sporting arms and ammunition (increased to 11 percent during World War II). The income generated, in excess of $146 million a year, goes to fund state wildlife programs.

1970 The Dingell-Hart Act imposes a 10 percent excise tax on handguns. Annual proceeds, currently in excess of $30 million annually, are directed to wildlife restoration, hunter safety courses, and the construction of public shooting ranges.

1972 The Goodling-Moss Act imposes an 11 percent excise tax on archery equipment, proceeds directed along the same avenues as those from the Dingell-Hart Act.

1976 The Federal Land Policy and Management Act designates 270 million acres as multiple-purpose public lands for fishing, hunting, and wildlife management.

1980 The Alaska Lands Act designates 80 million acres for national parks and refuge districts in Alaska.

1985 The Conservation Reserve Program protects 34 million acres as wildlife preserves.

1989 North American Wetlands Preservation Act is enacted to fund the North American Waterfowl Management Plan.

Now you know about the legislation that hunters and conservationists have spearheaded over the years. Look at the results of their efforts:

- The white-tailed deer population of North America was estimated at 500,000 in 1900. Today it is 14 million.

- In 1945, the pronghorn antelope population was 12,000. Today there are 1 million. The herd is culled as a result of regulated seasons in 16 states.

- In 1907, fewer than 40,000 elk or wapiti were estimated to populate the area around Yellowstone Park. Today that number is 500,000 in an area that covers 16 states.

- Wild turkey was virtually extinct in the early 1900s. Today that population is estimated at 3 million and increasing rapidly. Now 41 states often permit one- and two-season hunting periods for turkey.

Consider these facts from the U.S. Fish and Wildlife Service:

- Through their membership in and support of 10,000 organizations such as Ducks Unlimited, Pheasants Forever, and the Rocky Mountain Elk Foundation, hunters contribute $300 million to wildlife conservation activities.

- For every taxpayer dollar invested in wildlife conservation, sportsmen contribute nine dollars.

- Each day, sportsmen contribute more than $3 million to wildlife conservation, or $1.5 billion per year.

- Hunters and fisherman have contributed over $17 billion for wildlife conservation to date.

- Hunters contribute more than $14 billion to the U.S. economy each year, supporting more than 380,000 jobs. For every 50 hunters, enough economic activity is generated to create one job.

As Leopold points out, "We abuse land because we regard it as a commodity belonging to us. When we see land as a community to which we belong, we may begin to use it with love and respect." Wild game animals are likewise members of that community. Such love and respect as Leopold speaks of come with investment—not just in cash donations or license fees—but in time spent in the woods learning about nature's ways. It's a continuing self-education, often punctuated with revelations—and fulfillment.

Theodore Roosevelt and his son Kermit pose with Cape buffalo and Roosevelt's Holland & Holland .500/.450 double rifle on an East African safari, 1909-1910.

(PHOTO COURTESY OF T. ROOSEVELT COLLECTION, HARVARD COLLEGE/BUTTERFIELD & BUTTERFIELD)

Afterword

—

Three women join me on the cover of this book. They are my shooting partners. Don Hoffman photographed us in Center, Texas, at Hawkeye Hunt Club, the late Jerry Waters's terrific wingshooting preserve. Our upland attire, by C. C. Filson Company, Kaufman-Sorel, and Beretta Sport, is the kind of practical yet attractive clothing I discuss in chapter 3.

That's Sue King from chapter 10; the blonde is Sharon Borg Wall, who wrote the Foreword. The brunette is Cindy Marlenee, who with her husband, former U.S. congressman Ron Marlenee of Montana, is involved in legislative affairs for Safari Club International. These women are accomplished hunters and sporting clays enthusiasts. Sue's love for the out-of-doors was instilled in her by her grandfather. Cindy's father made shooting a family sport for her and her seven siblings. Sharon's husband taught her how to first shoulder a gun, just as mine taught me. Our combined experience as outdoorswomen exceeds a century, although none of us obviously looks a day over twenty-five.

We hail from different parts of the country. Sue's a native Texan, Cindy adopted Montana, Maryland is home for Sharon, and New Hampshire is mine. We are mothers and grandmothers, and our respective children are the fruit of devoted marriages. We're products of hardworking, middle-class parents that put a lot of stock in education and family values. Becoming career housewives was never an option; ours is the generation of professional women that partner two-income households. Leisure time is a precious commodity spent frugally, yet we lavish what we have on family and beloved friends. We do what we can to conserve natural resources and wildlife. More often than not our place of worship is a cathedral of lofty pines deep in the woods, baptized by a rippling stream. We've traveled roads that were seldom smooth and often treacherous, but even in the darkest times the way was clear, thanks to loved ones—and faith. This is who we are, and what we are. We are no different from you.

Now you've almost finished our book. Steve Smith has given you solid information on how to get into the shotgunning sports. He's a lifelong hunter and has passed the outdoors legacy his father handed down to him to his own fine children, as my husband did for ours. Smith has written extensively about wingshooting over the past few decades, and produced some definitive work on woodcock, grouse, and ducks. He's a rare bird himself: author, editor, former teacher, wildlife biologist, field dog trainer, wit. Learning from the best is important to your education as a new shooter. Now it's up to you to take what you've learned in our book and apply it, with assurance.

As for my part, I hope it serves you well. I was eighteen when I first shouldered a gun, a quarter century and several lifetimes ago, here in these woods that surround my home. Come October and November, the wind's like a Gaelic melody accompanied by rustling leaves, and an incandescent light at dusk casts a godly glow over the mountains. This is my time, this is my place, it is where I belong; and it is because you too are a lover of the out-of-doors, and hear and see these things, that I tell you this. Always remember, it's not for the gun, it's not for the game; it's something within, for which there are no words, and it's up to you to find it for yourself.

And so I leave you, now, with this story, which I give you so that you may know something about my own journey, and I wish you, with all my heart, godspeed on yours.

—Laurie Morrow
  April 1996

Lost

She knew the tears would come. They didn't come often, and she hated it when they did. But she was lost, really lost in the woods, and she was beginning to get frightened. She had never been frightened before, at least not like this; but it came from the same place, the fear. It came from within, that helpless place in her soul, the dark compartment she kept securely locked. She knew too well what it was to feel helpless.

Helpless, like the day she lost her only daughter.

She didn't want to think about that right now, she couldn't. She had to find her way out of the woods and get home. Home to her family. It was going to be dark in a couple of hours, and she was completely turned around. They would be getting worried. Even her little springer spaniel seemed concerned as she stood alongside her, looking up expectantly.

Her husband knew where she had gone, or at least where she was going. Her sons knew this place well, too. They learned to hunt here. That was . . . what? Ten years ago . . . *Don't worry,* her husband had assured her. *I'll take care of them. No, they're not too young. I was eight when my father took me bird hunting for the first time.* . . . Now their sons were at the cusp of adulthood, and yet it seemed like only yesterday. She wouldn't have been lost if they were with her; she shouldn't have gotten lost in the first place. After all, she learned to hunt here too, all those years ago. But then she gave it up, had the children, kept the homefires burning. Then the baby died. Afterwards, when she learned to live with the terrible emptiness in her heart and tried to get on with it, she took up hunting again. Bird hunting, and now this fall she was going after deer with her husband and their boys. She loved the woods, it was so peaceful. And the hunting, well, that was a good way to fill the place her daughter was meant to fill, to dull the loss, to understand that expectation always falls short when you want something so very, very much.

No, she shouldn't have gotten lost, but she did. These woods went on and on for miles, through swamps and hills and valleys and on to nowhere, for all anyone knew.

Once it had been a thriving New Hampshire village with home-steads and even a meeting house. You could still make out the road that led to it, but now it was only forested trail. Here and there lay founda-tions of old houses and barns. A stone corral for sheep had tumbled with time, barely an outline, bordered by ancient lilac bushes. Apple trees marked the foundation of an outlying farmhouse, one here, an-other there; they were overgrown and gnarled and shouldn't, but did, bear fruit, still, in the fall.

She picked a ruby red apple and pierced it lightly with her teeth, expecting bitter juice. But the apple was sweet, and she was hungry, and she ate it and picked another. Her pup jumped up begging for a bite and she gave her the core to devour. She stopped crying because the apple was comforting and she felt revived.

The leaves were brilliant, more brilliant against the blanket of dark-ening gray sky than they ever are on a cloudless, peacock blue day. Good artists never attempted to paint autumn, she thought, because only nature knew how to mix the right palette. She used to paint, but she had given it up. When the baby died she lost her inspiration. She couldn't deal with joy unrealized after she had been robbed of her only chance to raise a daughter. She wanted her so much. As time passed, it hurt more and she didn't understand why. Tears again pinched her eyes and she tried to fight them back.

Would she have raised her little girl to hunt? Probably not. When her sons and husband went hunting, she and her daughter would have gone shopping and done girlish things together. It would have become a joke. She would have threatened her husband with a big credit card bill as he and the boys took off for yet another weekend hunting deer. And he would have put her over his knee and pretended to spank her and the children would have laughed. Yes, he and the boys would have gone hunting, and she and their daughter would have gone shopping, and everyone would have had a good time and lots to tell over Sunday night supper.

But her husband couldn't hold her over his knee anymore, not since he got sick. That was just after the baby died, when his legs got weak and he couldn't go hunting anymore, at least not like he used to. Now that the boys were older, they would drive their dad to a promising place, and he'd sit and wait for a deer while his sons went stalking in the forest. Last year he took a fine buck that way, just under two hundred pounds dressed. Lately he felt better and he could walk a mile some-times. Last Sunday grouse season opened and they took their hot little springer pup out for her first opening day. She put up four grouse. It was such a delight to finally have a good dog to flush their favorite coverts that they missed every single shot; and laughed, like they used to.

How did she get so turned around? She hefted her shotgun, breech open, over her shoulder and headed out of the old orchard, away from the once-was town. Stupidly she left her compass in her other jacket, but the sun was setting and she made that her marker. Her dog became lively again, as if to say, *Good, let's go home.* But that wasn't it, she thought, that wasn't it at all. She brought her gun down, loaded a shell in each chamber, and no sooner had she closed the breech than her springer pounced on a fat grouse hen. The bird exploded from the forest floor with a *whirrrr,* hell-bent for a safe haven. She swung her gun to her shoulder, pointed the barrels and felled the bird with the second shot.

A sudden gust like a tailwind lifted the pup high over a crumbling stone wall as she bounded to retrieve the grouse. So majestic, the grouse, and she remembered the legend her husband told her of how Indians would say a prayer over their game, thanking their brother of the forest for sacrificing his life to sustain theirs. She whispered a tender prayer. She needed to speak to the silence; and the mighty pines arched overhead like a forest cathedral. The brisk evening wind blew her damp cheeks dry: It was at dusk eight Octobers ago today that her baby died in her arms.

Now she found herself in a fern-covered glen. The forest floor was awash with that golden cast peculiar to autumn sunsets. It reminded her of a happy time—how many years ago?—it must be going on twenty-five, when she and her husband first hunted together here. Here? Yes! She knew this place: She was at the beaver pond. They had brought a picnic and drank wine and then made love in the soft grass there, at the shoulder of the pond. The leaves shivered and shook loose the memory of a long-ago soft summer breeze that caressed their bare bodies, warmed by the sun, warmed from the loving. She wanted those days back, she wanted her daughter, she wanted to go home. . . .

She saw the hill beyond the beaver pond and knew that uphill was the forgotten cemetery and beyond that, the road. It was a hard climb but she was sure about it now, and it gave her renewed strength and hope. Her pup took the hill with trouble, for the ground was thick with brambles. She kept up with the little springer, her eye marking a birch tree that had splintered and fallen into the fork of a giant maple. Out of nowhere a limb suddenly slingshot and cut her above her chin. She felt it sting, and a drop of blood trickled onto her red turtleneck, against her black hair, and she grabbed at the branch that dared injure her and broke it off with a snap. High above she could see the horizon through the pines and she lunged forward, her arm bent to shield her face as tree limbs tore at her clothes as if trying to hold her back.

There it was, the little cemetery. Seven headstones, that's all. Only seven, but they told the whole story. *Their name was Eldridge,* her husband's voice spoke to her across the years, *and they owned that farm over there. Look. You can see the foundation.* She again turned her eyes in the direction he had pointed. It was still there, just a vestige of a place and a time that was no more.

A father, a mother, and their five children. See this little marker with the lamb. She was the first, she died at birth. Just like my daughter, she thought; just like my own baby. *And next to that,* the memory voice of her husband continued through the past, *three, all in a row. Two boys and a girl, ages two, three and five. All within a week. It was smallpox. The epidemic took the whole village.* She thought: Oh my God. I lost just one child. How did that mother survive? Then she saw the fifth stone and remembered the mother hadn't. *Within a year,* her husband's voice trailed, *the mother . . . they say she died from grief.* And the sixth? *The sixth tombstone was the last child, a son, killed in the first World War. Just turned eighteen.* The last stone, the seventh. It was less tarnished by years than the others, dated six years after the soldier-boy's. The father's. *He was helpless. There was nothing he could do but watch each of his loved ones die. They said he finally went mad from grief. . . .*

Helpless . . .

She didn't know how much time had passed, how long she sat pondering over the fate of the poor farmer and his family, how long she mourned for them, for herself. Her pup was asleep at her feet and the autumn air was now cold with damp, the sky dark. This was a good place to leave her grief, she thought. Let it go, get on with it, find the road. But she felt the weight of her soul heavy upon her as she stood up to go.

She left the cemetery through the stone posts, squeezing past a sapling that had grown smack between them. How tremendous, she thought, as she realized it was a Gilead tree. She picked a leaf and rubbed it on her hand, aching for some balm to heal the wound within.

Ahead was the road. After that she knew her way. Her pace quickened as each step brought her closer to familiar ground. It's time to get on with it, she thought. Not to sorrow. She had blessings to enjoy, far more blessings than sorrows.

And then, with utter disbelief, she saw them. Ahead of her on the road were three grouse, dancing up and down and beating their wings all for joy, dusting the dry dirt road with their tails. Even the pup paused to look at the pageant. The birds continued to whirl and flutter and the shiver of gold and red and orange leaves accompanied them like delicate music. All she could do was watch in wonderment.

The cover of night was gently descending upon the forest when, from a distance, there shone a light. Headlights. "Mom? Mom!" voices cried. "Are you all right?" Her sons raced toward her, scattering the grouse who then pirouetted high into the air like fireworks and disappeared into the woods. Not far behind was her husband.

"Yes . . . I'm here. . . . I'm all right!" she cried as she ran to her family. Each step felt lighter. Each step carried her closer to the shelter of her loved ones. Each step took her further and further from the burden she left behind. For she had finally unlocked the compartment in her soul, and gently, lovingly, laid her sorrow to rest in the holiness of the woods.

Directory

■

See page x for complete listing of Directory contents and page numbers.

Conservation Associations

These organizations spearhead and maintain programs that benefit wildlife and conserve its habitat. Sportsmen's dollars are a major source of funding for conservation activities.

Boone and Crockett Club
250 Station Drive
Old Milwaukee Depot
Missoula, MT 59801-2753
(406) 542-1888

Congressional Sportsmen's Foundation
1730 K Street, NW
Washington, DC 20006
(202) 785-9153

Ducks Unlimited
One Waterfowl Way
Memphis, TN 38120
(901) 758-3825

**Foundation for North American
Wild Sheep**
720 Allen Avenue
Cody, WY 82414
(307) 527-6261

Geese Unlimited
2820 South Highway 169
Grand Rapids, MN 55744
(218) 327-0774

**International Association of Fish
& Wildlife Agencies**
444 North Capitol Street, NW, #544
Washington, DC 20001
(202) 624-7890

**National Fish and Wildlife
Foundation**
1120 Connecticut Avenue, NW,
#900
Washington, DC 20036
(202) 857-0166

National Wild Turkey Federation
PO Box 530
Edgefield, SC 29824
(803) 637-3106

National Wildlife Federation
1400 16th Street, NW
Washington, DC 20036
(202) 797-6800

Pheasants Forever
PO Box 75473
St. Paul, MN 55175
(612) 481-7142

Pope and Young Club
PO Box 548
Chatfield, MN 55923
(507) 867-4144

Quail Unlimited
PO Box 610
Edgefield, SC 29824-0610
(803) 637-5731

Rocky Mountain Elk Foundation
PO Box 8249
Missoula, MT 59807
(800) CAL-LELK

The Ruffed Grouse Society
451 McCormick Road
Corapolis, PA 15108
(412) 262-4044

Safari Club International
4800 West Gates Pass Road
Tucson, AZ 86745
(602) 620-1220

Waterfowl USA
PO Box 50
Edgefield, SC 29824
(803) 637-5767

Whitetails Unlimited
PO Box 720
Sturgeon Bay, WI 54235
(414) 743-6777

The Wilderness Society
900 17th Street, NW
Washington, DC 20006
(202) 429-2637

Wildlife Management Institute
1101 14th Street, NW, Suite 801
Washington, DC 20005
(202) 371-1808

Shooting Sports Organizations

These sporting groups and shooting organizations will be helpful to you as you pursue your chosen shooting sport. These organizations can advise you of upcoming events and tournaments. Ask about memberships.

Amateur Trapshooting Association (ATA)
601 West National Road
Vandalia, OH 45377
(513) 898-4638

Hunter Education Association
PO Box 347
Jamestown, CO 80455
(303) 449-0631

National Rifle Association
1600 Rhode Island Avenue, NW
Washington, DC 20036
(800) 368-5714

National Shooting Sports Foundation
11 Mile Hill Road
Newtown, CT 06470-2359
(203) 426-1320

The NSSF is responsible for a wide variety of programs in the shooting sports. One is the Chevy Truck Sportsman's Team Challenge, sponsored by Chevrolet, where the average shooter and the world's top professionals can compete over the same courses of fire against shooters of comparable skill in action-oriented rifle, handgun, and shotgun events. The NSSF assists sportsmen and outdoor groups in observing National Hunting and Fishing Day, held the fourth Saturday of each September.

National Skeet Shooting Association (NSSA)
5931 Roft Road
San Antonio, TX 78253
(210) 688-3371

National Sporting Clays Association (NSCA)
5931 Roft Road
San Antonio, TX 78253
(210) 688-3371

Sporting Clays of America (SCA)
33 South Main Street
Norwalk, CT 06854
(203) 831-8483

Women's Shooting Sports Foundation (WSSF)
1505 Highway 6 South, Suite 101
Houston, TX 77077
(713) 584-9907

Conducts Ladies Charity Classics events. Mixed couples tournaments and other events sponsored by the WSSF have attracted male membership in significant numbers. Each year, the WSSF organizes a number of special shooting and hunting opportunities for its members.

Dog Clubs & Associations

American Kennel Club
5580 Centerview Drive
Raleigh, NC 27606
(919) 233-9767

Bird Dog Foundation, Inc.
PO Box 774
505 West Highway 57
Grand Junction, TN 38039
(901) 764-2058

Hunting Retriever Club, Inc.
United Kennel Club, Inc.
100 East Kilgore Road
Kalamazoo, MI 49001-5592
(616) 343-9020

National Shoot-to-Retrieve Field Trial Association (NSTRA)
226 North Mill Street, #2
Plainfield, IN 46168
(317) 839-4059
Fax: (317) 839-4197

North American Hunting Retriever Association (NAHRA)
PO Box 1590
Stafford, VA 22555
(703) 221-4911

North American Versatile Hunting Dog Association (NAVHDA)
PO Box 520
Arlington Heights, IL 60006
(708) 255-1120
FAX: (708) 253-6488

Shooting Schools

Proper instruction is the best investment you can make in your sport.

Instructors and Schools

Addieville East Farm
Instructor: Jack Mitchell
Contact: Mr. Geoff Gaebe
200 Pheasant Drive
Mapleville, RI 02839
(401) 568-3185

Aspen Outfitting Company/ Wingshooting America
Jon Hollinger
520 East Cooper Avenue
Aspen, CO 81611
(303) 925-3406

Wingshooting America can be booked through Aspen Outfitting Company for on-site, multiday shotgunning clinics for private clubs and groups of 9 to 12 students. Instructors: Jon Hollinger, Dan Carlisle, and Michael McIntosh.

Carlisle Shotgun Sports
Dan and Kathryn Carlisle
1747 Ridgecrest Avenue
Aiken, SC 29801
(803) 641-2228

Chesapeake Clays Shooting School
15890 Oakland Road
Bridgetown, MD 21640
(800) 787-0037

Dowtin Gunworks
7815 West Bridle Trail
Flagstaff, AZ 86001
(602) 779-1898

Dunn's Shooting School
Route 3, Box 39D4
Holly Springs, MS 38635
(800) 564-1396

Griffin & Howe Shooting School
33 Claremont Road
Bernardsville, NJ 07924
(908) 766-2287

Holland & Holland Shooting School
Instructor: Ken Davies
PO Drawer 2770
Avon, CO 81620
Call (800) 323-4386 for dates and locations

The Homestead Shooting School
PO Box 2000
Hot Springs, VA 24445
(540) 839-7787

Joshua Creek Ranch
PO Box 1946
Boerne, TX 78006
(210) 537-5090

Mt. Blanca Wingshooting & Sporting Clays Seminars
PO Box 236
Blanca, CO 81123
(719) 379-3825

Michael Murphy & Sons
6400 SW Hunter Road
Augusta, KS 67010
(800) 843-4513

National Rifle Association
11250 Waples Mill Road
Fairfax, VA 22030
(703) 267-1390

Certified firearms safety and marksmanship instruction available nationwide.

Paul Nelson Farm
Contact: Mr. Paul Nelson
119 Hilltop Drive
PO Box 183
Gettysburg, SD 57442
(605) 765-2469

Instructional clinics for women and couples are conducted by well-known outdoor writer Michael McIntosh and international shotgun champion Shari LeGate in a small, private luxury hotel setting.

Optimum Shotgun Performance Shooting School
15020 Cutten Road
Houston, TX 77070
(713) 897-0800

Orvis Shooting Schools
Historic Route 7A
Manchester, VT 05254
(800) 235-9763
and
Orvis Sandanona Shooting School
Sharon Turnpike, Route 44a
PO Box 800
Millbrook, NY 12545
(800) 554-5899

The Orvis Shooting Schools have women-only and mixed couples instructional programs. I have participated in Orvis Sandanona's one-day course, and found it to be comprehensive, excellently run, and well worth the time and expense.—L.M.

Gary Phillips Shooting Instruction
1210 Shallcross Avenue
Wilmington, DE 19806
(302) 655-7113

Pinehurst Gun Club Shooting School
PO Box 4000
Gun Club Road
Pinehurst, NC 28374
(919) 295-8464

The Remington Shooting School
Remington Arms Company, Inc.
14 Hoefler Avenue
Ilion, NY 13357
(315) 895-3574

Royal Berkshire Shooting School at Timberdoodle
The Timberdoodle Shooting Club
One Webster Highway
Temple, NH 03084
(603) 654-9510

SKAT Shooting School
PO Box 137
New Ipswich, NH 03071
(603) 878-1257

Westervelt Turkey School
PO Box 2362
Tuscaloosa, AL 35403
(205) 556-3909

White Oak Plantation Shooting Schools
5215 B County Road 10
Tuskegee, AL 36083
(334) 727-9258

Wings & Clays Shooting School at Bald Mountain Gun Range
2500 Kern Road
Lake Orion, MI 48360
(810) 814-9193

Women's Shooting Sports Foundation (WSSF)
1505 Highway 6 South
Suite 103
Houston, TX 77077
(713) 584-9907

WSSF-certified instructors are among the best-trained in the country and will work with you to improve your technique. I have studied under Lou Ann Daniels, New York WSSF chairwoman, and the quality of her instruction is outstanding. I understand that all WSSF instructors are of her caliber, and therefore highly recommend you contact one in your area code. They can either instruct you or refer you to a qualified instructor near where you live.

WSSF Senior Instructors
Susan Carter   (303) 356-5148
Shari LeGate   (719) 495-9793
Judy Woolley   (406) 826-5789

WSSF Certified Shotgun Instructors
Deb Cleverdon   (713) 530-3754
Lou Ann Daniels   (315) 343-4734
Jency Daugherty   (713) 207-6294
Jimmie Dexter   (603) 448-5552
Dee Dee Dury   (210) 633-2644

Connie Kieckhefer-Harris
              (609) 351-0078
Jim Harris   (713) 556-1597
Johnny Meitzen (409) 234-2247
Michael Murphy (319) 775-2137
Dan Moseley   (713) 530-1620
Glynne Moseley (713) 584-9907
Stephanie Schultz
              (713) 584-9586
Steve Schultz   (713) 342-1908
Teresa Selby   (217) 662-2497
Peggy Siler   (417) 443-3093
Carleen Stevens (603) 878-2786
Don Stoner   (717) 697-2243
Pat Thompson   (401) 539-4028

Alice Tripp   (512) 310-8382
Charlie Wilson (800) 877-5338

Woodcock Hill, Inc.
PO Box 363
Benton, PA 17814
(717) 864-3242

Woodcock Hill offers a shooting school, gun fitting, teaching, coaching, and practice by a certified British Association of Shooting & Conservation shotgun coach.

Professional Gunsmiths

A good gunsmith is worth his weight in gold. Here are a just a few. We recommend the following from personal experience.

The American Custom Gun Makers Guild
P O Box 812
Burlington, IA 52601
This trade association will be able to connect you with a qualified professional gunsmith in your area.

Briley Manufacturing
1230 Lumpkin
Houston, TX 77043

Frank L. Conroy, Master Engraver
2 Pomfret Road
PO Box 76
West Hartford, VT 05084

Conroy is a master engraver and can execute a custom design or recut worn checkering. He is a specialist in gold inlay and Bolino-style engraving.

Paul Jaeger, a division of Dunns Supply, Inc.
1 Madison Avenue
Grand Junction, TN 38039

Galazan/Connecticut Shotgun Manufacturing
PO Box 1692
New Britain, CT 06051

Griffin and Howe
33 Claremont Road
Bernardsville, NJ 07924

Kirk Merrington, Master Gunsmith
207 Sierra Road
Kerrville, TX 78028

Trained at Churchill's in Birmingham, England, Kirk specializes in rebuilding and refurbishing barrels for high-grade shotguns.

Tom Morrow, Professional Gunsmith
P O Box 328
Freedom, NH 03836

Morrow specializes in the restoration of fine shotguns and rifles and is well-known as a custom rifle maker.

New England Arms
P O Box 27
Lawrence Lane
Kittery Point, ME 03905

New England Arms has been described by *Forbes* and *Field & Stream* magazines as "the best gunshop in the world." It is the largest importer of fine Italian shotguns. A full-time English-trained gunsmith is on-site for repairs and alterations.

New England Custom Gun Service, Ltd.
Brook Road
Rural Route 2, Box 122W
West Lebanon, NH 03784

This firm specializes in fine gun repair and restoration, and offers a selection of fine gun accessories.

Doug Turnbull Restoration, Inc.
PO Box 471
Bloomfield, NY 14469

Woodcock Hill/Thomas Bland and Sons Gunmakers
RD #1, Box 147
Benton, PA 17814

Gun Dealers, Manufacturers, and Importers

These are just a few of the many reputable dealers, manufacturers and importers of fine quality firearms in the United States today. We recommend their products based upon personal knowledge or experience.

Arnold Arms Company, Inc.
PO Box 10011
6914 204th Street NE, Suite C
Arlington, WA 98223
(800) 371-1011

This relatively new company is already, in our estimation, one of the finest U.S. manufacturers of precision-made rifles. Varmint rifles, *African* and *Alaskan* series big-game and dangerous-game hunting rifles, and competition models are available. Call for a dealer near you.

Beretta

Beretta is the world's oldest firearms manufacturer. Their retail stores in Manhattan and Alexandria, Virginia, offer a comprehensive selection of Beretta shotguns and feature the company's own line of hunting clothing and accessories. Beretta's field and sporting models S686 and S687 Over and Under shotguns are very popular; their premium grade SO6 and SO9 shotguns are among the finest made today. Beretta is one of the few gunmakers that produce classic double-barreled rifles. Call their corporate office for a Beretta dealer nearest you.

Beretta Gallery
718 Madison Avenue
New York, NY 10021
(212) 319-6614

Beretta Gallery
317 South Washington Street
Old Town, Alexandria, VA 22314
(703) 739-0596

Beretta U.S.A. Corporation
17601 Beretta Drive
Accokeek, MD 20607
(301) 283-2191

Richard L. Beauchamp
PO Box 181
Richmond, MA 01254
(413) 698-3822

Beauchamp offers a full line of guns, accessories, and parts and distributes Davide Pedersoli of Italy black powder and breech-loading guns.

Browning
One Browning Place, Route 1
Morgan, UT 84050
(800) 333-3288

This American firearms manufacturer is named after John Browning, who developed many of Winchester's finest guns during the 1880s and 1890s, and the A-5 auto-loading shotgun in 1905 for Fabrique Nationale. Women looking for a general-purpose hunting rifle may wish to consider Browning's A-bolt II Micro-Medallion lightweight rifle, a down-sized version of the original model A-Bolt hunting rifle. The

Browning Citori Over and Under shotgun maintains an almost fanatical following among hunters and target shooters: and, of course, there's the Women's Shooting Sports Foundation WSSF 425 Sporting Clays shotgun, designed with the assistance of Sue King. Browning also offers an extensive line of clothing, gun luggage, gun safes, and accessories. Contact them for a dealer near you. Literature available.

Cabela's
115 Cabela Drive
Sidney, NE 69161
(308) 254-6560

Classic antique, collectible, and fine sporting firearms are only some of the extensive merchandise carried by Cabela's, whose sporting-goods catalogue is one of the best available. Call for catalogue.

Cape Outfitters
599 Co. Road 206
Cape Girardeau, MO 63701
(314) 335-6260

Cape Outfitters is a dealer in American and imported firearms, gun cases, accessories, and books that often are advertised at discount prices.

Chadicks, Ltd.
119 East Moore Avenue
Terrell, TX 75160

This well-known dealer in fine American, English, and Europan firearms also offers a gun stock and finish restoration service.

Cherry's Fine Guns
3402-A West Wendover Avenue
Greensboro, NC 27435-0307
(910) 563-7577

Cherry's is known for its large selection of modern, antique, and historic reproduction firearms. Call for a free copy of *Cherry's Sporting Goods News.*

Colt Manufacturing Co., Inc.
PO Box 1868
Hartford, CT 06144
(800) 962-COLT

Since Samuel Colt designed the first single barreled, revolving, multiple-shot, breech-loading gun, or *revolver,* in the 1830s, the company he founded has primarily been a hand-gun manufacturer. Today Colt also makes hunting and sporting rifles, such as the Colt Match Target Rifle. New Colt Wear, a line of rugged outdoor clothing and accessories, is also available. Call for a dealer near you.

**Connecticut Shotgun
Manufacturing Company**
35 Woodland St.
PO Box 1692
New Britain, CT 06051-1692
(860) 225-6581

Maker of new A. H. Fox double shotguns and A. Galazan Over and Under full sidelock shotguns. Our opinion is that Tony Galazan shotguns are the finest designed and crafted guns made in America today and come precious close to works of art.

Connecticut Valley Arms, Inc.
5988 Peachtree Corners East
Norcross, GA 30071
(800) 251-9412

CVA makes modern and traditional black powder rifles, accessories, kits, and leather goods.

David's Firearms, Ltd.
PO Box 6039
Falmouth, ME 04105
(207) 657-4706

David Bichrest, past president of the Winchester Arms Collectors Association, is one of the most knowledgeable and respected dealers of collectible Winchesters and other American firearms in the United States. Catalogue available.

Game Fair, Ltd.
99 Whitebridge Road, No. 105
Nashville, TN 37205
(615) 353-0602

Game Fair sells sporting firearms, Barbour clothing, accessories, and collectibles, and specializes in fine upland guns.

Rod Fuller, Inc.
Route 1, Box 177
Grant, NE 69140
(308) 352-4080

Specializes in Browning Belgium Superposed shotguns and previously owned Browning semiautomatic shotguns and rifles.

Griffin & Howe
36 West 44th Street, Suite 1011
New York, NY 10036
(212) 921-0980
and
33 Claremont Road
Bernardsville, NJ 07924
(908) 766-2287

Martha Bichrest actively assists her husband, David Bichrest of David's Firearms, with his business. David, a past president of the Winchester Gun Collector's Association, specializes in selling collectible firearms and fine sporting guns. Martha herself is highly knowledgeable about the field. "You can't be in this business without learning something," she points out. Martha is a retired Chief Petty Officer in the Coast Guard, where she learned to shoot an M16 and a .45. In 1975 her husband introduced her to sporting guns. She developed an interest in black powder guns and went on to win medals in 50 and 100 yards as a Maine State champion.

(LAURIE MORROW)

Griffin & Howe sporters were the finest American-made bolt-action rifles available between the World Wars. Today the company deals in other fine American guns, as well as previously owned English and European firearms. The Griffin & Howe rifle side mount is a specialty. The company's showroom is in New York, and its gunsmith facility and shooting school are located in Bernardsville.

Holland & Holland, Ltd.
31–33 Bruton Street
London, W1X 8JS, England
(011-44-171) 499-4544

Since 1835, one of England's *best* Best gunmakers. The Royal side-by-sides and Royal Over and Unders are among the finest ever crafted. The Holland & Holland Sporting Over and Under model is available in 12- and 20-gauge. Upland hunting clothing and accessories are also available. The company has announced plans to open a Manhattan shop. (See Holland & Holland Shooting School under Shooting Schools, pages 218–221).

Jaqua's Fine Guns, Inc.
900 East Bigelow Avenue
Findlay, Ohio 45840
(419) 422-0912

One of the finest and most extensive selections of fine firearms in the Midwest. Call for free gun list.

James W. King
PO Box 70577
Albany, GA 31708
(912) 436-0397

Jimmy travels to gun shows throughout the country with his diverse selection of high quality collectible firearms. Gun list available.

William Larkin Moore & Co.
31360 Via Colina
Westlake Village, CA 91361
(818) 889-4160
and
8227 E. Via de Commercio, Suite A
Scottsdale, AZ 85258
(602) 951-8913

One of the best-known West Coast dealers, and an importer of Piotti, F.lli. Rizzini, B. Rizzini, and Garbi shotguns.

Krieghoff International, Inc.
7528 Easton Road
Ottsville, PA 18942
(610) 847-5173

German manufacturer of competition shotguns for trap, skeet and sporting clays, European-style hunting guns, and gun care products.

Marlin Firearms
100 Kenna Drive
North Haven, CT 06473
(203) 239-5621

One of America's legendary rifle makers and still one of the best, since 1880. A solid performance hunting rifle is the Marlin MR-7 bolt action. We recommend Marlin's Model 2000L target rifle. It is not made especially for women, but at 8 pounds it is the lightest new production target rifle made today and dead-on accurate.

New England Arms Co.
Lawrence Lane
PO Box 278
Kittery Point, ME
(207) 439-0593

NEACo has been described as the best gun shop in the world by *Field & Stream* and *Forbes* magazines because of its extensive inventory of fine American, British, and European shotguns and rifles. Arrizabalaga, B. Rizzini, and Arrieta shotguns, made-to-order to the customer's specifications, are stocked in hand-selected Turkish walnut specially imported by NEACo. Gun cases, shotshells, Bismuth shot, and Barbour clothing are also sold. Catalogue $5.

Orvis
Historic Route 7A
P.O. Box 798
Manchester, VT 05254
(802) 362-3622

One of America's premier fly rod makers and outdoor catalogue companies has entered the shooting sports field with its own line of custom shotguns. Complete gunsmithing services and a selection of classic American and European shotguns are also available at its flagship store. Orvis operates a shooting school near its Manchester, Vermont, headquarters, and at Sandanona Shooting Grounds, which the company acquired in 1995 (see Shooting Schools, pages 218–221). Call for information, catalogue, and an Orvis dealer near you.

Pachmayr, Ltd.
1875 South Mountain Avenue
Monrovia, CA 91016
(818) 357-7771

This long-established West Coast gun dealer is the maker of Pachmayr recoil pads and other gun accessories.

Perazzi USA Inc.
1207 South Shamrock Avenue
Monrovia, CA 91016
(908) 469-0100

One of Italy's finest shotguns makers offers a full line of hunting, trap, skeet, and sporting clays guns ranging from standard grade to Extra-Extra Gold Grade. Brochure available; call for the dealer nearest you.

James Purdey & Sons, Ltd.
57–58 South Audley Street
London, WlY 6ED England
(011-44-171) 499-1801

One of England's oldest, most famous Best gun makers also offers a selection of clothing and accessories. If you own a Purdey shotgun you conceivably drive a Rolls Royce, and the two cost about the same. Catalogue available.

Remington Arms Company, Inc.
B-6217, 1007 Market Street
Wilmington, DE 19898
(302) 773-5291

Modern rifles and shotguns, ammunition, gun safes, clothing, and accessories from another one of America's oldest and most reputable firearms dealer. The company recently introduced the new Remington 1816 flintlock, a true reproduction of the first Remington rifle ever made, and a high-grade Over and Under shotgun known as the *Peerless*.

Safari Outfitters, Ltd.
Washington Hollow Plaza
R.D. 1, Box 2
Salt Point, NY 12578
(914) 677-5444

Some of the most magnificent collectible and sporting firearms can be seen—and obtained—here.

Sturm, Ruger & Company
217 Lacey Place
Southport, CT 06490
(520) 778-1217

Known primarily as a handgun manufacturer, Sturm Ruger also manufactures rifles and shotguns: the Ruger Red Label, a favorite among the clays crowd; and the Woodside Over and Under sporting clays model is the company's most recent addition and is available in 12- and 20-gauge.

Thompson/Center Arms Company
PO Box 5002
Rochester, NH 03867
(603) 332-2394

Makers of field-grade muzzle loading rifles and shotguns. Thompson/Center's Contender single shot carbine in 7-30 Waters is an excellent rifle for women—light, handy, and powerful enough for deer. Call for a dealer near you.

U.S. Repeating Arms Co.
(makers of Winchester firearms)
275 Winchester Avenue
New Haven, CT 06511
(203) 789-5000

This company has been America's premier longarms manufacturer since 1866; Winchester firearms made before 1964 and after 1993 are of comparable high quality. A few years ago the company was taken over by new management, and the operation was retooled with state-of-the-art equipment. The result is superb quality. There's the classic Model 94 carbine, the legendary model 70 rifle, the 1001 Over and Under shotgun (new in field-grade and sporting clays models), the 1300 in many configurations, and America's all-time favorite pump shotgun, the Model 12. Call for a dealer near you.

James Wayne
2608 North Laurent
Victoria, TX 77901
(512) 578-1258

James Wayne is another reputable dealer of quality and collectible shotguns and rifles.

Weatherby
2781 Firestone Boulevard
South Gate, CA 92080
(800) 227-2016

Best known for hunting rifles, Weatherby also makes Over and Under shotguns in Orion-, Athena-, and higher grade models.

Woodcock Hill, Inc./Thomas Bland & Sons Gunmakers, Ltd.
PO Box 363
Benton, PA 17814
(717) 864-3242

Dealer in fine English sporting guns, handcrafted English gun cases, wax clothing, and shell bags. The company also offers gunsmithing services (see Professional Gunsmiths, page

221), operates a shooting school (see Shooting Schools, pages 218–221) and arranges shooting trips to Scotland (see Shooting Travel/Outfitters, page 243).

About Used Guns

We've listed only a few of the many dealers of previously owned, older guns. Chances are your local gunshop or sporting goods store carries an assortment of used guns. As we discuss in Chapter 4, choose a reputable dealer—that is, someone who is knowledgeable and honest about what he is selling. *No used gun should ever be fired until it is carefully inspected by a qualified professional gunsmith.*

Here are some of the older makes and model guns you're likely to find. One in good condition will most likely offer you years of careful use. A gun in good condition has a brilliant or shiny bore, no bulges in the barrel of any kind, a stock with no cracks or chips, and is in mechanically sound condition. For argument's sake, we define an older gun as one made before 1965. Our comments do not reflect upon production guns made after 1990.

- Winchester Model 1894 and 94 rifle, made before 1964 (serial numbers up to 2,586,000), in .30-30 caliber

- Winchester Model 1886 in .45-70 only (it will be tough to find ammunition for any other caliber)

- Winchester Model 70 rifle in any caliber, preferably prior to serial number 581,470

- Winchester Model 21 double-barreled shotgun in any caliber

- Winchester Model 12 pump shotguns (Model 12s with Cutts compensators attached to the muzzle of the barrel are distinctly less desirable than guns without, but do not affect the gun's performance)

- Double-barreled shotguns made by A. H. Fox of Philadelphia and Parker Brothers. *Early guns that have Damascus barrels are not suitable for modern ammunition and can be dangerous if fired.* We do not recommend L. C. Smith shotguns, and chances are a Lefever may be too old to safely shoot.

- The classic Savage 99 lever-action rifle—one of the most underestimated guns ever made

- Savage 101 bolt-action rifle

- Remington model 870 pump shotgun

- Remington model 760 pump rifle

- Browning Superposed shotguns in any caliber

- Browning A-5 (made in Belgium or by Fabrique Nationale)

- Remington 720 series bolt-action rifles

- Griffin and Howe sporter (if you're lucky enough to find one)

- Most British, German, Belgian, French, and Italian guns by known makers (too many to list—but this is where the fine gun dealers we've mentioned can be helpful)

Beware of:

- Sporterized military rifles. Some are fine, such as the Griffin & Howe sporter, but more often than not basement gunsmiths have tampered with such conversions, resulting in guns that will not work well and possibly are unsafe.

- Shotguns with cut barrels should be avoided. The choke invariably has been removed.

- Shotguns with barrels less than 18 inches are illegal.

- Any rifle with a barrel less than 16 inches is illegal.

- Avoid guns with replaced barrels unless you are certain they are factory replacements. Otherwise you won't know whether the headspace is correct until it is checked by a professional gunsmith. Excessive headspace is extremely dangerous to the shooter.

- Guns with replacement stocks, unless the restocking is by a reputable stockmaker or by the factory. Otherwise, wood-to-metal fit is probably incorrect, and the gun will not shoot well.

Buying or inheriting a good older gun is a pleasure only if the gun is mechanically sound and safe to shoot.

Shotgun Shells

Bismuth Cartridge Company
3500 Maple Avenue
Dallas, TX 75219
(800) 759-3333

Eley Ammunition
(Tomart, Inc.)
122 Lafayette Avenue
PO Box 610
Laurel, MD 20725
(301) 953-3301

Estate Cartridge Company
2778 FM 830
Willis, TX 77078
(409) 856-7277

Federal Cartridge Company
900 Ehlen Drive
Anoka, MN 55303
(612) 323-2300

Fiocchi of America, Inc.
5030 Fremont Road
Ozark, MO 65721
(417) 725-4118

Gamebore Cartridge Co., Inc.
New England Arms Co.
Box 278, Lawrence Lane
Kittery Point, ME 03905
(207) 439-0593

Polywad Shotgun Shell
PO Box 7916
Macon, GA 31209
(912) 477-0669

Remington Arms Company, Inc.
Delle Donne Corporate Center
1011 Centre Road, 2nd floor
Wilmington, DE 19805-1270
(800) 243-9700

Winchester Ammunition
Olin/Winchester
427 North Shamrock
East Alton, IL 62024
(618) 258-2000

Gun Care and Security

Birchwood Casey
7900 Fuller Road
Eden Prairie, MN 55344
(800) 328-6156 (#7933)

A complete line of high quality gun-care products to clean, protect, and refinish your guns.

Break-Free, Inc.
1035 South Linwood Avenue
Santa Ana, CA 92705-4396
(714) 953-1900

Solvents, lubricants, and gun cleaning products.

Browning (See Clothing)

Hornady Mfg. Co.
PO Box 1848
Grand Island, NE 68802
(308) 382-1390

"One Shot"—gun cleaner and dry lube.

Kleen-Bore, Inc.
16 Industrial Parkway
Easthampton, MA 01027
(800) 445-0301

Quality gun care products and accessories; deluxe cleaning set.

Remington Arms Company, Inc.
Delle Donne Corporate Center
1011 Centre Road, 2nd floor
Wilmington, DE 19805-1270
(800) 243-9700

Complete shotgun firearm care kits; oils and lubricants; cleaning fluids and supplies; gun parts and accessories.

Shooter's Choice Gun Care
Venco Industries, Inc.
16770 Hilltop Park Place
Chagrin Hills, OH 44023
(216) 543-8808

Cleaners, lubricants, and preventatives.

Gun Cases

Americase Incorporated
1610 East Main
PO Box 271
Waxahachie, TX 75165
(800) 972-2737

Beretta U.S.A. (See Clothing)

Custom-designed Beretta gun cases from simple soft to molded and aluminum cases.

Briley Manufacturing
Warrior Luggage by Briley
1230 Lumpkin
Houston, TX 77043
(800) 331-5718

Lightweight stainless-steel case to English trunk case quality standards. Briley also manufactures choke tubes, bore gauges, and other shotgun products.

Browning (See Clothing)

Huey Handbuilt Gun Case
PO Box 22456
Kansas City, MO 64113
(816) 444-1637

Deluxe oak and leather trunk cases, custom fitted, no two alike.

New England Arms
Lawrence Lane, PO Box 278
Kittery Point, ME 03905
(207) 439-0593

Remington Arms Company, Inc.
(See Gun Care)

Gun Safes and Cabinets

Browning (See Clothing)

Crystal Vault
Matrix Technical Engineering
PO Box 11
Greencastle, IN 46135
(800) 678-7233

Fort Knox Security Products
1051 North Industrial Park Road
Orem, UT 84057
(800) 821-5216

National Security Safe Co., Inc.
PO Box 755
American Fork, UT 84003
(800) 544-3829

Remington Arms Company, Inc.
(See Gun Care)

Winchester Safes
Meilink Safe Co.
111 Security Parkway
New Albany, IN 47150
(800) 4WI-NSAF

Clothing, Footwear, and Protective Gear

Clothing and Footwear
Barbour, Inc.
55 Meadowbrook Drive
Milford, NH 03055
(800) 338-3474

Waxed cotton jackets, shooting vests, and country clothing and accessories.

Bob Allen Sportswear
214 SW Jackson Avenue
Des Moines, IO 50315
(800) 347-8048

Chimere, Inc.
3435 Enterprise Avenue, #44-7
Naples, FL 33942
(813) 643-4222

Competition clothing and accessories; vests, shirts, rainwear, sweaters, gloves, glasses.

Columbia Sportswear
6600 North Baltimore
Portland, OR 97203
(800) MAB-OYLE (Retail)

Outdoor apparel and footwear.

Christopher Dawes Countrywear
Chapel Field Barn, 2 Old Bank
Ripponden, Sowerby Bridge
West Yorkshire, HX6 4DG, England
011-44-1-42-282-4600

Distributed in America by Dunn's Supply, Inc. (see below). Ladies' country clothing for all field sports.

Dunn's Supply, Inc.
1 Madison Avenue
Grand Junction, TN 38039
(800) 228-3006

Simply the best upland and waterfowl bird hunting mail-order catalogue. Everything from clothing to hunting accessories (see Christopher Dawes).

C.C. Filson Company
PO Box 34020
Seattle, WA 98124
(206) 624-4437

Outdoor clothing, luggage and hats. C.C. Filson clothing is among the most durable and well-designed outdoor clothing in America. Small men's sizes in jackets fit women very comfortably. However, Filson's also offers women-sized jackets and pants.

Hunting World, Inc.
PO Box 5981
Sparks, NV 89432
(702) 331-0414

Clothing, accessories, and luggage. Stores worldwide. Catalogue available.

Johnson Garment Corp.
3115 South Maple Avenue
PO Box 603
Marshfield, WI 54449
(715) 384-5272

Women's hunting/outdoor clothing.

Kaufman/Sorel of Canada
410 King Street, West
Kitchner, Ontario N2G 4J8
(800) 265-2760

Sorel Boots come in a variety of sizes and styles, including many expressly for women. I wear the Forester for upland hunting (as I do on the cover of this book) and in the spring. The Forester with a liner is the most effective boot against the cold that I have ever owned.—*L.M.*

LaCrosse Footwear, Inc.
1319 St. Andrew Street
PO Box 1328
LaCrosse, WI 54603
(800) 323-2668

General outdoor and hunting footwear.

Lewis Creek Company
2065 Shelburne Road
Shelburne, VT 05482
(800) 336-4884

Outerwear, shooting apparel and accessories.

Mossy Oak
Haas Outdoors, Inc.
PO Box 1427
West Point, MS 39773
(601) 494-8859

Camouflage hunting apparel and accessories.

Red Head
1935 South Campbell
Springfield, MO 65898-0300

Wide selection of clothing and gear.

Shoot the Moon
11450 Salem Court
Peyton, CO 80831
(719) 495-9793

Women's jackets, shirts, shooting and hunting vests.

Spartan-RealTree Products, Inc.
1390 Box Circle
Columbus, GA 31904
(404) 569-9101

Hunting clothes: RealTree camouflage clothing in RealTree All-Purpose pattern. Fabrics include 100 percent cotton ripstop, 50/50 brushed twill, 100 percent cotton knits, Polar Tuff, several types of netting, among others; products include 100 percent cotton tees, coats, pants, shorts, netting items, hats, sports shirts, western shirts, and bib overalls.

Suzy Smith Outdoor Sportswear
PO Box 185
29130 West Highway 160
South Fork, CO 81154
(800) 824-5930

Women's hunting and fishing clothing.

Tox
2915 LBJ Freeway, Suite 133
Dallas, TX 75234
(214) 243-4016

Extensive line of outdoor clothing. Call for a dealer near you.

Tiemann's
PO Box 130
Priddy, TX 76870
(915) 966-3523

Women's riding, hunting, and safari clothing.

Timberland Company
PO Box 5050
Hampton, NH 03842
(800) 445-5545

Outdoor footwear.

Wathne
4 West 57th Street
New York, NY 10019
(212) 262-7100

Elegant hunting attire.

Woolrich, Inc.
One Mill Street
Woolrich, PA 17779
(800) 995-1299

Hunting, shooting, and fishing clothing.

Zanika
(Formerly Beyond Sportswear)
PO Box 11943
Minneapolis, MN 55411
(612) 529-1785

Women's outdoor/hunting under- and outerwear. Informational flyer available.

Ear Protection

E.A.R., Inc.
Insta-Mold Division
PO Box 2146
Boulder, CO 80306
(800) 525-2690

Hoppe's
Airport Industrial Mall
Coatsville, PA 19320
(610) 384-6000

Pettor Inc.
41 Commercial Way
East Providence, RI 02914
(401) 434-1708

Eye Protection

Bausch & Lomb Sports Optics Division
9200 Cody
Overland Park, KS 66214
(913) 752-3400

Binoculars, rifle scopes, sporting scopes, and shooting glasses.

Bushnell Corporation
9200 Cody
Overland Park, KS 66214

Cabot Safety Corporation
90 Mechanic Street
Southbridge, MA 01550
(800) 327-3431

Polycarbonate lenses provide protection against debris from discharged powder and spent shell/cartridge particles; clear, gray, and yellow.

Decot Hy-Wyd Sport Glasses
PO Box 15830
Phoenix, AZ 85060
(800) 528-1901

Leupold & Stevens, Inc.
PO Box 688
Beaverton, OR 97075
(503) 646-9171

Peltor Inc.
41 Commercial Way
East Providence, RI 02914
(401) 438-4800

Remington Shooting Glasses
14760 Santa Fe Trail Drive
Lenexa, KS 66215
(913) 492-3200

Silencio/Safety Direct
56 Coney Island Drive
Sparks, NV 89431
(702) 359-4451

Carl Zeiss Optical, Inc.
Sports Optic Division
1015 Commerce Street
Petersburg, VA 23803
(800) 338-2984

Mail Order Catalogs

Bass Pro Shops
1935 South Campbell
Springfield, MO 65898-0400
(800) BAS-SPRO

L.L. Bean, Inc.
Casco Street
Freeport, ME 04033-0001
(800) 221-4221

Brownells, Inc.
200 South Front Street
Department 910
Montezuma, IA 50171
(515) 623-5401

Cabela's
812 13th Avenue
Sidney, NE 69160
(800) 237-4444

Dunn's Supply, Inc.
One Madison Avenue
Grand Junction, TN 38039
(800) 223-8667

C. C. Filson Company
PO Box 34020
Seattle, WA 98124
(206) 624-4437

Gander Mountain
Box 248, Highway West
Wilmot, WI 53192
(800) 558-9410 (customer service)

Happy Jack
PO Box 475
Snow Hill, NC 28580
(800) 326-5225

Herter's
Waterfowling & Outdoor Specialists
PO Box 1819
Burnsville, MN 55337-0499
(800) 654-3825

The Orvis Company
Historic Route 7A
Manchester, VT 05254
(800) 548-9548 (orders)

Scott's Dog Supply, Inc.
9252 Crawfordsville Road
Indianapolis, IN 46234
(800) 966-3647

Wingset
61 Central Street
PO Box 178
Woodstock, VT 05091
(800) 356-4953

Hunting and Shooting Preserves

Alabama

Rockfence Station
4388 Chambers
County Road 160
Lafayette, AL 36862
(800) 627-2606
Contact: Mr. Raymond McClendon

Located 100 miles southeast of Birmingham, Rockfence Station offers dove, quail, pheasant, chukar, turkey, and deer hunting, as well as sporting clays on 8,000 family-owned and privately controlled acres for 2 to 16 guns.

Westervelt Lodge
PO Box 2362
Tuscaloosa, AL 35403
(205) 556-3909
Contact: Mr. John Roboski

Located 50 miles southwest of Tuscaloosa, Westervelt Lodge offers dove, quail, and turkey hunting, as well as sporting clays and skeet. This 14,000-acre preserve offers personalized hunting packages for 1 to 12 guns.

White Oak Plantation
5215 B Country Road 10
Tuskegee, AL 36083
Contact: Mr. Robert Pitman
(334) 727-9258

Located 35 miles east of Montgomery, White Oak Plantation offers quail, turkey, duck, deer, and rabbit hunting, as well as sporting clays, on over 16,000 acres, and takes pride in its special brand of southern hospitality.

Alaska

Eagles' Ridge Ranch
HC 62, Box 5780
Delta Junction, AK 99737
(907) 895-4329
Contact: Mike Crouch

Arizona

Wingshooters Lodge
1305 North Grand Avenue,
Suite 20-122
Nogales, AZ 85621
011-52-641-49934 (Mexico)
Contact: Ruben Del Castillo

California

Rock Springs Ranch
11000 Old Hernandez Road
Paicines, CA 95043
(800) 209-5175
Contact: Ken Range

Colorado

J.M.L. Outfitters
Marie Haskett
8563 East Davies Avenue
Englewood, CO 80112
(303) 795-8091

Mt. Blanca Game Bird & Trout
PO Box 236
Blanca, CO 81123
Contact: Mr. Bill Binnian
(719) 379-3825

Mt. Blanca Game Bird & Trout is located 100 miles southwest of Colorado Springs in a spectacularly beautiful valley near the Sangre de Cristo Mountains, and offers dove, quail, pheasant, chukar, ducks, geese, and a sporting clays course. The staff at Mt. Blanca are hospitable and attentive to your needs, designing a hunt that suits you and your party in every way. They keep a fine kennel of dogs and offer a choice of several breeds to hunt over, from the classic English setter and pointer to the lesser-known field cocker spaniel. The lodge is comfortable, the food is excellent, the atmosphere is relaxed and the hunting and fishing are first-rate.

—L.M.

Connecticut

Blue Trail Range
316 N. Branford Road
Wallingford, CT. 06492
(203) 269-3280
Contact: Dave and Deb Lyman

Connecticut Woods & Water
6 Larson Street
Waterford, CT 06385
(203) 442-6343
Contact: Capt. Dan Wood

Florida

Big D Plantation
Route 2, Box 294-C
Lake City, FL 32055
(904) 752-0594
Contact: Charlie Parnell

Fin & Feather Guide Service
6551 12th Avenue, NW
Naples, FL 33999
(813) 597-6020
Contact: Steve Ambrose (5 to 9 P.M.)

Jennings Bluff Hunting Preserve
Route 2, Box 4250
Jennings, FL 32053
(904) 938-5555
Contact: Troy Tolbert

Palm Beach Sporting Clays
5309 Hood Road
Palm Beach Gardens, FL 33418
(407) 622-7300
Contact: Warren Woody

Georgia

Ashburn Hill Hunting Preserve, Inc.
PO Box 128
Moultrie, GA 31776
(912) 985-1507
Contact: F. R. Pidcock, III

Barksdale Bobwhite Plantation
Route 4, Longstreet Road
PO Box 851
Cochran, GA 31014
(912) 934-6916
Contact: Ronnie Wright

Bevy Burst Hunting Preserve
Route 2, Box 245
Edison, GA 31746
(800) 447-9389
Contact: Kathy Gray

Burnt Pine Plantation
2941 Little River Road
Madison, GA 30650
(706) 342-7202
Contact: Mr. Steve Spears

Located 60 miles east of Atlanta, 6,000-acre Burnt Pine Plantation offers a wide assortment of tailor-made hunting packages that include whitetail deer, bobwhite quail, dove, pheasant, chukar, duck, and turkey.

Live Oak Plantation
Route 2, Box 308
Adel, Georgia 31620
(800) 682-4868

Located 35 miles northwest of Valdosta, Live Oak Plantation offers pheasant and quail hunting from custom mule-drawn hunting buggies—and true southern hospitality.

Llewellin's Point Hunting Preserve & Kennel
4897 Salem Road
Pine Mountain, GA 31822
(800) 636-9819
Contact: Floyd Clements

Mountain Creek Quail Farm Hunting Preserve
121 Barker Road
Molena, GA 30258
(706) 495-5894
Contact: Tony Benefield

Myrtlewood Hunting/Sporting Clays
PO Box 199
Thomasville, GA 31799
(912) 228-0987
Contact: Bob or John

Oakie Sink Shooting Preserve
Camilla, GA
(904) 561-1230
Contact: Tanya Gibbens

Pine Hill Plantation
255 Kimbrel Road
Colquitt, Georgia 31737
(912) 758-6602
Contact: Mr. G. J. Kimbrel III

Pine Hill Plantation, located 60 miles northwest of Tallahassee, offers quail hunting in the traditional manner for small parties of 3 to 6 guns.

Riverview Plantation
Route 2, Box 515
Camilla, GA 31730
(912) 294-4904
Contact: Mr. C. B. Cox III

Located 30 miles southwest of Albany, Riverview is a bobwhite quail hunting preserve in the traditional manner, with a kennel of 200 pointers and English setters.

Southpoint Plantation
PO Box 4309
Albany, GA 31706
(912) 888-6598
Contact: Darryl E. Pinkston

Hawaii

Ulupalakua Hunting Club
191 Mano Drive
Kula, HI 96790
(808) 878-6632
Contact: Patrick Fisher evenings

Idaho

Flying B Ranch
Route 2, Box 12C
Kamiah, ID 83536
(208) 935-0755
Contact: Steve Evans

Illinois

Olde Barn Sporting Clays
Bill and Mark McQueen
R.R. 2, Box 143A
Oakland, IL 61943
(217) 346-3211

Kansas

Ringneck Ranch
H.C. 61, Box 7
Tipton, Kansas 67485
(913) 373-4835
Contact: Keith and Debra Houghton

Located 75 miles northwest of
Salina, Ringneck Ranch offers dove,
quail, pheasant, turkey, prairie
chicken, duck, and geese hunting on
9,000 acres of land and can accommodate 26 guns.

Claythorne Hunting Lodge
Frieda Lancaster
Route 1, Box 13
Hallowell, KS 66725
(316) 597-2568

Locust Point Gun Club
Doug and Janice Koehler
R.R. 2, Box 122
Lyndon, KS 66351
(913) 828-3406

Ravenwood Hunting Preserve
Ken Corbet
10147 S.W. 61st Street
Topeka, KS 66610
(913) 256-6444

Maryland

Alexander Sporting Farm
James R. Alexander
13503 Alexander Road
Golt, MD 21637
(410) 928-3549

J & P Hunting Lodge, Inc.
John George
11054 Benton Corner Road
Sudlersville, MD 21668
(410) 438-3832

Pintail Point Sporting Clays
Doug Davis
511 Pintail Point Farm Lane
Queenstown, MD 21658
(410) 827-7029

Michigan

Deer Creek Hunt Club
George Daniels
180000 Basswoods Road
Three Oaks, MI 49128
(616) 756-6600

Saginaw Gun Club, Inc.
Cora Gorsuch
PO Box 6054
9540 Gartiot Road
Saginaw, MI 48608-6054
(517) 781-2260

Pheasant Ridge Hunting & Conservation Club

Wingshooting did not originate as a gentleman's sport. It was the pastime of peasants willing to degrade themselves by crawling on their hands and knees to surprise a flock of geese or roust about, waving their arms to flush "longtails" from their cover. It was not until a paltry two or three centuries ago that *shooting-flying*, as it was called, became the passionate sport of gents and gentlewomen. Its acceptance by aristocrats was a direct result of improvements in, and elaborations to, firearms, and a fascination for purebred hunting dogs. The result was "country house" society.

A shooting fortnight at a country estate was a blueblood gathering whose paraphernalia included pureblood horses, Best guns, bespoke Norfolks, and waterproofs worn over Saville Row breeches—all washed down with fine brandy and Scotch. Catering to the whims and wants of the aristocracy was a household staff of butlers, manservants, and ladies' maids. Down at the hunting lodge, the game keeper—commander-in-chief of the upland drives—drilled his army of gun-bearers, beaters, and ghillies.

Hey-ho, halcyon days. Such things are the stuff dreams—and coffee-table picture books—are made of. But the lure remains.

One woman has delved into the past to grasp the flavor of the golden era of shooting. She's a real lady, dressed in ankle-length tweed skirt and feathered hat, and her name is Virginia Mallon. She owns and operates Pheasant Ridge Hunting and Conservation Club, a 100-acre estate manicured "in the wild" as a prime pheasant-shooting habitat. Pheasant Ridge is located in Greenwich, New York, 13 miles north of Saratoga Springs and 35 miles from Manchester, Vermont.

Ms. Mallon, formerly in charge of international labor negotiations for Pan Am Airlines, began to transform her property into a British-style shooting preserve in 1990, shortly after the airline folded. Her commitment to creating a first-rate operation shows: from the selective cutting of the forests surrounding Pheasant Ridge, to the restrained elegance of its nineteenth-century farmhouse.

Shoots at Pheasant Ridge can be booked for individuals, couples, or groups from September through November by calling Virginia Mallon at (518) 692-9464 or (518) 692-9459.

—L.M.

Missouri

Devil's Ridge Sporting Clays
JoAnn Hatch
209 NW 1771
Kingsville, MO 64061
(816) 597-3886

New York

Friar Tuck Inn
Ross Caridi
4858 Route 32
Catskill, NY 12414
(518) 678-2271

North Carolina

Deep River Sporting Clays
Bill Kempffer
3420 Cletus Hall Road
Sanford, NC 27330
(919) 774-7080

Ohio

Hidden Haven Shooting Preserve
Ronald Blosser
9257 Buckeye Road
Sugar Grove, OH 43155
(614) 746-8568

Pennsylvania

Hillside Hunting Preserve
James and Jane Scurfield
228 Main Street
Berlin, PA 15530
(814) 267-4484

Rhode Island

Addieville East Farm
Contact: Mr. Geoff Gaebe
200 Pheasant Drive
Mapleville, RI 02839
(406) 763-4900

Addieville East Farm is considered one of the finest preserves in New England and offers pheasant shooting in as close to wild hunting conditions as possible, which is quite an accomplishment since it is located less than an hour from Providence, an hour from Boston, and three hours from New York City. Addieville is a popular place for field-dog trials, dog-training classes, sporting clays and clays competitions and offers club memberships for those who wish to make use of its extensive facilities year-round. It has a comfortable clubhouse and a real sporting ambience.—L.M.

South Carolina

Hermitage Farm Shooting Sports
Joe B. Cantey, III
2362 Tickle Hill Road
Camden, SC 29020
(803) 432-0210

South Dakota

High Brass
RR1, Box 4X
Chamberlain, SD 57325
(605) 734-6047
Missouri River Adventures
Bill Dillion
Pickstown, SD
(605) 487-7262

I had a great time in South Dakota with High Brass in Chamberlain and Bill Dillion's Missouri River Adventures in Pickstown. The birds—pheasants—were unbelievable. Both of these outfits put on top-quality hunts with fine meals, lodging, and guides. The pheasant numbers were astounding—we saw up to *a thousand a day!* High Brass likes larger groups early in the season, smaller groups later on. Bill Dillion prefers groups of five or fewer and has some fine French Brittanys who know the score on running roosters. You can bring your own dogs if you want. This is 12-gauge country, so don't bother packing a smaller gun. —S.S.

Valley West Hunting Preserve
Cyndi Phillips
809 West 10th Street
Sioux Falls, SD 57104
(800) 424-2047

Texas

American Shooting Centers
Bill Bacon
16500 Westheimer Parkway
Houston, TX 77082
(713) 556-1597

Blue Goose Sporting Clay Range
John Fields
PO Box M
Altair, TX 77412
(409) 234-3597

Hawkeye Hunt Club
PO Box 27
Center, TX 75935
(409) 598-2424

La Paloma Sporting Club
Henry Burns
PO Box 436
7110 FM 1863
Bulverde, TX 78163
(210) 980-4424

Rio Grande Valley Shooting Center
Mary Jo Janovsky
PO Box 2425
3418 Spy Glass Hill
Harlingen, TX 78550
(210) 421-4233

Virginia

Primland Hunting Reserve
Johnny Lambert
Route 1, Box 265-C
Claudville, VA 24076
(540) 251-8012

I'd like to recommend a place called Primland in Virginia. It has great flighted mallard shooting as well as British-style driven pheasants. They also have traditional quail-wagon hunts for bobwhites or quail-pheasant combinations. The food is great and the driven pheasants are as challenging as anything you'll see in the States. I had decent luck shooting a 16-gauge, even though some of the pheasants were pretty tall. The mallard shooting requires steel shot, but Primland has guns available if you don't want to take your own for ducks.—S.S.

Walnut Hill Shooting Center
Ruther Allen
PO Box 177
Route 624
Caret, VA 22436
(703) 788-3567

Shooting Travel/Outfitters

Addieville Adventures
200 Pheasant Drive
Maplevile, RI 02839
(401) 568-3185

Argentina Wings
207 Temelec Drive
Sonoma, CA 95476
(800) 946-4486

Dunn's Adventure Travel
One Madison Avenue
Grand Junction, TN 38039
(800) 228-3006

Frontiers International Travel
PO Box 959
Wexford, PA 15090
(800) 245-1950

Griffin & Howe
36 West 44th Street
New York, NY 10036
(212) 921-0980
and
33 Claremont Road
Bernardsville, NJ 07924
(908) 766-2287

Hendry, Ramsay & Wilcox
415 Madison Avenue, 20th floor
New York, NY 10017
(212) 768-3272

Holland & Holland, Ltd.
32 Bruton Street
London, W1X 8JS, England
011-44-1-71-499-4411

The Orvis Company
Historic Route 7A
Manchester, VT 05254

Sporting Holidays International
1701 Northwest Cookingham
Kansas City, MO 64155
(816) 734-4044

Woodcock Hill
R.D. #1, Box 147
Benton, PA 17814
(717) 864-3242

Publications

These publications are among many that will keep you aware of what's going on in your sport.

American Hunter
National Rifle Association
11250 Waples Mill Road
Fairfax, VA 22030
(703) 267-1300

CADA Gun Journal
Blue Book Publications, Inc.
One Appletree Square
Department WC
Minneapolis, MN 55425
(800) 877-GUNS

An excellent source for the fine firearms collector or anyone with an appreciation for classic collectible guns. Available by subscription or on newsstands.

Double Gun Journal
PO Box 550
East Jordan, MI 49727
(800) 447-1658

A classy magazine that features fine shotguns and double rifles. Available by subscription and at select bookstores and sporting goods stores.

Ducks Unlimited
One Waterfowl Way
Memphis, TN 38120
(901) 758-3825

Field & Stream
Times Mirror Magazines, Inc.
2 Park Avenue
New York, NY 10016
(212) 779-5000

The granddaddy of outdoor magazines, *Field & Stream* celebrated its 100th anniversary in 1995. Primarily for the big-game hunter and fisherman. Available by subscription or on newsstands.

Gray's Sporting Journal
725 Broad Street
Augusta, GA 30901
(706) 722-6060

A beautiful magazine for the all-around hunter. Available by subscription and at select bookstores and sporting goods stores.

Gun List
Krause Publications
700 East State Street
Iola, WI 54990
(715) 445-2214

Issued twice a month, this publication lists over 8,000 guns for sale in every issue. Available by subscription.

National Rifle Association
Women's Issues
11250 Waples Mill Road
Fairfax, VA 22030
(703) 267-1390
Brochures, books, and videos. Catalogue available.

Hunting
Petersen's Publishing Company
6420 Wilshire Boulevard
Los Angeles, CA 90048
(213) 782-2185

Outdoor Life
Times Mirror Magazines, Inc.
2 Park Avenue
New York, NY 10015
(212) 779-5000

Like *Field & Stream,* one of America's longest running outdoor publications. Available by subscription and on newsstands.

Pheasants Forever
PO Box 75473
St. Paul, MN 55175
(612) 481-7142

The Pointing Dog Journal
The Retriever Journal
PO Box 968
Traverse City, MI 49685
(616) 946-3712

The best magazines for people that are owned by pointing dogs and retrievers. Available by subscription.

Quail Unlimited
PO Box 610
Edgefield, SC 29824-0610
(803) 637-5731

RGS—The Ruffed Grouse Society Magazine
451 McCormick Road
Coraopolis, PA 15108
(412) 262-4044

Shooting Sportsman
Down East Enterprises, Inc.
PO Box 1357
Camden, ME 04843
(800) 666-4955

A beautiful magazine that focuses on upland bird shooting and fine guns. Available by subscription and at select bookstores and sporting goods stores.

Shotgun Sports
PO Box 6810
Auburn, CA 95604
(800) 676-8980

An information-packed magazine on the various shotgun sports. Available by subscription and at sporting-goods stores.

Sporting Classics
PO Box 1017
Camden, SC 29020
(800) 849-1004

A quality magazine for the shotgunner. Available by subscription and at select bookstores and sporting-goods stores.

Sporting Clays
Patch Communications
5211 South Washington Avenue
Titusville, FL 21780
(800) 677-5212

A superb magazine chock-full of valuable information, a calendar of events and more for the sporting-clays enthusiast. Available by subscription and at sporting-goods stores.

Sports Afield
250 West 55th Street
New York, NY 10019
(212) 649-4302

Like *Field & Stream* and *Outdoor Life, Sports Afield* is one of America's oldest and most popular outdoor magazines. Available by subscription and on newsstands.

Turkey & Turkey Hunting
Krause Publications, Inc.
700 East State Street
Iola, WI 54990
(715) 445-2214

Varmint Hunter
Box 759
Pierre, SD 57501
(800) 528-4868

Waterfowl Magazine
Waterfowl U.S.A. National Headquarters
PO Box 50
Edgefield, SC 29824
(803) 637-5767

Black's Wing & Clay
43 West Front Street, Suite 11
PO Box 2029
Red Bank, NJ 07701
(908) 224-8700

Issued once a year, this is the definitive source listing for anyone involved in the shotgun sports.
Available at sporting-goods stores,
bookstores.

Women & Guns
267 Linwood Avenue
PO Box 488, Station C
Buffalo, NY 14209
(716) 885-6408

Booksellers (also see Suggested Reading)

Angler's & Shooter's Bookshelf
PO Box 178
Goshen, CT 06756
(203) 491-2500

Judith Bowman Books
Pound Ridge Road
Bedford, NY 10506
(914) 234-7543

Gary L. Estabrook, Books
PO Box 61453
Vancouver, WA 98666
(360) 699-5454

Fair Chase, Inc.
S1118 Highway HH
Lyndon Station, WI 53944
(800) 762-2843

Gunnerman Books
PO Box 214292
Auburn Hills, MI 48321
(810) 879-2779

**Wilderness Adventures Sporting
Books**
PO Box 1410
Bozeman, MT 59771
(800) 925-3339

Willow Creek Press
No. 1, 51 Centre
PO Box 881
Minocqua, WI 54548
(715) 358-7010

Suggested Reading

Wingshooting

Whispering Wings of Autumn by Gene Hill and Steve Smith, published by Wilderness Adventures Press (800-925-3339), is a book to cherish by two of the best: Gene Hill, one of America's most beloved outdoor writers, and Steve Smith, whose insights into the habits and habitat of woodcock and grouse are invaluable to anyone who hunts these native gamebirds; $29.

Outdoor Yarns & Outright Lies, also by Hill and Smith ($18.95), gives you more of the wit and wisdom of these popular writers.

Many readers of *Field & Stream* consider Gene Hill's column, "Hill Country," the heart of the magazine. Other books by Hill include *Mostly Tailfeathers: Stories About Guns and Dogs and Birds and Other Odds and Ends* ($15.95); *A Listening Walk and Other Stories* ($15.95); *A Hunter's Fireside Book* ($15.95); *Shot-*

gunner's Notebook: The Advice & Reflections of a Wingshooter ($24.50); and *Sunlight and Shadows* ($24.50). All are available in bookstores and sporting-goods stores nationwide or direct from Safari Press (800-451-4788) or Wilderness Adventures Press (800-925-3339).

Other books by Steve Smith include *Just Labs* (see Field Dogs), *Hunting Ducks and Geese* (see Waterfowl Hunting), and *Just Mutts*.

Corey Ford: Trickiest Thing in Feathers, compiled and edited by Laurie Morrow ($29), is a collection of upland bird-hunting stories by the beloved outdoor writer, Corey Ford, who wrote "The Lower Forty" column in *Field & Stream.* Sometimes witty, often poignant, each story includes an introduction by Morrow, Ford's official biographer.

A Hunter's Road by Jim Fergus ($25), follows one of the most captivating outdoor writers on a bird-hunting journey throughout the United States. His chronicle is worth reading not only for the information on wingshooting, but also for the way Fergus shows the reader the soul of the hunter.

The books of George Bird Evans are modern classics, available through Wilderness Adventures Press (800-925-3339): *From My Covers; Grouse on the Mountain; Living with Gun Dogs; George Bird Evans Introduces People & Dogs; An Affair with Grouse;* and *Troubles with Bird Dogs.*

Fool Hen Blues: Retrievers & Shotguns, and the Birds of the American West by E. Donnall Thomas, Jr. ($30), follows the author and his versatile retriever on captivating bird-hunting excursions across America, from the Kenai Peninsula of Alaska to the high plains of central Montana. *Doc Hall's Journal: The Ramblings of a Sportsman* by Dr. James Whitney Hall ($29) chronicles an avid outdoorsman's travels around America and abroad.

Regional, United States

The following guides are published by Wilderness Adventures Press (800-925-3339):

Wingshooters Guide to Montana: Upland Birds and Waterfowl by Chuck Johnson and Ben O. Williams ($26) is indispensable for anyone planning to hunt in this beautiful state; includes maps, graphs, tips, techniques, and advice on where to hunt. A companion Montana atlas and gazetteer are available as well.

Wingshooters Guide to South Dakota by Chuck Johnson and Ben O. Williams ($26) is an excellent handbook for those who plan to hunt pheasants, prairie chickens, sharp-tailed grouse, Hungarian partridge, mourning doves, turkeys, and waterfowl in South Dakota, one of the richest states for upland bird shooting. Ask about the companion South Dakota atlas and gazetteer when you call.

Kicking Up Trouble: Upland Bird Hunting in the West by John Holt ($29) is a funny, intimate book by an author who adopted Montana as his home state in order to bask in the splendor of the outdoors and enjoy hunting.

Waterfowl Hunting

Hunting Ducks and Geese: Hard Facts, Good Bets, and Serious Advice from a Duck Hunter You Can Trust by Steve Smith ($20) is the book you'll need to learn more about the sport of waterfowl hunting. Autographed copies are available through Wilderness Adventures Press (800-925-3339).

Wildfowler's Season: Modern Methods for a Classic Sport by Chris Dorsey, editor of *Ducks Unlimited* magazine and expert duck hunter ($37.95) is a must-read, and includes 182 photos.

Waterfowl: An Identification Guide to the Ducks, Geese and Swans of the World by Steve Madge and Hilary Burn ($24.95) is a careful study of the various types of ducks, the regions they populate, migratory habits and routes, and other information that every responsible waterfowl hunter should know; includes 150 maps.

Other excellent books on waterfowl hunting include the following: *Ducks, Geese, and Swans of North America* by Frank C. Bellrose ($49.95) is a profusely illustrated guide to help you identify native American waterfowl in flight and on the water.

American Duck Shooting by George Bird Grinnell ($17.95) is the classic American book on the subject, available in softcover and a cornerstone of a good waterfowl hunting library.

Autumn Passages: A Ducks Unlimited Treasury of Waterfowling Classics ($27.50), issued by America's foremost waterfowling conservation foundation, is a collection of duck hunting stories by some of the best outdoor writers in the country.

The Gordon MacQuarrie Trilogy: Stories of Old Duck Hunters by Gordon Mac-Quarrie, published by Willow Creek Press (800-850-WILD; $49) is a fireside reading at its best; no one captures the essence, even passion, of duck hunting like MacQuarrie.

Field Dogs

Just Labs by Steve Smith, photographs by Dale Spartus (Willow Creek Press, $35) tells the story of the Labrador retriever; anyone who loves Labs will love this book.

Warm Hearts & Cold Noses, compiled by Laurie Morrow, is a collection of short stories about dogs by such famous authors as E. B. White, Robert Benchley, James Thurber, D. H. Lawrence, Ring Lardner, William Faulkner, and others. Each story is introduced by Laurie Morrow, who closes the book with the never-before-published original version of the Corey Ford story "The Road to Tinkhamtown."

A Field Guide: Dog First Aid by Randy Acker, D.V.M., with Jim Fergus ($15) is a handy, pocket-size book that covers just about every emergency situation that may crop up when hunting with a dog. A must for every wingshooter, this book could save your dog's life.

Training the Versatile Retriever to Hunt Upland Birds by Bill Tarrant ($29) tells you how to train your retriever to hunt upland birds. Other books by Tarrant, one of the finest field-dog trainers in the United States, include *How to Hunt Birds with Gun Dogs* ($21); *Bill Tarrant's Gun Dog Book: A Treasury of Happy Trails* ($25); *Pick of the Litter,* a collection of dog stories ($25); *Hey Pup, Fetch It Up! The Complete Retriever Training Book* ($25); *Problem Gun Dogs: How to Identify and Correct Their Faults* ($20); *Best Way to Train Your Gun Dog: The Delmar Smith Method* ($20).

Turkey Hunting

Better on a Rising Tide: Tales of Wild Turkeys and Rural Folk by Tom Kelley ($25) describes a turkey hunter's experiences and enjoyment of the sport.

America's Greatest Game Bird: Archibald Rutledge's Turkey-Hunting Tales, edited by Jim Casada ($24.95).

Illumination of the Flatwoods: A Season with the Wild Turkey by Joe Hutto ($25).

Deer Hunting

Hunting Trophy Whitetails by David Morris ($29.95) is a 483-page book by the former editor of *North American Whitetail* magazine; available from Safari Press (800-451-7888).

Stalking Trophy Mule Deer by Walt Prothero (Safari Press, $18.98) discusses the methods and strategies that will help you successfully hunt mule deer. Also by Prothero, *Stalking the Big Game* ($19.95) covers successful hunting techniques for pronghorn antelope, bighorn sheep, and all other major native American big game.

Whitetail Autumn, Whitetail Winter, and *Whitetail Spring* by John J. Ozoga (Willow Creek Press) are magnificent photographic journals that depict the life of the whitetail deer. Although these are not how-to books on hunting, they are valuable to the aspiring deer hunter for the information they provide on the deer's habits and habitat.

Big Game Hunting

The Life of the Hunt by John Barsness (Wilderness Adventures Press, $29) is one of the most captivating and enchanting new books about hunting big game in America. Barsness captures the life—and the heart—of the hunt in a Hemingwayesque style of writing that pulls the reader deeply into the author's world.

The Jim Corbett Collection A set of books that provide unequaled insight into the soul of a hunter. Corbett lived in British India and later in Africa; throughout his life, he conducted himself with a compassion and modesty that earned the respect of the hunting world. Five volumes, slipcased, include *Jungle Lore,*

The Man-eating Leopard of Rudraprayag, My India, Man-eaters of Kumaon, and *The Temple Tiger;* available from Safari Press (800-451-4788) and Wilderness Adventures Press (800-925-3339); $90.

African Twighlight: The Story of a Hunter by Robert F. Jones (Wilderness Adventures Press, $29) imparts the majesty of hunting in twelve stories that set the imagination on fire.

African Hunter by James Mellon ($110) is a definitive book on hunting over 200 species in 20 countries in Africa. A worthy volume for expert and beginning big-game hunters alike, it includes practical advice about preparing for safari.

Spiral-Horn Dreams by Terry Wieland (see Firearms).

Hunting, General

The Best of Field & Stream: 100 Years of Great Writing from America's Premiere Sporting Magazine ($24.95), available through Safari Press (800-451-4788) and in bookstores nationwide, includes more than 50 stories by some of the great outdoor writers published in *Field & Stream* over the past century.

Firearms

American Hunting Rifles: Their Application in the Field for Practical Shooting by Christopher Boddington ($35) is a handy and comprehensive book for anyone who hunts with a rifle. Boddington, considered one of the most authoritative writers in the field, provides important information on game and guns.

Also by Boddington is *Shots at Big Game* ($15.95), a valuable technical book on shooting techniques, rifle accuracy, and essential equipment for hunting big game; available from Safari Press (800-451-4788).

Spanish Best: The Fine Shotguns of Spain by Terry Wieland ($50) explores the world of Spanish gunmaking, its history, its traditions, and its industry. If you are considering buying a Spanish gun, you'll want to read this book by a fine outdoor writer who hails from Canada.

Also by Terry Wieland is *Spiral-Horn Dreams,* one of the best books on African antelope, including bongo, kudu, and mountain nyala. A limited edition is available for $90 through Wilderness Adventures Press (800-925-3339).

Good Guns Again: A Celebration of Fine Sporting Arms by Steve Bodio ($29) is the best book for seasoned and new firearms enthusiasts alike—easy to understand and a delight to read.

The gun books of Michael McIntosh include *Best Guns* ($39.50), a comprehensive overview of the finest shotguns ever made in America and Europe; *Shotguns and Shooting* ($30), which delves into the art of shooting and gun making; *A. H. Fox: The Finest Gun in the World* ($49.95), which tells the story of

Ansley H. Fox, one of America's finest shotgun makers; and *The Big Bore Rifle* ($40), which examines large caliber double and magazine rifles, their history, development, and use. McIntosh also is listed under Shotgun Instructors in the Directory (see Paul Nelson Preserve and Wingshooting America). His books are available from both Wilderness Adventures Press (800-925-3339) and Safari Press (800-451-4788).

The Sporting Craftsmen by Art Carter, editor of *Sporting Classics* magazine ($95), introduces the many craftsmen throughout the country who produce wonderful custom-made outdoor equipment in this valuable source book.

Shooting Technique

Positive Shooting by Michael Yardley ($30) offers sound advice about shooting technique, gun fit, and much more for the hunting and nonhunting shooting sportsman and sportswoman.

Wild Game Cookery

The following books are available from Willow Creek Press (800-850-WILD):

The Wild Menu by Chef Christopher Ray with Greg Linder ($24.50) features award-winning recipes that take you every step of the way in preparing the game you shoot for the gourmet table.

500 Wild Game & Fish Recipes ($12.95) is devoted to the entire spectrum of game cookery, with terrific easy-to-follow recipes.

Glossary

——

action. That part to which the barrel is attached, and where all the mechanisms or working parts are housed. It is often called the receiver and is also used to indicate the different forms of gun locks.

ammunition. Cartridges, shotshells, powder, shot, bullets, slugs, primers—all the components used in the discharge of firearms.

barrel. The steel tube of a rifle or shotgun through which the projectile (bullet, shotshell, slug) is given motion and travels in its line of flight.

binocular vision. Sighting with both eyes open, which is the correct method of aiming a firearm.

blueing or bluing. A black-blue metal finish applied to the barrels to prevent rust.

bolt. The sliding bar in a bolt-action rifle that works part of the action to lock the cartridge in the chamber.

bore. The interior of the barrel through which the charge or projectile passes.

boxlock. A type of shotgun action in which the metal parts are hung in a self-contained, boxlike arrangement.

breech. The end of the barrel closest to the action.

broken, or break-open, gun. A side-by-side or Over and Under shotgun that opens by means of a hinge in the action to permit loading and discharging of shotshells.

browning. An acid-applied oxidation process, used primarily on Damascus barrels, that colors the steel brown and protects the outside of the barrels from rust.

butt. The part of the gunstock that fits against the shoulder.

buttplate. A plate that is fitted to the butt to protect the wood from damage. It is usually made of metal, horn, hard rubber, or plastic.

buttstock or stock. The large wooden part of the gun that supports the action, which is gripped by the hand and pressed against the shoulder.

caliber. The diametrical measurement of the bore of a rifle barrel.

cap. The primer placed on the nipple of a muzzleloader to ignite the charge.

carbine. A short rifle with a barrel length of 20 inches or less. Rifles with barrels that measure less than 16 inches are illegal, unless they are registered by the U.S. Bureau of Alcohol, Tobacco and Firearms (BATF). Originally, carbines were popular among cowboys and other people who carried guns on horseback.

cartridge. The fixed ammunition for a firearm.

case-hardening. A chemical process applied to certain metal parts of the gun, particularly the receiver, that results in an attractive finish of deep, mottled colors.

cast-off. A measurement crucial to proper gun fit, which is the distance the stock is offset at the heel to the right from a straight line with the axis of the bore.

cast-on. A measurement crucial to proper gun fit, which is the distance the stock is offset at the heel to the left from a straight line with the axis of the bore.

centerfire. A cartridge case that has the primer placed directly in the center of the base.

chamber. The recess in the breech of a barrel where the cartridge is placed.

checkering. A fine cross-hatch pattern cut into the forend and/or wrist of a gunstock that matts the surface and affords a more secure grip. The butts of fine guns are often checkered. Steel buttplates are sometimes checkered, but checkering on smaller gun parts is usually called knurling.

choke. The degree to which the constriction at the muzzle limits the spread of the shot. Chokes are measured in this country as Full, Modified, Improved Cylinder, and Cylinder.

choke bore. A shotgun bore slightly constricted at the muzzle that limits the spread of the shot.

comb. The part of the gunstock where the cheek rests at the time of firing.

cylinder bore. A shotgun bore with no constriction at the muzzle.

Damascus. Barrels, usually made prior to 1900, produced by twisting steel and iron strips and welding them together. Damascus barrels were replaced by fluid steel barrels in the 1890s. Modern ammunition should, under no circumstance, be fired in a gun with Damascus barrels. Black powder may be fired in guns with Damascus barrels, but you must consult a professional gunsmith about the soundness of *any* antique gun and have him determine the black powder load. A good rule of thumb is to assume that early Damascus barrels are unsafe with any ammunition until proven otherwise.

ejector. An automatic device in shotguns that ejects the fired, or spent, shell upon opening the breech of the gun.

extractor. A hook that draws the spent case from the chamber of a gun.

forearm or forend. The wooden part of a stock the shooter grips under the gun barrel. The most common types of forends are splinter, Schnabel, semi-beavertail, and beavertail.

front sight. The sight located at the muzzle of the barrel. In a shotgun it is a bead. In a rifle, it may be any one of a variety of types.

gauge. The term used for shotgun bore sizes, indicating the number of bore-size lead balls it takes to weigh one pound. Modern gauges are 10, 12, 16, 20, and 28. The smallest shotgun size is the .410, which is actually a caliber.

grip. The part of the buttstock the shooter grips when he or she shoulders a rifle or shotgun.

hammer. The striking part of the action. A hammer gun has this part on the outside of the action. The hammers of a hammerless gun are concealed inside the action.

hang fire. Delayed ignition in modern ammunition, which can be very dangerous. Be exceedingly careful removing the spent cartridge, and do not fire a gun that has delayed ignition until it has been carefully checked by a gunsmith.

Kentucky, muzzleloader, or flintlock rifle. Early types of breech-loading, single-shot rifles that were used by American pioneers. Today they are popular in historic re-creations and with shooters who enjoy this type of firearm. All states offer special muzzleloading deer seasons, and it is recommended you use modern manufacture muzzleloaders for this purpose.

magazine. The receptacle cartridges are kept in until they are fed, one at a time, into the chamber for firing.

Monte Carlo. A type of buttstock that has a high comb that is preferred in certain types of shooting.

mounts. The metal cradle that holds the scope of a rifle.

muzzle. The exit end of a gun barrel.

N.R.A. National Rifle Association.

Over and Under. A shotgun in which the barrels are placed one over the other. Be careful of very early guns with stacked barrels. The Over and Under was not mechanically perfected until the 1940s.

pistol grip. A downturning in a gunstock just behind the wrist, like the handle of the pistol. (Shooters that favor a pistol grip claim it gives them better control. Those who do not claim it hinders gun movement. It's all personal preference.)

pitch. The angle of the buttstock in relation to the line of sight.

pump gun. A type of action. A pump gun loads and ejects shells when the forend is pumped, or *shucked,* back and forth.

recoil. The backward force of a firearm after it is fired. Most recoil is absorbed in the stock. The degree of recoil in a rifle or shotgun is a function of the power of the ammunition and the weight of the gun.

rimfire. A cartridge in which the priming mixture is placed in a fold at the head of the shell.

safety. The mechanical device on many (but not all) guns that prevents it from firing. A safety is never, under any circumstances, to be trusted.

semi-automatic. A type of action that uses either the recoil of the gun or the gas produced by the cartridge to eject the spent cartridge and feed in a new one. It fires one shot with each pull of the trigger.

shot. Lead or steel spherical projectiles designed for use in shotshells.

shot pattern or patterning. The dispersion of shot at a given range, usually measured by the proportion placed in a 30-inch circle at 40 yards.

shotshell or shell. Shotgun ammunition. The five components of a shotshell are the case, the primer, powder charge, wad, and shot. Only the shot is expelled when a shotshell is fired.

side-by-side. A two-barreled gun whose barrels are soldered together alongside each other.

trigger. The small finger lever under the action which, when pressed or pulled, releases the main spring and allows the hammer to descend, thereby causing the process that results in the discharge of the cartridge.

Index

———